Withdrawn

Healing the Bereaved Child

Grief Gardening, Growth Through Grief and Other Touchstones for Caregivers

Also by Alan Wolfelt:

The Child's Experience of Grief: The Caregiver's Role
(videotape)

A Child's View of Grief
(book and videotape)

Creating Meaningful Funeral Ceremonies: A Guide for Caregivers

The Experience of Grief: Helping Oneself and Others
(videotape)

Healing Your Grieving Heart: 100 Practical Ideas

Healing The Grieving Heart:
100 Practical Ideas for Families, Friends and Caregivers

Helping Teens Cope with Grief
(videotape)

Interpersonal Skills Training: A Handbook for Funeral Home Staffs

The Journey Through Grief: Reflections on Healing

Sarah's Journey: One Child's Experience with the Death of Her Father

Self-Care for the Bereavement Caregiver: The Codependent Syndrome
(videotape)

Understanding Grief: Helping Yourself Heal

What Bereaved Children Want Adults to Know About Grief
(booklet and audiocassette)

Companion
PRESS

Companion Press is dedicated to the education and support of both the bereaved and bereavement caregivers. We believe that those who companion the bereaved by walking with them as they journey in grief have a wondrous opportunity: to help others embrace and grow through grief—and to lead fuller, more deeply-lived lives themselves because of this important work.

For ordering information, write or call:

Companion Press
The Center for Loss and Life Transition
3735 Broken Bow Road
Fort Collins, CO 80526
(970) 226-6050

Healing the Bereaved Child

Grief Gardening, Growth Through Grief and Other Touchstones for Caregivers

Alan D. Wolfelt, Ph.D.

Companion
PRESS

An imprint of the Center for Loss and Life Transition

Companion Press is an imprint of the Center for Loss and Life Transition, 3735 Broken Bow Road, Fort Collins, Colorado 80526.

Manufactured in the United States of America.

05 04 03 02 01 00 99 98   7 6 5 4 3

ISBN: 1-879651-10-6

Dedication
In memory of
Vincent Rubertino,
killed at age four by a drunk driver May 5, 1993

I met Vinnie's mother, Judy, at a talk I gave on grief gardening this summer. After my presentation she shared with me the story of her family's loss and "Vinnie's Sunflower." You see, before he was killed Vinnie planted a sunflower in a paper cup at preschool. Sadly, Vinnie never had the chance to see his sunflower grow to maturity.

But grow it did. By the end of the summer—when the Rubertino family was deep in the throes of early grief—the sunflower stood eight feet, five inches tall. The family harvested the sunflower head and stored it over the winter. In the spring they planted the seeds and by fall were rewarded with a garden of bright yellow sunflowers turning their faces to the heavens.

In memory of Vinnie and as a positive drunk driving deterrent, the Rubertinos have since shared Vinnie's story and sunflower seeds with many others. Judy sent me some, and I plan to plant them with my children next spring. What a wonderful, life-affirming idea!

When I first decided to develop the grief gardening concept and weave it throughout this book, I could never have guessed how literally grief gardening might help to heal mourners. But it does—and did long before I came along to coin the term.

Contents

Preface

Please take pause for a moment to reflect on your own childhood losses and your struggles to understand your experiences with these losses. As you do so, I hope you recognize the need for resources intended to help adults artfully *companion* children in the journey into grief and mourning.

It was in 1983 that I wrote the following: "Any child old enough to love is old enough to grieve." Since that time I've attempted to continue to learn from many bereaved children and their families. I've also had the privilege of teaching and learning from thousands of caregivers to bereaved children throughout North America. I have certainly changed and, I like to think, grown both as a caregiver and as a human being in these last 11 years.

To "companion" bereaved children means to be an active participant in their healing. When you as a caregiver companion grieving children, you allow yourself to learn from their unique experiences. You let them teach you instead of

When you as a caregiver companion grieving children, you allow them to teach you instead of the other way around.

On a personal level this growth is largely attributable to the births of my three lovely children, Megan, Christopher and Jaimie. They, along with the children and adolescents I have companioned as a [coun]selor, are my constant teachers. I hope the following pages [reflect] some maturity and wisdom gained over the last decade. As I [get o]lder, my inner child keeps reminding me that I must stay in [touch] with that little boy inside myself. Every day my own children [remind] me that play is the focus of their world. (This reminder [usually c]omes around 6:00 a.m. each morning!)

[Profes]sionally, I am more and more convinced that working with [griever]s, particularly children, is more art than science. Each of us as [caregivers to ber]eaved children must, in part, find our own way. We must [integrate our] experiences with knowledge, skill and a creative, intuitive, [heartfelt way of] joining the world of the hurting child. For me, counseling [bereaved childr]en has evolved into a more intuitive, spiritual process than the traditional medical model of mental health care supports. I have left my clinical doctoring behind to become the grief gardener that I am today, and I hope the grief gardening model I offer in this book invites you on a similar journey of professional growth. ("What in the world is 'grief gardening'?" you're probably asking yourself right now. "Has Wolfelt finally lost it?" I assure you that I have not "lost it," but instead have gained much, personally and professionally, through the development of this model. But to understand what I mean by "grief gardening," you must read this book, particularly the parable on pp. iv-v, Chapter 1 and the Grief Gardening Model on p. 315.)

When I started to create this book about two years ago, I told myself I didn't want to add another academic textbook to the library shelves of educators and clinicians. While I must admit that I occasionally find myself thinking I should fill these pages with a multitude of research-based references, I have resisted the urge. I'm proud to be an academician and respect the need to draw on research in my work with bereaved children. However, I wanted this book to be about what I think and feel about companioning bereaved children: what I do and how I do it. If this sounds interesting to you, please read on! If it doesn't, you may find other books more suited to your needs.

I have left my clinical doctoring behind to become the grief gardener I am today.

I have found that many people who work with bereaved children are burdening themselves with thoughts that they should always know what to say and do. Many seem to want a cookbook, prescriptive approach to *treating* the child. I have found that the need to fill silences and treat bereaved children as patients results from contamination by a medical model of mental health caregiving. This model teaches us to study a body of knowledge, assess patients and treat them with hopes of resolving issues and conflicts. In my experience, there is one major problem with this model as it applies to caring for bereaved children—it doesn't work!

I have come to realize that the true expert in the counseling relationship is the bereaved child. This seems so obvious to me now, almost too elementary to write down. Yet this simple realization has proved profound to me in my work with kids. Bereaved children are our finest teachers about grief and mourning. They are naturals! They don't play psychological games or hide out in efforts to repress genuine thoughts and feelings. They instinctively move toward it in manageable doses, even when they fear the pain. As they mourn the death of someone loved, they tutor us in walking not behind them, not in front of them, but beside them. They know about the need to mourn, they just need safe places in which to do it in their own way and time.

The author at three years old.

If you work with bereaved children, you will at times feel uncertain, even helpless. I don't always know why I'm responding the way I do when I'm with a bereaved child; my reactions are never scripted. Usually I'm following the lead of the unique child. I like to say, "I invite children to the dance, but I allow and encourage them to lead." When I work with bereaved kids, sometimes we actively embrace pain, but more often we laugh and have fun. Techniques I might use are merely in response to the evolving process. I want the child to come to know me as someone who accepts and respects him for who he is and where he is in his grief journey. Not every moment is filled with some therapeutically profound insight, but I realize something is happening all the time. And, some of the deepest communication comes during our silences.

I remember being a child—at times a happy child, at times a sad or angry child. I remember feeling deeply (as I still do). I wondered about life and death. Sometimes I was scared and uncertain about my future and the future of my family. I loved to play with other children (I still do that, too). I think my ability to remember my childhood provides me a view of children that children respond to. Yes, it's easier to be around children when they are happy. Yet we must also be present to them in their pain and loneliness. I hope this book helps you use your gifts to "be with" and learn from bereaved children.

Acknowledgments

Healing the Bereaved Child is the result of literally thousands of hours of work by many different people. Though I authored the text, many others contributed their gifts and professional abilities to its development and completion. My deepest thanks to:

- my parents, Don and Virgene Wolfelt, who brought me into this world, and my brother, Gary, and my sister, Kay, for growing up with me from childhood into adulthood.

- my childhood friends, with whom I learned to play, to fight, to love and to mourn.

- my wife, Sue, who has supported my time commitment to this project. Her love gives me strength to share my life with others. Her understanding frees me to travel and help others learn how to companion bereaved children and families.

- my three darling children—Megan, Christopher and Jaimie. They have helped me find heaven on earth! They give me the gift of love, the inspiration to remember my own childhood and a deep understanding of the importance of giving and receiving love.

- my editor, Karla Oceanak, who responded with enthusiasm to my initial gardening concept. Without her support, guidance, contributions and suggestions, this book would still be pages in a folder. She is a wonderful wordsmith who has greatly enriched what I feel a need to share with the world.

- this book's photographer and my friend, Patrick Dean, who responded with excitement when invited to be a part of this work of love. He far surpassed my expectations, presenting me with hundreds of rich, poignant photos of children and gardens. (Alas, we had to whittle his pile down considerably when choosing what we could realistically include in the book.) Thanks, too, to the families and children who agreed to be photographed by Patrick for the book.

- my office manager, Bridget Tisthammer, who anchored the Center for Loss while my energies were directed toward this book.

✻ landscape architect Sandy Schlicht and artist Cathy Goodale, who worked to bring to life my visual image of a gardening model to help bereaved children. Their watercolor (see the full color section) ties the many elements of this text together and was the perfect finishing touch for the project.

✻ Susie Cannon and Launie Korth of Companion Press, who designed and coordinated the printing of this book.

✻ Andrea Gambill of *Bereavement* magazine, who provides me with a forum to regularly write about the important needs of bereaved children. She is a true friend who shares my commitment to helping bereaved people of all ages in the healing process.

✻ Lois Pearson and Lori Stahl, who contributed the valuable artwork from bereaved children on pp. 164-165.

✻ Jeffrey Kauffman, who wrote of the special needs of mentally retarded bereaved children on p. 31.

✻ Leslie Delp, who provided the model for grief camps for bereaved children on p. 223.

✻ the bereaved children and adolescents who so generously contributed their artwork and writings to this book in the hopes that other children might be helped.

✻ my seminar participants, who honor me in allowing me to teach and be taught.

✻ the bereaved children and families with whom I have had the privilege to grief garden, for they are truly the inspiration behind this book.

Bless all of you!

Alan D. Wolfelt

October, 1995

The Gardener and the Seedling
A Parable

One spring morning a gardener noticed an unfamiliar seedling poking through the ground near the rocky, untended edge of his garden. He knelt to examine its first fragile leaves. Though he had cared for many others during his long life, the gardener was unsure what this new seedling was to become. Still, it looked forlorn and in need of his encouragement, so the gardener removed the largest stones near the seedling's tender stalk and bathed it in rainwater from his worn tin watering can.

The gardener believed in the seedling's natural capacity to adapt and survive.

In the coming days the gardener watched the seedling struggle to live and grow in its new, sometimes hostile home. When weeds threatened to choke the seedling, he dug them out, careful not to disturb the seedling's delicate roots. He spooned dark, rich compost around its base. One cold April night he even fashioned a special cover for the seedling from an old canning jar so that it would not freeze.

But the gardener also believed in the seedling's natural capacity to adapt and survive. He did not water it too frequently. He did not stimulate its growth with chemicals. Nor did he succumb to the urge to lift the seedling from its unfriendly setting and transplant it in the rich, sheltered center of the garden. Instead the gardener watched and waited.

Day by day the seedling grew taller, stronger. Its slender yet sturdy stalk reached for the heavens and its blue-green leaves stretched to either side as if to welcome the gardener as he arrived each morning.

Soon a bud appeared atop the young plant's stem. Then one warm June afternoon the tightly wrapped, purple-blue petals unfurled, revealing a creamy white ring of petals inside and a tiny bouquet of yellow stamens at its center.

The gardener knew that the columbine would continue to grow and flourish.

A columbine—the gentle wildflower whose name means "dovelike." A single, perfect columbine.

The gardener smiled. He knew then that the columbine would continue to grow and flourish, still needing his presence but no longer requiring the daily companionship it had during its tenuous early days.

The gardener crouched next to the lovely blossom and cupped its head in his rough palm. "Congratulations," he whispered to the columbine. "You have not only survived, you have grown beautiful and strong."

The gardener stood and turned to walk back to his gardening shed. Suddenly a gust of wind lifted his straw hat and as he bent to retrieve it, a small voice whispered back, "Without your help I could not have. Thank you."

The gardener looked up but no one was there. Just the blue columbine nodding happily in the breeze. . .

1

My Guiding Model: Growth-Oriented Grief Gardening with Bereaved Children

The more bereaved children I have the privilege to work with, the more I see myself not as a *counselor* but as a *counselor-gardener*.

Too often, counselors are taught (and subsequently internalize) the medical model of bereavement care, which suggests that bereaved children are "sick" and need to be "cured." This same mindset implies that the goal in bereavement caregiving is to help the child "resolve" or "recover from" the illness that is grief.

The medical model of understanding human behavior actually damages bereaved families because it takes responsibility for healing away from the bereaved person (child, adolescent or adult) and puts it in the hands of the doctor or caregiver who "treats" the "patient." Look up the word "treat" in the dictionary and you'll find it derives from the Latin *tractare*, which means, interestingly enough, to drag. The word patient, defined as a noun, refers to a sick person who is being cured by a professional. As compassionate caregivers, we cannot (and should not try to) drag our "patients" into being "cured."

"Now the gardener is the one who has seen everything ruined so many times that (even as his pain increases with each loss) he comprehends— truly knows— that where there was a garden once, it can be again . . ."

Harry Mitchell,
The Essential Earthman (1981)

Grief gardeners believe that grief is organic—as natural as the setting of the sun and as elemental as gravity.

Grief gardeners, on the other hand, believe that grief is organic. That grief is as natural as the setting of the sun and as elemental as gravity. To us, grief is a complex but perfectly natural—and necessary—mixture of human emotions. Grief gardeners do not cure the grieving child; instead we create conditions that allow the bereaved child to mourn. Our work is more art than science, more heart than head. The bereaved child is not our patient but instead our companion.

The seedling in the parable that precedes this chapter represents, of course, the bereaved child. The seedling is struggling to live in its new, hostile environment much as a bereaved child struggles to cope with her new, scary world. A world without someone she loved very much. A world that does not understand the need to mourn. A world that does not compassionately support its bereaved.

This child needs the love and attention of caring adults if she is to heal and grow. It is the bereavement caregiver's role to create conditions that allow for such healing and growth. In the parable, the gardener removes stones near the seedling's tender stalk and offers it life-sustaining water. In the real world, the grief gardener might simply listen as the child talks or plays out her feelings of pain or sadness, in effect removing a heavy weight from her small shoulders. Instead of water, the grief gardener offers his empathy, helping quench the child's thirst for companionship.

The gardener in the parable also dug out weeds that threatened to choke the young seedling; the grief gardener might attempt to squelch those who threaten the child's healing, such as a dysfunctional or grief-avoiding family member. Dispelling prevalent grief myths (described between every chapter in this book) is another weeding task for the grief gardener. The grief gardener's compost is the nourishment of play—that necessary work that feeds the souls of all children.

The grief gardener does not seek to rescue the bereaved child from her pain.

But notice, too, that the gardener in the parable does not take complete control of the seedling's existence, but rather trusts in the seedling's inner capacity to heal and grow. The gardener does not water the seedling too frequently; the grief gardener does not offer companionship to the point of codependency. The gardener does not use chemical fertilizers; the grief gardener does not advocate the use of pharmaceuticals (unless made necessary by a medical condition, of course) or other inorganic therapies for bereaved children. The gardener does not transplant the seedling but instead allows it to struggle where it has landed; the grief gardener does not seek to rescue the bereaved child from her pain.

The greatest joy of grief gardening is witnessing the growth and new beauty in bereaved children who have learned to reconcile their grief.

Largely as a result of its own arduous work, the seedling in the parable grows into a beautiful columbine. Bereaved children, with time and the loving care of adults, also have inside themselves the potential for this same kind of transformation. The greatest joy of grief gardening, in fact, is witnessing this growth and new beauty in bereaved children who have learned to reconcile their grief.

Mourning and Gardening: A Historical Connection

"We find no fault with those who like to bustle through life in a whirl of steam: but for our own part we love to dally on the road, to pluck a flower here, and plant one there, and while away a little of our time in the pursuit of pleasure, among sanctified creations of nature."

You might never guess that this 1841 quote from the *New York Daily News* describes Green-Wood, a public cemetery in Brooklyn. Indeed, in the mid-1880s in America, cemeteries began to be seen as ideal places for combining burial grounds with public gardens.

Massachusetts' Mount Auburn Cemetery/Horticultural Garden, which opened in 1931, was America's first rural cemetery. The grounds at Mount Auburn were designed in the newly fashionable "pastoral" style—emphasizing the use of native materials in a natural-looking landscape.

Green-Wood Cemetery followed suit a decade later. It, too, gained acclaim as a beautiful place for quiet contemplation and relaxation—a "pastoral refuge." Newspaper accounts of the time tell of large numbers of people visiting the cemetery daily for "excursions of pleasure and health."

This style of cemetery remained in vogue until the late 1800s, when public parks (sans burial grounds) began springing up around the country. It's too bad cemeteries and parks parted company. What a healthier outlook on mourning our society might have if we zigzagged through graves on our way to a soccer game or picnicked among headstones.

What a healthier outlook on mourning our society might have if we zigzagged through graves on our way to a soccer game or picnicked among headstones.

Growth through Grief

Grief gardeners provide a nurturing environment in which bereaved children can not only heal, but grow. Like the columbine seedling in the parable, grieving kids can—after time and with the compassionate care of the adults in their lives—adapt to their new, often hostile surroundings and go on to not just survive, but thrive.

Growth in bereaved children is as exquisite as the rosebud's explosion into bloom.

Bereaved children can and do grow through grief. I have been privileged to witness this transformation many times. And when it happens, it is as jubilant, as exquisite, as awe-inspiringly *natural*, as the butterfly's crawl from the chrysalis or the tiny rosebud's explosion into bloom.

In fact, it is the potential for this type of growth that guides me in my work with bereaved children. It is, at bottom, why I am a grief counselor. If I did not believe that grieving kids can heal and eventually flourish, I could not do the work I do.

But what precisely do I mean by growth through grief? I mean many things, the most important of which I will explore here:

The marigold after the hailstorm

Growth means change

The marigold shredded by a fierce June hailstorm is never quite the same. It will likely grow new buds and leaves—and go on to flower in profusion later in the season. But the plant's growth habit may be different than its unharmed cousins'. It may be shorter or taller or jauntier. In any case, it will have been permanently affected by the hurt.

My experience has taught me that we as human beings are also forever changed by the death of someone we love. To talk about resolving someone's grief, which denotes a return to "the way things were" before the death, doesn't allow for the transformation I have both personally experienced and witnessed in others who have mourned. Mourning is not an end, but a beginning.

The marigold shredded by a fierce June hailstorm is permanently affected by the hurt.

By using the concept of growth, I can go beyond the traditional medical model of bereavement care that teaches that the helping goal is to return the bereaved person to a homeostatic state of being. A return to inner balance doesn't reflect how I, or the children and families who have taught me about their grief journeys, are forever changed by the experience of bereavement. In using the word growth, I acknowledge the changes that mourning brings about.

Drought and aphids in the garden...

Growth means encountering pain

The role of suffering continues to be misunderstood in this culture. We seem to lack any understanding of how hurting is part of the journey on the way to healing. The painful yet normal thoughts and feelings that result from loss are typically seen as unnecessary and inappropriate. The bereaved child who, because of his grief, has trouble with concentration is at risk for being mislabeled "attention deficit disordered." The bereaved child who tries to elicit caregiving through acting out is at risk for being mislabeled "undersocialized-aggressive behavior disordered."

Our culture lacks an understanding of how hurting is part of the healing journey.

"Buck-up therapy" messages in the face of pain are alive and well in North America. The messages we continue to give bereaved children include, "You have to be strong for your mother," "You need to take care of your little brothers and sisters," or "Your grandpa wouldn't want you to cry." And combined with these messages is often an unstated but strong belief that "You have a right not to hurt. So do whatever is necessary to avoid it." In short, we continue to encourage bereaved families to deny, avoid or numb themselves to the pain of grief.

As our culture moves away from embracing the pain of grief, our children are trying to get our attention. We must listen, learn and respond in helpful ways. When bereaved children internalize messages that encourage the repression, avoidance, denial or numbing of grief, they become powerless to help themselves heal. They may instead learn to act out their grief in destructive ways. Ultimately, not learning to mourn well results in not loving or living well.

But encountering the pain of loss all at once would overwhelm the child; therefore she must have a "safe place" for embracing pain in "doses." Sometimes bereaved children need to distract themselves from the pain of loss, while at other times they need a "safe harbor" to pull into and embrace the depth of the loss. (Obviously, this concept of valuing pain is contrary to the tenets of traditional medicine, which advocates the diminishing of pain.)

Grief gardeners understand that pain is a natural, necessary part of life, much as bad weather and troublesome insects are a part of gardening. And while we certainly do not revel in the havoc wreaked by drought and aphids, we come to accept their role in nature's plan.

Grief is like the rain... **Growth means a new inner balance with no end points**

While the bereaved child may do the work of mourning to recapture in part some sense of inner balance, it is a new inner balance. My hope is that the term growth reflects the fact that children do not reach some end point in their grief journeys.

No one ever totally completes the mourning process. People who think you get over grief are often continually striving to "pull it all together," while at the same time they feel that something is missing. And adults who think people should "get over grief" will project this message onto the children they help. The paradox is that the more we as adults try to "resolve" a child's grief, the more the child will resist us.

A participant in one of my recent training seminars wrote me the following note upon her return home:

The concept of reconciliation can free mourners from the need to judge themselves.

I know that in my own work of grief and mourning (dating back to childhood), I have always judged myself and secretly believed I was "wrong" for not being able to "resolve" my sense of loss and bring my various grief experiences to completion. . . I continued to judge myself, to perceive myself as deficient or "less than." The concept of reconciliation freed me from the need to judge myself. It also permitted me to experience a remarkable sense of healing in my sense of "self" and in my belief in my ability to "handle" events in appropriate ways.

Children and Grief: Then and Now

In early American history, death was much more familiar to children—indeed to all of us—than it is today. Because several generations of a family often lived in the same household, even very young children learned the naturalness of birth, aging, illness and death. They heard their siblings' first cries from their parents' bedroom-turned-delivery room. They saw some of those same siblings, cousins and friends die early deaths from then-deadly diseases like polio and smallpox. They watched, firsthand, their grandparents grow old, and they gathered to mourn with other family members when grandma or grandpa died. And because the wake and the funeral were typically held in the home, the children (who slept just upstairs from the dead body in the parlor) played intimate roles in these important rituals.

Children of yesteryear were also much more likely to live on or near farms, where everyday they witnessed the natural cycle of birth, life and death. They watched as calves slipped out of their lowing mothers and took their first wobbly steps. They giggled as chicks pecked their way from the shell. Later they grieved as those barnyard friends went to market.

For our grandparents and their grandparents, death was something that just happened. And because it happened all around, children came to know it gradually, in their own way and in their own time. Death was not a mystery, but an accepted fact of life. That was then.

This is now. Today's children have become the world's first "grief-free" generation. Modern medical discoveries have resulted in drastic reductions in infant and child mortality as well as prolonged life expectancy. As a result, the average American experiences a death in the family only once every twenty years. Plus, the much-discussed "mobility" of our society has scattered the extended family. And even when children and their grandparents remain in the same area, the increased use of hospitals and nursing homes—many of which have visitation policies excluding children—reduces the chances that children will witness the aging and dying of those they love and experience the normal grief that follows.

Our mourning-avoiding culture continues to make it hard for children to mourn in healthy ways, as well. Unfortunately we still believe that grief is shameful and should be "gotten over" as quickly as possible.

Still, grief gardeners around the globe are working to make this world a more compassionate place for bereaved children. I have seen our successes in hospices, in schools, in special grief centers all across North America. If you haven't already, I hope you'll join us. It is my fervent hope that the children of the next century will mourn in healthy, appropriate ways with the help of caring adults—who are but children themselves right now. In helping today's bereaved child, we leave a legacy of emotional well-being for future generations.

This woman's experiences nicely illustrates how there is no end point to the grief journey—for people of any age, including children.

Grief gardeners understand that grief is like the rain. During the spring of loss it may come down in torrents, but by summer it tends to taper off and by fall our gardens may be dry day after day. But the rain never stops altogether. At any moment a thunderstorm may drench us, sending us running for cover. Or a week-long drizzle may, now and then, dampen our spirits.

Grief gardeners and the morning glory...

Growth means exploring our assumptions about life

Grief gardeners are a philosophical bunch. Each time we meet a new bereaved child, we tend to rethink the whys of human existence and, ever so slightly, amend our life philosophy so that it incorporates what we learn from this child. We open our souls to grief's lessons, much as the morning glory eagerly spreads its petals to the dawn.

Grief gardeners tend to rethink the whys of human existence each time we meet a new child.

Growth in grief is a lifelong process of exploring how death challenges us to examine our assumptions about life. When someone loved dies, we naturally question the meaning and purpose of life. Religious and spiritual values also come under scrutiny. Bereaved children may ask questions like, "If God is good, why did he make Mommy go away?" or simply, "Why do people have to die?"

Finding answers to these questions is an ongoing process for the bereaved child. Indeed, children often don't form such philosophical stances until long into adulthood. Initially, we as caregivers can best help by not providing pat answers ("God knows best") but instead allowing the bereaved child to explore her unique, appropriately child-like thoughts and feelings about life and death.

Plants grow naturally...

Growth means actualizing our losses

The concept of "actualization" was first used in the counseling literature as it related to the growing process of an organism. The idea was then expanded on by such noted people as Abraham Maslow, Rollo May, Frederick Perl and Carl Rogers. As I will describe it in this book, the actualizing of loss emphasizes that experiencing and expressing one's potentials is essential to living.

The encounter of grief awakens us to the importance of utilizing our potentials—our capacities to mourn our losses openly and without shame, to be interpersonally effective in our relationships with others, and to continue to discover fulfillment in life, living and loving. Rather than "dragging us down," loss often helps us grow. Loss seems to free the potential within. Then it becomes up to us as human beings to embrace and creatively express this potential.

In the garden, plants naturally grow to their fullest potential. If we provide them with the proper light, water and nourishment, and tend to weeds and other pests, our horticultural charges will thrive. Children, because of their straightforward optimism, also possess this innate tendency to flourish in a nurturing environment.

Rather than dragging us down, loss often helps us grow.

Still, not every bereaved child or adult experiences actualizing growth. Unfortunately, some people do not seem to know how to grow or have conditions surrounding them that prevent such growth. They may remain emotionally, physically and spiritually crippled for years. For children, this is strongly influenced by what the helping adults in their lives do or don't do to help them with their grief.

In fact, in our mourning-avoiding culture, more and more people are invited *not* to grow in their grief journeys. Our challenge as grief gardeners, then, is to fight this cultural tendency and instead extend bereaved children this invitation: Teach me about your grief and let me help you discover how this experience can enrich your life. A large part of the "art" of caregiving to the bereaved child is to free them to grow and live until they die.

A not-so-secret hope of mine is that this growth model will eventually replace the medical model of bereavement care, which teaches that grief's goal is a movement from illness to normalcy. The growth model helps people understand the human need to mourn and discover how grief has forever changed them. It understands the normalcy of drowning in your grief before you tread water, and that only after treading water do you go on to swim. This growth model also frees helpers from thinking they have to "cure" a "sick patient." Instead, the helper is responsible for creating conditions that allow the bereaved child to do the work of mourning.

Now you've read the principles that guide my work with bereaved children. What are yours? I believe that every counselor must eventually develop his *own* theory about what helps bereaved children heal and grow. The effective counselor cannot and should not simply adopt the same ideas of another helper. Why not? Because she has not had the same life experiences and ways of perceiving and understanding the needs of bereaved children.

I challenge you to write out your personal philosophy of counseling bereaved children. You might start by asking yourself: What conditions do I believe help bereaved children heal?

_____

_____

_____

_____

_____

_____

_____

1. *It is my helping responsibility to create a safe environment for the bereaved child to do the work of mourning. (A bereaved child does not have an illness I need to cure.)* I *collaboratively* work with the bereaved child. I do not assess, diagnose or treat her. The traditional doctor-patient model of mental health care is grossly inadequate. Why? Because it creates expectations of external cures that involve the bereaved child and family only minimally in the helping process. To be effective with bereaved children, I must see them as *active participants* in the work of mourning. I'm a caregiver, not a curegiver!

2. *A bereaved child's perception of his reality is his reality.* A "here and now" understanding of that reality allows me to be with children where they are instead of trying to push them somewhere they are not. I will be a more effective helper if I remember to enter into a child's feelings without having a need to change those feelings.

3. *Each bereaved child I meet is a unique human being.* A child's intellectual, emotional and spiritual development is highly complex and is shaped by many inter-related forces.

4. *While I believe children are able to experience feelings similar to adults', their thought processes are quite different.* A child's understanding of death depends upon his developmental level. As children mature, they may need to mourn in a new way based on these normal developmental changes. Therefore, helpers to bereaved children must stay available to help them for years after the event of the death. Mourning is a process, not an event.

The relationship between counselor and child forms the foundation for the work they will do together.

5. *The relationship developed between counselor and child forms the foundation for all the work they will do together.* Empathy, warmth and acceptance are essential qualities for the counselor working with bereaved children.

6. *Play is the child's natural method of self-expression and communication.* To work effectively with bereaved children I must keep my own inner child alive and well.

7. *Bereaved children use behaviors (regressive behaviors, explosive emotions, etc.) to teach me about underlying needs (for security, trust, information,*

etc.). I have a responsibility to learn what those underlying needs are and help the child get those needs met.

8. *Children are not only thinking, feeling and doing beings, they are also spiritual beings.* Not everything we observe in children can be precisely measured or construed. As a helper to bereaved children, I must remain open to the mystery that children keep alive in their young worlds.

9. *While the major focus in working with bereaved children is on the present and future, I must encourage them to remember their past.* This historical approach aids in understanding the nature of the relationship with the person who died. It is in embracing memories of the person who died that the child discovers hope for a new tomorrow.

10. *While much of the bereaved child's behavior and view of the world is determined by personal history and influences beyond her control, the growth process requires a hope for healing.* I have a responsibility to help the bereaved child not simply reach "homeostasis" but to discover how the death changes her in many different ways. As a growth-oriented grief gardener, I work to help bereaved children not just survive, but learn how they are changed by this experience.

11. *I must work to create a social context that allows bereaved children to mourn openly and honestly.* It is through this social context that the child can work on the six reconciliation needs of mourning (see Chapter 5).

Grief gardeners must work to create a social context that allows bereaved children to mourn openly and honestly.

12. *Some children do the work of mourning well in the safety of a group experience.* The commonality of shared experience that comes from a support group provides a sense of belonging and helps normalize the grief process.

13. *While I am responsible for creating conditions for healing and growth in bereaved children, the ultimate responsibility for healing lies within them.* I must remind myself to be responsible to bereaved children, not to be totally responsible for them.

14. *Right-brain methods of healing and growth (such as intuition) should be used more with bereaved children than in the past and integrated with left-brain methods (intentional, problem-solving approach)* if counseling bereaved children is to become more growth-oriented than historical mental health models of care.

15. *This grief gardening approach to counseling bereaved children sees children as possessing a wealth of strength, assets and resources. As I companion the bereaved child, I help her discover and make use of these strengths as she begins the lifelong process of mourning losses.*

In the space below, you may want to write out your own beliefs about what helps bereaved children heal. Put your pen to paper and see what comes out.

_____

_____

_____

_____

_____

_____

_____

_____

_____

_____

_____

_____

_____

_____

_____

_____

_____

_____

_____

_____

_____

_____

Between every chapter in this book you'll find a common myth about children and grief. Sometimes these myths seem harmless, but I have found that when adults (and subsequently the children in their care) internalize them, they quickly become hurdles to healing. You might think of them as weeds in the grief garden. If they are allowed to grow unchecked, their aggressive habits will soon overtake the garden, choking out the impressionable seedlings. As a fellow grief gardener, I hope you'll join me in helping to dispel these myths.

Grief Myth

Grief and mourning are the same experience.

Grief is internal; mourning is external.

People tend to use the words "grief" and "mourning" interchangeably. However, there is an important distinction between the two—a distinction that becomes all the more critical for those who work with bereaved children.

Grief represents the thoughts and feelings that are experienced within children when someone they love dies. Grief is the internal meaning given to the experience of bereavement. Mourning, on the other hand, means taking the internal experience of grief and expressing it outside oneself. Another way to think of mourning is "grief gone public," or "sharing one's grief with others." Because bereaved children mourn more through their behaviors than they do through words, mourning for them is not expressed in the same ways it is for adults.

We often refer to children as "forgotten mourners." Why? Because though children grieve, we as a society often do not encourage them to mourn. We as grief gardeners, on the other hand, have the responsibility and the privilege to create conditions in which children can mourn.

Have you seen this myth carried out? When and how?

_____

_____

_____

_____

_____

_____

2

Mourning Styles: What Makes Each Child's Grief Unique

No two gardens are alike. Each gardener determines the size, shape and composition of his plots. Climate also has a fundamental influence. Here along northern Colorado's front range, gardens receive a scant 15 inches of precipitation each year. It's dry and it can be windy. The dense, clay soil is relatively poor. And the sun, which shines about 300 days a year, is much stronger at this elevation of 5,000 feet than in lower areas.

Such are the influences that make each garden unique.

In much the same way, each person's grief is uniquely her own. No one, adult or child, grieves exactly as anyone else does, nor does one person grieve the deaths of different people in her life in the same way. Grief is never the same twice.

The grief gardening counseling model I use when working with bereaved children assumes that they know best about their own personal grief experiences. As caring adults and professional caregivers, our job is to observe their behaviors and listen to what they have to say—and to learn from them. Our job is never to prescribe what a bereaved child should be thinking or feeling. Instead, it is our job to listen and watch as he teaches us what his grief journey is like.

The factors that influence a child's grief are important things to listen and watch for. At times children themselves teach us about these influences, while at other times we can glean this information from significant adults in the bereaved child's world. This chapter explores some of the main factors that influence the grief of children (though all influence the grief of adults, as well). Following the discussion of each influence is a list of questions that you might ask yourself as you companion a bereaved child as well as space to jot down thoughts that occur to you as you read about each influence.

"The garden had to be put in order, and each sister had a quarter of the little plot to do what she liked with...Meg had roses and heliotrope, myrtle and a little orange tree in it. Jo's bed was never alike two seasons, for she was always trying experiments...Beth had old-fashioned, fragrant flowers in her garden—sweet peas and mignonette, larkspur, pinks, pansies...Amy had a bower in hers... with honeysuckles and morning glories hanging their coloured horns and bells in graceful wreaths all over it; tall white lilies, delicate ferns and as many brilliant, picturesque plants as would consent to bloom there."

Louisa M. Alcott,
Little Women (1868)

Of course, you will want to keep in mind that children do not enter our offices announcing, "Today I would like to discuss some of the influences on my mourning." Nonetheless, it is my responsibility to patiently, compassionately and gently encourage them to teach me about these influences.

I find it helpful to remember the grief gardening concept as I learn about these many influences over time. I use my rake, hoe or sometimes even my shovel as we dig gently around the edges of the child's pain. The concept of gardening pulls me back from a more traditional model of assessment, in which I might be tempted to ask too many direct questions of the child.

As you consider how you will learn about these important influences with each new child in your care, you may find it helpful to keep the following in mind:

- *Too many informational questions tend to push the child away from teaching me.* If I am patient, the child will trust me enough to naturally begin teaching me about these influences. I'm always telling myself, "I must join the child where he is before I can in any way move with him."

- *Watch for doors that lead to understanding these influences.* As the bereaved child learns to trust me, she will teach me both verbally and nonverbally about these influences (e.g., through emotion in the face, body posture, repetitive themes in play, etc.) Responding to these cues at a feeling level as opposed to an intellectual level often will lead us to mutually deeper levels of understanding.

- *Avoid premature interpretations of why a child acts or feels a certain way.* This is a trap the medical model of assessment may invite you into. ("But I have to assess so I can treat!") Premature interpretation is often an unconscious way for the counselor to control, and therefore feel less anxious. Yet, the paradox is you must give up control to companion and be taught by the child.

Now, let's review some of the many influences on the bereaved child's grief:

Relationship with the person who died

Each child's response to a death depends largely upon the relationship he had with the person who died. For example, children will naturally grieve differently the deaths of a parent, a grandparent or a sibling.

Perhaps more important than the familial tie, however, is the closeness the child felt to the person who died. The death of a nearby but emotionally distant uncle may mean much less to a child than the death of a pen-pal cousin states away. Even within the same family, different siblings will respond differently to the death of a relative based on each child's attachment to the person who died.

Also keep in mind that children are sometimes very close to non-family members, such as a teacher or daycare provider. When I was young, I would stop by a neighbor lady's house after school. We had a ritual that became very dear to me: while she cleaned my glasses, I would tell her what happened at school that day. It didn't matter that we weren't related; she was still my good friend.

I was 11 when my neighbor died. Though I struggled with a multitude of thoughts and feelings about her death, no one thought to talk to me about it. Neither my parents nor other adults allowed me to teach them what her death meant to me. Because my neighbor and I weren't related, my grief became disenfranchised. I was a forgotten mourner.

A child's response to a death depends upon the relationship he had with the person who died.

Just as you shouldn't assume that kinship ties determine the magnitude of grief, you shouldn't assume that attachment doesn't exist even in ambivalent relationships. I see several children in my work who have had parents die of alcohol dependency-related causes. Consistently they teach me that while they loved the person who died, they hated the disease that killed that person. They hated the way the alcohol-dependent person's behavior was influenced by the chemical abuse. They also teach me that they don't so much mourn the loss of a good relationship as they mourn the loss of a relationship they wish they could have had.

Questions to ask yourself as grief gardener:

- What was the relationship between the bereaved child and the person who died?
- What was the level of attachment in the relationship?
- What functions did this relationship serve in the child's life?
- Have you observed any ambivalence in the child's feelings for this person?

Notes _____

_____

When a Parent Dies

The death of a parent is, without a doubt, one of the most painful experiences in a child's life. It leaves a permanent imprint on the child. Even when reconciliation unfolds, this profound loss will never be forgotten.

Perhaps the most important influence on the child's grief journey will be the response of the surviving parent or other important adults in the child's life. Obviously, the surviving parent will be less available to the child than she was prior to the death. We don't want to shame her for this but instead encourage her to seek support for her own work of mourning. As her mourning progresses she will become more available to the child. If, on the other hand, the surviving parent (or other significant caregiving adult) continues to be immobilized by her own grief, the bereaved child may suffer not only from the death, but from the feeling of being isolated emotionally from the surviving parent.

Many bereaved children wonder if they are still part of a family after the death of a parent.

The death of a parent also frequently results in numerous accompanying losses for the child, such as changed financial status, moves requiring changes in friends, schools, etc. At a time when the child's world has been turned upside down by the death of a parent, these additional losses may overwhelm the child and put him at risk for retreating from life.

Another important lesson many bereaved children have taught me after the death of a parent is that they wonder if they are still a family without a mom or dad. The child needs help in redefining herself as she searches to find meaning in going on without the dead parent. Maintaining faith in her future may be a real struggle. The child may in effect ask herself, "What meaning will my life have without this important person?"

Sometimes children act out their wish to be reunited with a dead parent through fantasizing their own deaths. Some "death play" is normal, but adult caregivers must be careful not to make heaven seem so attractive that the child would prefer to die and be with her dead parent.

Helping a child who has a parent die is the epitome of good preventive mental and spiritual health care. The potential long-term effects of not being companioned well at this time are many, including difficulties with future intimate relationships, vocational success and general joy of life.

When a Sibling Dies

The death of a sibling can be among the most traumatic events in a child's life. Why? Because not only has a family member died, but a family member for whom the child probably had very strong and ambivalent feelings. As those of us who have brothers and sisters know, sibling relationships are characterized by anger, jealousy and a fierce closeness and love—a highly complex mélange of emotion. This complexity colors the surviving child's grief experience.

I have had the privilege to counsel hundreds of bereaved siblings. Among many other special lessons, they have taught me they often feel:

• *Guilt.* For a number of reasons, bereaved siblings often feel guilty. Their power of "magical thinking"—believing that thoughts cause actions—might make them think they literally caused the death. "John died because I sometimes wished he would go away forever" is a common response among children who haven't been given the concrete details of the sibling's death and who haven't been assured that they were not at fault.

The death of a sibling can be among the most traumatic events in a child's life.

• *Relief.* A child may also feel relief as well as pain when a sibling dies. Responses such as "Now no one will take my things" or "I'm glad I have a room to myself" are natural and do not mean the child didn't love his sibling. It is important that you provide an atmosphere in which the child feels safe to express whatever he may be feeling.

• *Fear.* When a child's brother or sister dies, another young person has died. So, for a child, confronting this reality can mean confronting the possibility of one's own death. Be prepared to honestly but reassuringly answer questions such as "Will I die, too?" The death of a sibling can also make a bereaved child fear that one or all of her other family members will die, too, leaving her alone.

• *Confusion.* One eight-year-old girl I counseled after the death of her brother asked me, "Am I still a big sister?" This little girl was obviously struggling with the confusing task of redefining herself, both within the family unit and the world at large. The answer to her question, of course, is both yes and no, but ultimately it is a question the child must answer herself. Adults can help, however, by letting the child teach them what this confusion is like.

The nature of the death

The circumstances surrounding a death have a tremendous impact on a child's grief. As you help bereaved children do the work of mourning, be aware of the following four influences:

1) anticipated vs. sudden death
2) the age of the person who died
3) the child's sense of culpability for the death
4) the stigma surrounding the death

1) Anticipated vs. sudden death

Anticipating a death, such as one caused by prolonged illness, has the potential of assisting the child in adapting to the death. All too often, though, children are excluded from anticipatory grief by adults who want to protect them from pain.

Children who are allowed to participate in anticipatory grief may still be in great pain after the death.

If, for example, Uncle Jeff has been dying of cancer for two years but his nine-year-old nephew Eric has been "protect-ed" from this fact, Eric will be shocked when Uncle Jeff dies—and certainly less prepared than he would have been if the adults in his life had sooner talked to him about the impending death. To outsiders, then, what sometimes looks like an anticipated death is really a sudden death to an uninformed child.

Also keep in mind that children who are truly allowed to participate in anticipatory grief may still be in a lot of pain after the death. The fact that they were somewhat "pre-pared" for the death shouldn't minimize their need to mourn.

Sudden death, on the other hand, does not allow the child to emotionally prepare for grief's impact. The more sudden the death, the more likely the child is to mourn in doses and to push away some of the pain at first. Following an unex-pected death, bereaved children may even respond with an apparent lack of feel-ings. Don't be surprised, for example, if the little girl whose mother just died responds to the news by going outside to play on the swingset. She is protecting herself from this painful reality in the only way she knows how. You may see even less outward mourning in the child who experiences a sudden death than in the child who experiences an anticipated death.

Sudden, Traumatic Death and the Bereaved Child

Unfortunately, today's children are exposed to violent deaths in many forms. They have been taught, through the media and through the realities of their own day-to-day lives, that people die senselessly. That people often kill other people. That people kill themselves. That people take drugs or alcohol and then drive, often killing others.

But when a child is personally impacted by sudden or accidental death, homicide or suicide, she is not often taught about her unique grief and its healthy expression. You can help by understanding the special needs of survivors of sudden and traumatic death.

• *Sudden, traumatic deaths often leave survivors feeling numb and shocked for weeks and even months.* Whether the death was natural (as in a heart attack) or accidental (as in a car crash), the bereaved child will probably have a hard time acknowledging the reality of the death. She will probably need extra support in the first weeks and months following the death.

• *Death by homicide also creates overwhelming grief for survivors.* Murder results in survivors grieving not only the death, but how the person died. A life has been cut short through an act of cruelty. The disregard for human life adds overwhelming feelings of turmoil, distrust, injustice and helplessness to the child's normal sense of loss and sorrow.

Survivors of murder victims enter into a world that is not understood by most people. A sad reality is that members of a community where a tragic murder has occurred sometimes blame the victim or survivors. Out of a need to protect themselves from their own personal feelings of vulnerability, some people reason that what has happened has to be somebody's fault. This need to "place blame" is projected in an effort to fight off any thoughts that such a tragedy would ever happen to them.

• *Death by suicide is stigmatized in our society.* In general we believe that suicide is wrong and talking about it makes us uncomfortable. If a child's father dies of a heart attack or is killed in a random shooting, he may receive lots of loving support from those around him. But if his father completes suicide, the child may be left to grieve in isolation.

A child's grief following a sudden, traumatic death is always complex. Don't be surprised by the intensity of her feelings. Accept that she may be struggling with a multitude of emotions more intense then those experienced after other types of death. Confusion, disorganization, fear, vulnerability, guilt or anger are just a few of the emotions survivors may feel.

For child survivors of sudden or violent death, the world no longer feels as safe as it once did.

A child survivor of sudden or violent death may also feel intense anger. His sense of injustice about the nature of the death turns the normal anger of grief into rage. Remember—anger is not right or wrong, good or bad, appropriate or not appropriate. Do not try to diminish the anger, for it is in expressing rage that it begins to lose some of its power. Ultimately, healthy grief requires that these explosive emotions be expressed, not repressed.

Feelings of anxiety, panic, and fear are also normal. The child may feel threatened and unprotected. The world no longer feels as safe as it once did. Fear of what the future holds, fear that more sudden deaths might occur, an increased awareness of one's own mortality, feelings of vulnerability about being able to survive without the person, an inability to concentrate and emotional and physical fatigue all serve to heighten anxiety, panic and fear.

The unanswerable question, "But, why?" naturally comes up for survivors of a traumatic, violent death. The bereaved child is searching to understand how something like this could happen. This doesn't mean you must answer the "why?" question. Bereaved children need a safe place to think, talk and play out their feelings about this question more than they need a pat answer.

2) Age of the person who died

The age of the person who died can impact the child's psychological and spiritual integration of the death. The natural order of the world says that older people die first: grandparents, then parents, then their children (when they have become grandparents themselves). Like many of us, children often believe that only old people die, or that only old people *should* die. The older a person is, the more acceptable the death.

For a child, the death of a parent seems "out of order." Not only does the child lose a primary caregiver, but he also loses the chance to spend time with the parent later in life and to enjoy the prospect of having grandparents around for his own children. Moreover, the child whose parent has died can feel a sense of awkwardness or anger because most other children his age still have parents. This grief-borne form of peer pressure only underscores the child's sense that his parent died "too young." (For more on the death of a parent, see p. 21.)

Of course, if a parent is too young to die, another child is much too young to die. What's more, when a child's sibling or friend dies, another young person has died; confronting this reality can mean confronting the possibility of one's own death—a very scary prospect for children.

3) The child's sense of culpability for the death

Due to the developmental concept of "magical thinking," in which children sometimes believe that thoughts cause action, the bereaved child might feel a sense of responsibility for a death. What child, for example, hasn't wished that her sibling would just go away and leave her alone? If this sibling dies, then, the bereaved child may well feel guilty. Giving children accurate information about why and how a death occurred can help ease their consciences and allow them to move forward in their grief journeys.

On the other hand, in our increasingly violent society, children sometimes actually are responsible for the death of someone else, intentionally or not. Almost every day in our metropolitan newspapers we read about the accidental shooting death of a child at the hands of another child, for example. In these cases, the bereaved child will most certainly feel overwhelming guilt. I recommend that these children receive professional guidance in exploring their culpability and how it will change their lives.

4) The potential stigma surrounding the death

Sometimes there is a stigma surrounding the nature of the death. The greater the stigma, generally the less the support available to the child and family as they mourn. Examples of stigmatized deaths include those from AIDS, suicide, homicide and drug overdose. My colleague Ken Doka has described losses that cannot be openly acknowledged, socially sanctioned or publicly mourned as "disenfranchised grief" experiences. The potential of stigma should always be kept in mind as you companion bereaved children and their families.

When a Grandparent Dies

When a grandparent dies, the grandchildren may or may not actively mourn.

Some children are extremely close to their grandparents; they may see them frequently and even overnight with them. In some cases grandparents even assume a primary parenting role for their grandchildren. When a grandparent to whom a child is close dies, the child can be profoundly affected. On the other hand, in our highly mobile culture some grandchildren rarely, if ever, see their grandparents. Naturally, these children may not express a need to mourn when a long-distance grandparent dies.

Still, don't assume that distance in child-grandparent relationships determines the depth of feelings. A child who lives down the street from his grandmother may feel less close to her than a child whose far-away grandmother writes, calls or visits often.

We also know that many children feel disenfranchised after the death of a grandparent if the death is not openly acknowledged, publicly mourned or socially supported. You may have heard people say, "Well, it was only his grandparent. The child has to have known that the grandparent would die someday." Obviously, these kinds of comments don't allow for the "teach me" philosophy emphasized throughout this book.

In families where grandparents were strong matriarchs or patriarchs, there is often a ripple-effect across generations as the family unit struggles to redefine itself. Perhaps the family doesn't get together as often as it did before grandma's death. Now the children may not see their cousins and aunts and uncles as often as they did before.

The personality of the grandparent (see p. 32) also influences children's responses. Some older adults are naturals with children and the kids feel very close to them. Other older adults may have a difficult time relating to young children. Therefore, they may be around the children but still not create any kind of emotional bond. Think about your own grandparents. Did you find yourself relating differently and feeling closer to one grandparent over another?

As always, the key in companioning children through grief after the death of a grandparent is to let the children teach you about what the death means to them. Then, support them non-judgmentally in their need or lack of need to mourn the death.

Death of my Grandpa

My Grandpa was a kind and loving person. I was six when my Grandpa died and I only remember a few things about him. He was very proud of me and took me places. He always took me across the street and bought me candy.

The day my Grandpa died we got a phone call and they said my Grandpa was very sick and in the hospital. My family drove to Jasper and before my mom got to the hospital my Grandpa was already dead. Once my whole family found out we all started crying.

My Grandpa knew me at times when he couldn't remember other people. The last words he said to me were, "Goodnight, Sweetheart." I know my Grandpa is happy now because he is in heaven.

Essay written by a sixth grader about the first death she ever mourned. Thanks to teacher Dave Harris, Newburgh, Indiana, for this submission.

Questions to ask yourself as grief gardener:

- Was the death anticipated or unexpected?
- If the death was anticipated, was the child given information about the nature of the illness at his level of understanding?
- How old was the person who died?
- How has the age influenced the child's perception of the timeliness of the death?
- Does the child feel guilty about the death?
- Was the child in any way actually responsible for the death?
- Is there any stigma surrounding the nature of the death?
- What helping resources are available in my community that match up well with the nature of the death experience?

Notes _____

_____

_____

_____

_____

_____

The child's unique personality

Each child has a unique personality that affects the ways in which he mourns. Some kids are talkative while others are quiet. Some are boisterous while others are gentle. These personality styles, which existed long before the death, will influence the child's mourning style.

For example, the naturally retiring child may be accustomed to working through stresses on her own. For her, temporarily withdrawing from others may help her do her work of mourning. Another child may tend to wear his feelings on his sleeve. This child may let everyone know that he is in pain after someone he loves dies.

As kids move toward adolescence, their personalities may seem to change somewhat and it may be harder to distinguish between behaviors brought about by

AIDS Deaths and the Bereaved Child

When someone a child loves dies of AIDS (acquired immune deficiency syndrome), the social stigma surrounding the death may make the child unsure about how or where or even *if* she should express her grief. The child's family members may not openly acknowledge the death. The child's peers may tease her or avoid her altogether for fear they, too, will "catch" the disease.

If you are in a position to help such a child, help him make sense of his grief. Help him understand:

- *what AIDS is.* Some child AIDS survivors have not been adequately or appropriately educated about the disease itself. They may harbor painful fears and misconceptions about who contracts the disease and how.

- *that his feelings about the death are normal.* He might feel sad, relieved (particularly if the person with AIDS was ill for a long time), angry, numb or many other emotions.

- *that he is not wrong or bad for loving someone with AIDS.* Many children are torn between their love for the dead person and society's hate and fear of people with AIDS.

- *that he needs to express his grief if he is to heal.* This may be hard for him if he has been taught that AIDS is shameful and should be kept a secret. Help him find people with whom and places in which he can mourn safely.

You can help a child AIDS survivor understand that his feelings about the death are normal.

developmental stresses and behaviors associated with grief. My experience suggests that it doesn't really matter which is which. All behaviors are multiply-determined anyway, and trying to separate their causes is beside the point.

There is no right way to mourn.

The important thing to note here is that there is no right way to mourn. All mourning styles are OK, provided that the child hasn't changed dramatically due to the death. If, for instance, a formerly gregarious child withdraws completely from friends and family, this is a sign that she needs extra bereavement help. The opposite is also true. If a formerly withdrawn child starts getting in fights, that's a symptom of an underlying grief need that's not being met. In adolescents, look for red flag behaviors such as suicidal actions, sexual acting out and eating disorders.

Questions to ask yourself as grief gardener:

- What was the child's personality like prior to the death?
- How has the child responded to previous crises in his life?
- Does the child seem to be a dramatically different person than she was prior to the death and if so, is this a cry for help?

Notes _____

_____

_____

_____

_____

Caring for the Mentally Retarded Bereaved Child

by Jeffrey Kauffman, M.A., M.S.S., L.S.W.

Mentally retarded children have the same feelings as non-mentally retarded children, and have the same needs for support, understanding and caring to affirm and facilitate the expression of their grief.

The differences in the thought and communication patterns of mentally retarded people may lead us to underestimate their sensitivity, emotional intelligence and implicit understanding of human interaction. My impression is that regardless of the cognitive deficits of the mentally retarded, they are no less attuned to basic human emotion in themselves and in interactions with others. In fact, they are often quite perceptive of the "emotional language" of normal human discourse.

Still, mentally retarded bereaved children do have special needs and typical mourning patterns that caregivers should be aware of:

- *Like all children, mentally retarded kids form very strong attachments to their primary caregivers and other significant people in their lives.* But for mentally retarded children, feelings of security, identity and self-worth are more deeply dependent on the caring presence of caregivers. When the caregiver relationship is broken—due to death or other reasons—the mentally retarded child's feelings of helplessness and loss of self are typically very deep and enduring.

- *Mentally retarded children frequently express their grief through acting-out behaviors.* It is important that these behaviors be recognized as expressions of grief. If the child runs around screaming, she may be searching for the dead person, she may be literally trying to "run away" from the loss or she may be angry and frustrated over being abandoned. Don't seek to modify the behaviors; instead try to understand the feelings that underlie them.

- *Mentally retarded people have strong, obsessive characteristics to their processing of thoughts and feelings.* As they grieve, troubling thoughts and affective disturbances tend to be especially persistent. We sometimes see a repetition of the same thought or feeling over and over again, suggesting the child is having great difficulty in acknowledging and integrating the death.

Mentally retarded bereaved children, like all bereaved children, deserve our utmost compassion and support. Watch, listen and try to understand as they teach you what grief is like for them.

Jeffrey Kauffman is writing a book about the grief of mentally retarded people. If you would like to talk to him about this topic, call him at 610/789-7707.

Unique characteristics of the person who died

Just as the personality of the bereaved child is reflected in her expression of grief, so too are the unique characteristics of the person who died. While some people have personalities that allow children to be close to them, others can make it difficult for children to connect.

A personal example might help illustrate here. When I was growing up, I had very different relationships with—and feelings for—my two grandmothers. One grandma was nurturing and supportive; in her eyes I could do no wrong. When she died and her loving personality was gone, I felt a deep sense of loss and sadness. My other grandmother was hypercritical and a strict disciplinarian. Often she made me feel ashamed. When she died, I had more mixed feelings. I still missed her and grieved her death, but I did not miss her personality and the way she sometimes made me feel.

Another aspect of personality is the role the person who died played within the family system. If, for example, the family patriarch dies—perhaps the grandfather—the child may feel a compounded sense of loss when the family no longer gathers at grandpa's house. Not only has the child lost a grandfather, but perhaps contact with her aunts, uncles and cousins, as well.

Questions to ask yourself as grief gardener:

- What was the person who died like?
- What role did he or she play within the family?
- What does the bereaved child miss most or least about the person who died?

Notes _____

_____

_____

_____

_____

_____

_____

The child's age

Over the past 50 years, a number of researchers have studied the ways in which chronological age affects the child's response to loss. In general, these studies found that children five and under tend not to fully understand death, particularly death's finality. For children older than five, the studies had divergent findings. One found that children six and older may understand that death is final, while another found that only children nine and older have realistic perceptions of death.

Having worked with thousands of bereaved children, I believe that we as grief gardeners must let each child teach us about his understanding of death. Yes, as they get older, children appear to proceed from little or no understanding of death to, finally, a realistic recognition of the concept. But I could line up ten six-year-olds and we would find that each one attaches a very different meaning to the word "death."

That difference in meaning is a product of each child's life experiences to date. Those who at a young age have already had several people they love die are more likely to fully understand death, for example. On the other hand, children who have never experienced the death of someone loved or, just as important, haven't been lovingly taught by adults about death, are more likely to harbor inaccurate notions of the concept. Moreover, other factors such as self-concept and intelligence also have an important role in the individual child's understanding of death.

Questions to ask yourself as grief gardener:

- What does death mean to this child?
- How have other factors influenced his understanding of death?
- How can I allow this child to teach me about his understanding of death?

Notes _____

_____

_____

_____

_____

Grief Gardening: Ages and Stages

I am not a believer in the theory that bereaved children of a certain age grieve in a certain way. Each child's responses—cognitive, emotional, spiritual and physical—to the death of someone loved are different.

Still, it is true that a child's developmental level affects her mourning. The chart that follows tries to capture some of the most common grief responses of children in different age categories. But remember—an individual child should not be stuffed into a textbook category. As grief gardeners, we must let each bereaved child teach us what grief is like for him.

	Typical grief responses	Grief gardening tips
Infants and toddlers (Baby - age two) *Loss may be understood as an* absence, *particularly of a primary caregiver.*	"I'm upset" behaviors (e.g. crying, more, thumb sucking, biting.)	Offer physical comfort.
	Changes in normal patterns. May sleep more or less, eat more or less, be fussier.	Accept the changes while still trying to adhere to some kind of routine. Infants and toddlers are typically comforted by the structure of routines.
Preschoolers (Ages 3-6) *Death may be thought of as temporary and/or reversible.*	May not understand their new, scary feelings and may not be able to verbalize what is happening inside them.	Provide them with terms for some of their feelings: grief, sadness, numb.
	May ask questions about the death over and over again. During play may reenact the death .	Answer concretely and lovingly. Be honest. Don't tell half-truths. Death play is fine and helps children integrate the reality of the death. You may want to join in and offer your guidance.
	May regress: cling to parents, suck thumb, lose potty training, baby talk, etc.	Short-term regressive behaviors are normal. Offer your presence and support.

	Typical grief responses	Grief gardening tips
Grade schoolers (Ages 6-11) *A clearer understanding of death develops. Older kids in this age group may have an "adult" understanding of what death is.*	Children in this age group continue to express their grief primarily through play.	Use "older kid" play therapy techniques, especially for 10-12-year-olds.
	May "hang back" socially and scholastically.	Children need permission to concentrate on mourning before they can be expected to forge ahead with the rest of their lives. Give them time.
	May act out because they don't know how else to handle their grief feelings.	Offer constructive "venting" alternatives. Support groups can be very helpful.
Adolescents (Ages 12 and up) *Understand death cognitively but are only beginning to grapple with it spiritually.*	May protest the loss by acting out and/or withdrawing.	Acting-out behaviors should be tolerated if the teen or others is not being harmed. Withdrawal is normal in the short-term. (Long-term withdrawal is a sign the teen needs extra help.)
	May feel life has been unfair to them, act angry.	A teen's normal egocentrism can cause him to focus exclusively on the effect the death has had on him and his future. After he has had time to explore this issue, encourage him to consider the death's impact on the larger social group: family, friends, etc.
	May act out a search for meaning. May test his own mortality.	Teens begin to really explore the "why" questions about life and death. Encourage this search for meaning unless it may harm the teen or others.

Helping Infants and Toddlers When Someone They Love Dies

Many adults think that because very young children are not completely aware of what is going on around them, they are not impacted by death. We must dispel this myth. I say it simply: Any child old enough to love is old enough to mourn.

True, infants and toddlers are not developmentally mature enough to fully understand the concept of death. In fact, many children do not truly understand the inevitability and permanence of death until adolescence. But understanding death and being affected by it are two very different things. When a primary caregiver dies, even tiny babies notice and react to the loss. They might not know exactly what happened and why, but they do know that someone important is now missing from their small worlds.

This section contains practical tips for primary caregivers to bereaved infants and toddlers. If you are counseling a parent or other caregiver to a bereaved infant or toddler, you may want to photocopy this section for their use.

The special needs of bereaved infants

As anyone who has been around infants knows, babies quickly bond with their mothers or other primary caregivers. In fact, studies have shown that babies just hours old recognize and respond to their mothers' voices. Many psychologists even believe that babies think they and their mothers are one and the same person for a number of months.

This powerful and exclusive attachment to mommy and daddy continues through most of the first year of life. When a parent dies, then, there is no question the baby notices that something is missing. She will likely protest her loss by crying more than usual, sleeping more or less than she did before or changing her eating patterns.

- *Offer comfort.* When they are upset, most infants are soothed by physical contact. Pick up the bereaved infant when he cries. Wear him in a front pack; he will be calmed by your heartbeat and motion. Give him a gentle baby massage. Talk to him and smile at him as much as possible. And do not worry about spoiling him. The more you hold him, rock him and sing to him, the more readily he will realize that though things have changed, someone will always be there to take care of him.

- *Take care of basic needs.* Besides lots of love, an infant needs to be fed, sheltered, diapered and bathed. Try to maintain the bereaved baby's former schedule. But don't be surprised if she sleeps or eats more or less than usual. Such changes are her way of showing her grief. If she starts waking up several times a night, soothe her back to sleep.

Any child old enough to love is old enough to mourn.

The most important thing you can do is to meet her needs—whatever they seem to be—quickly and lovingly in the weeks and months to come.

The special needs of bereaved toddlers

Like infants, bereaved toddlers mostly need our love and attention. They also need us to help them understand that though it is painful, grief is the price we pay for the priceless chance to love others. They need us to teach them that death is a normal and natural part of life.

• *Offer comfort and care.* The bereaved toddler needs one-on-one care 24 hours a day. Make sure someone she loves and trusts is always there to feed her, clothe her, diaper her and play with her. Unless she is already comfortable with a certain provider, now is not the time to put her in daycare.

Expect regressive behaviors from bereaved toddlers. Those who slept well before may now wake up during the night. Independent children may now be afraid to leave their parents' side. Formerly potty-trained kids may need diapers again. All of these behaviors are normal grief responses. They are the toddler's way of saying, "I'm upset by this death and I need to be taken care of right now."

• *Model your own grief.* Toddlers learn by imitation. If you grieve in healthy ways, toddlers will learn to do the same. Don't hide your feelings when you're around children. Instead, share them. Cry if you want to. Be angry if you want to. Let the toddler know that these painful feelings are not directed at him and are not his fault, however.

Sometimes you may feel so overwhelmed by your own grief that you can't make yourself emotionally available to the bereaved toddler. You needn't feel guilty about this; it's OK to need some "alone time" to mourn. In fact, the more fully you allow yourself to do your own work of mourning, the sooner you'll be available to help the child. In the meantime, make sure other caring adults are around to nurture the bereaved toddler.

• *Use simple, concrete language.* When someone a toddler loves dies, he will know that person is missing. He may ask for Mommy or Uncle Ted one hundred times a day. I recommend using the word "dead" in response to his queries. Say, "Mommy is dead, honey. She can never come back." Though he won't yet know what "dead" means, he will begin to differentiate it from "bye-bye" or "gone" or "sleeping"—terms that only confuse the issue.

• *Keep change to a minimum.* All toddlers need structure, but bereaved toddlers, especially, need their daily routines. Keeping mealtimes, bedtime and bathtime the same lets them know that their life continues and that they will always be cared for. And try not to implement other changes right away. Now is not the time to go from a crib to a bed, to potty train or to wean from a bottle.

Social expectations based on the child's gender

This influence on grief stems from the different ways in which boys and girls are taught to express their feelings. Generally, boys are encouraged to be strong and exercise restraint in expressing painful feelings. Because of this, boys often have more difficulty in allowing themselves to feel helpless and express their grief.

Girls, too, may encounter socially-engendered difficulties in expressing their grief. While they may have been taught to show sadness, they are often also taught that for them, anger is bad — especially physical expression of that anger. So, sometimes in little girls, appropriate grief-borne anger gets repressed.

Girls are often taught that for them, anger is bad.

We as caregivers must stay sensitive to this gender conditioning. Unfortunately, we can't control how children have already been conditioned, but we can help them express those feelings they sometimes feel ashamed to have. For example, you might encourage both boys and girls to physically release pent-up emotions by participating in sports.

Questions to ask yourself as grief gardener:

- Based on his or her gender, how has this child been socially influenced to respond to loss?
- How can you help the child release emotions he or she may be repressing due to gender conditioning?
- How do the child's family role models influence his or her concept of gender?

Notes _____

_____

_____

_____

_____

Availability of support systems

Yet another factor influencing a child's grief is the support system surrounding him. Some unfortunate children literally do not have a support system. Most often these are children from homes in which the adults haven't been emotionally available to them.

When bereaved children do have familial support systems, this does not automatically mean family members help them with the work of mourning. Some families have a closed family system that doesn't allow members to talk openly about death. In these homes, the (stated or unstated) rules about death are: we take down photos of the dead person, we don't allow children to go to funerals, we don't talk about the person who died, etc. It's as if there's an elephant in the living room but no one's acknowledging it.

Some bereaved children are lucky enough to be surrounded by loving adults who support them in their grief.

At the other end of the spectrum are lucky children who are surrounded by loving adults who encourage them to talk openly about their grief. These bereaved children are invited to participate in the funeral or other ritual, are encouraged to remember the person who died and are able to ask questions about death without feeling shame or embarrassment. (For more on the family's influence on the bereaved child's mourning, see Chapter 7.)

The availability of support systems to the bereaved child is only half the story here. The child's capacity to make use of that support is the other half. In my experience, younger children are generally more responsive to support. Helping adults will generally find their efforts well-received if they make themselves available to young children.

As children get older though, especially when they enter adolescence, they sometimes find it hard to accept help. Their primary developmental task—separating from their parents and other adult caregivers—runs contrary to seeking help from these same people.

Finally, children tend to imitate what goes on around them. If the adults in their lives model healthy support-seeking behaviors, the bereaved child will most likely do the same. On the other hand, if the bereaved child's parents tend not to seek out or accept help from others in times of need, the child won't either.

Questions to ask yourself as grief gardener:

- Does the child have a positive support system available?
- Does this support system allow and encourage her to mourn?
- Is the child able to accept the support of others?
- Does the child have adults around him who model healthy help-seeking?

Notes _____

_____

_____

_____

_____

Cultural / ethnic background

The grieving child's response to death is impacted by her cultural and ethnic backgrounds. Different cultures are known for the various ways they express or repress their grief. As caregivers we must remember to be careful about defining "normal" responses of both bereaved children and adults. Normal mourning (means of expression, length considerations, etc.) varies widely from culture to culture.

Keening, for example, is a process of lamenting for the dead. It is usually expressed in a very loud, wailing voice or sometimes in a wordless crying out. Some cultures encourage and legitimize keening while others don't understand it and sometimes perceive it as "pathological." Ireland, Crete, China and Mexico are among those countries where you are more likely to see the bereaved keening.

The grieving child's response to death is impacted by her ethnic background.

Cultures that encourage outward expressions of grief such as keening are more likely to instill healthy mourning practices in the bereaved child. Mourning-avoiding cultures, on the other hand, like those prevalent in American Anglo society today, often make a child's grief journey more difficult. As we know, the repression of grief can have negative repercussions long into the bereaved child's adulthood. We can find another example in

Latino cultures. For Latin Americans, it is important to "take care of your own"—which means the bereaved child may not be able to seek outside help. Emotional outlets such as bereavement support groups may not be seen as "necessary."

Questions to ask yourself as grief gardener:

- What is this child's cultural/ethnic background?
- What do I need to know to better understand his background?
- How does that background influence the child's expression/repression of grief?

Notes _____

_____

_____

_____

_____

Staying Sensitive to the Bereaved Child's Culture and Religion

Once upon a time, there lived a Chinese servant whose uncle had recently died. The servant asked his American employer for the day off to attend the funeral. "My family will leave bowls of rice at my uncle's graveside so that he will have plenty to eat where he has gone," the servant explained.

"Yes, you may go to the funeral," his employer begrudgingly replied. Then, giving voice to his disgruntlement at the work-week's interruption added, "When exactly do you expect your uncle to eat the rice?"

The servant turned to hide the smile creeping across his face. "About the same time your aunt who died last week will smell the flowers you left on her grave."

Throughout history, every culture has had its own way of mourning. Unlike today, however, different cultures were once isolated from one another. Geographic boundaries were more distinct and modern technology hadn't yet made the world the global community it has now become. Now bereavement care professionals, especially those in the diversely populated cities of the U.S. and Canada, must stay sensitive to multiculturalism and its impact on mourning practices.

Throughout history, every culture has had its own way of mourning.

Because the beliefs, values and practices surrounding death are so diverse, we as bereavement caregivers must be careful about what we say is "normal" as we help bereaved people from different cultures do their work of mourning. We often have our own personal notions of what constitutes "healthy mourning." We each have our own set of social norms for who mourns, how they should mourn as well as how long they should mourn. We must be careful not to assume that we know what is best or most appropriate for others in the work of mourning.

Let's explore some key questions you can ask yourself when you need to better understand a particular culture's rituals and traditions surrounding death:

Are there any specific things families do when someone is dying? For example, is it traditional for the family to care for the person who is dying in their own home or do they entrust that care to a hospital, in-patient hospice or nursing home?

What specific rituals are used to recognize that someone has died? (And what are the reasons for these rituals?)

What traditions surround disposal of the body? Cremation is obligatory in some cultures and forbidden in others, for instance.

What belief systems surround what happens after death? For example, will survivors be reunited with the deceased when the survivors die?

What cultural norms surround who has the right to mourn? Is this distinction based on kinship ties or on broader perceptions of who might grieve when someone dies?

How long is it considered appropriate to mourn? (And is it "appropriate" to discuss one's response to death?)

Are there any specific rituals tied to acknowledging "milestones" in the healing process?

Are mourning clothes worn, and if so, for how long after the death?

Are social stigmas associated with some types of deaths? (e.g., suicide, murder, death of a child)

Is death considered to be the most important life cycle transition? (If so, how does it influence the ritual "send off"?)

Some of the Burial Rites and Beliefs of Different Faiths

The doctrine of Baha'i (a predominantly middle eastern religion) stipulates that the deceased's body may not be transported more than one hour's journey from the place of death to the place of interment.

Judaism dictates that the children of the deceased recite prayers three times a day for eleven months.

Traditional Buddhist funeral rites require that a bowl of uncooked rice be placed by the family altar, with the deceased's chopsticks stuck upright in the bowl.

Some sects of the Eastern Orthodox church, particularly those in the Mediterranean, bury their dead for a few years and then disinter the bones, which are subsequently placed in special receptacles called ossuaries.

Seventh-day Adventists believe that after death comes a period of unconscious sleep in the grave. This sleep culminates in a glorious resurrection upon Christ's return and the simultaneous end of the world.

For Indian Hindus, the body is usually cremated on an open bier on the banks of a river.

All those present at a Muslim funeral participate in filling the grave by throwing in three handsful of earth while reciting a short prayer from the Koran.

Religious / spiritual influences

Religious and spiritual backgrounds, which are of course very closely tied to cultural and ethnic backgrounds, also influence the child's grief response. I truly believe that to be a growth-oriented grief gardener to bereaved children, I must be sensitive not only to the psychological dimensions of the child's world, but to the religious and spiritual dimensions as well. Children by their very nature are spiritual beings! If we ignore this, we don't allow them to teach us about this vital part of themselves.

Many of us trained in traditional mental health settings were literally taught to ignore religious and spiritual issues in the lives of those we work with. Some of us may have even been taught that "religious or spiritual problems" are merely symptoms of deeper, psychological problems. But in my growing experience, I find there to be a spiritual dimension to every life crisis, particularly death. If we allow it, death penetrates the defensive shell of (assumed) invulnerability that most North Americans wear. Fortunately, most children have not yet donned this defensive armor and openly enter into teaching us adults about religious and spiritual experiences.

We must ask ourselves what belief systems undergird and give meaning to the life of this child and family. Even though these beliefs may be different than my own, how can I understand and acknowledge them in the life of this child? If the child tells me (as many have) that her mom or dad, grandma or grandpa, brother or sister is "watching over her," how do I understand this?

Do the belief systems I learn about from the child and family help or hinder the healing process? In other words, is their religion or spirituality crippling or creative?

In some belief systems, for example, mourning implies that you are not a true believer. After all, their doctrines reason, the dead person has gone to Heaven— the most wonderful place imaginable. Why be sad at this miraculous passage? Because, the bereaved child may say to himself, I am sad. I do feel bad/angry/guilty, etc. Religious systems that deny a child the healthy expression of these normal grief responses only cause the child to feel confused and emotionally and spiritually stifled.

On the other hand, many families recognize that having faith and mourning are not mutually exclusive. They allow and encourage children to be open to the mysteries of both life and death. **A personal goal for me as a grief gardener is to nurture in people of all ages a high level of spiritual wellness.** (This often is much easier accomplished with children than adults.) Growth-oriented grief gardening with children demands that we as caregivers be holistic, seeking to enable healing and growth in all dimensions—psychological as well as spiritual and religious.

I should note that I sometimes must gently confront religious or spiritual messages that I believe might complicate the child's healing journey (e.g., "We have faith, so we don't need to be sad.") This kind of message is growth-blocking, not growth-enhancing. With gentle respect and timely pacing, I attempt to help reframe for these families the need to mourn despite having faith. It doesn't always work, but I feel an ethical and spiritual obligation to try.

Questions to ask yourself as grief gardener:

- What is this child's religious or spiritual background?
- What do I need to know to better understand her background?
- Are there any messages that suggest open mourning is inconsistent with having faith?
- Does this child attend any organized religion of some kind? If so, are they supportive of the child's need to mourn?
- What is the family's faith history? How does it influence this bereavement process?
- What did my training as a caregiver teach me about these important parts of my being?
- How does my own religion or spirituality influence my caregiving?

Notes _____

_____

_____

_____

_____

The Faith and Spirituality of Bereaved Children

"Faith is a journey, not a destination." Joan Burney

To understand the bereaved child and the family from which the child comes, we as grief gardeners must strive to learn about the influence faith and spirituality have in their lives. In fact, nurturing a bereaved child's natural spirituality and questions about faith and God is every bit as vital as other aspects of caring for her. Along with physical, material, social and emotional needs, children have spiritual needs. They need to see themselves as good and capable of giving and receiving love. They need spiritual security and a sense of belonging in the world.

The child learns about faith in part from the adult models in his life. As I grief garden with a bereaved child, I ask myself: What is the child's parents' (or guardians') image of God? Habits of prayer? How do they struggle with difficult life and death questions? What parts do God, faith and spirituality play in the everyday lives of this child and family? How can I help this child and family embrace their faith in ways that will help them heal?

But I've also learned that children are innately spiritual beings. Regardless of their family's religious orientation, they are typically optimistic about life and living. They find deep joy in the discoveries of each day. They are eager to learn and to love.

Children are innately spiritual beings.

They are also inquisitive about all things spiritual. Bereaved children, like all of us, wrestle with questions of faith as they mourn. They are, at times, like struggling butterflies in a cocoon. As adult caregivers, we provide the cocoon: a safe place that will nourish the child's body and soul so she can develop wings mature enough to fly. Her wings grow strong by pushing against the walls of the cocoon as she questions life's purpose. We must not provide pat answers but instead lean into the pushing wings so the child grows strong of her own accord.

Children are also naturally attracted to rituals (which by their nature are spiritual). Simple traditions and rituals of loss, closings and grief nurture a child's spiritual life without necessarily teaching facts about death. We can embrace a child's faith-life by including him in ceremonies surrounding death.

As caring adults, we have the privilege of recognizing and supporting a child's spirituality by being the very best caregivers we know how to be. In doing so, we share the gifts of presence, love and faith in his capacity to heal.

Other crises / stresses in the child's life

Death and loss seldom occur in isolation. To understand the impact of a death on a child, you must also understand other losses the child is experiencing concurrently. Sometimes two or more people a child loves will die around the same time. This, of course, may overwhelm the child and may complicate his mourning.

Also stay sensitive to the impact of secondary losses on a child's grief journey. (See p. 48.) Secondary losses include the loss of friends and community due to a geographical move, loss of security if the breadwinner in the family has died, and loss of childhood if the child has been forced to "grow up" prematurely because of the death. In short, the death of someone loved will often cause a ripple effect of other losses.

On the other hand, sometimes additional stresses on the child at the time of the death are good stresses. Say, for example, a child's grandfather dies about the same time her mother gives birth to a new baby. In this case the birth of the baby may actually delay the child's mourning because the child (like most of us) will choose to focus on the happy event first.

Questions to ask yourself as grief gardener:

*   What other stresses are impacting the child at this time?
*   What additional losses —community, friendship, etc. — have resulted from the death?

Notes _____

_____

_____

_____

_____

Secondary Losses

When someone we love dies, we don't just lose the presence of that person. As a result of the death, we may lose many other connections to ourselves and our world. Children feel these secondary losses, too.

As you grief garden with the bereaved child, keep in mind the following common secondary losses that can make the grief experience more complex.

Loss of self

- self	("Part of me died, too, when my Mommy died.")
- identity	(The child may have to rethink her role as child or sibling.)
- self-confidence	(Child mourners often feel shame or a lessened sense of self-esteem.)
- health	(Physical symptoms of mourning)
- personality	("I'm just not myself . . .")

Loss of security

- emotional security	(Parent/caretaker is now gone, causing emotional upheaval.)
- physical security	(A bereaved child may worry who will take care of her physical needs.)
- fiscal security	(A bereaved child may be concerned about family finances.)
- lifestyle	(Child may be used to a boisterous and loving family life, but that life is now quieted due to the death of a family member.)

Loss of meaning

- goals & dreams	(Dreams for future can be shattered, goals can seem unreachable without person who died.)
- faith	(Mourners often question faith.)
- will/desire to live	("Why go on?")
- joy	(Life's most meaningful emotion—happiness—is compromised by the death of someone loved.)

Multiple Loss and the Bereaved Child

In recent years we have been seeing more and more children who are confronted with multiple losses, both death-related losses and non-death-related losses.

When a child is confronted with multiple deaths (the deaths of two or more significant people in the same event, or the sequential deaths of two or more significant people within a relatively short time period), the child's bereavement may be naturally complicated. The child may wonder:

- How do I begin to mourn?
- Can I mourn these deaths all at once?
- Whom do I mourn first?
- Can I trust enough to allow myself to love again?

Other manifestations of complicated mourning due to multiple loss include overwhelming, unbearable pain; lack of support if more than one primary caregiver dies; potential survivor guilt ("Why am I still alive?"); and a natural resistance to undertake the work of mourning. If, over time, the child isn't compassionately companioned through his complicated mourning journey, he is at risk for attachment disorders and other emotional problems.

So how best to grief garden with children who have experienced multiple loss? In my experience, what these children need most is to be very slowly helped to mourn and to trust in the world again. Expect more intense, longer lasting grief in these kids. You might also see more extensive acting-out and long-term complications with attachment. Be patient, firm and compassionate.

When a child is confronted with multiple loss, the child's bereavement may be naturally complicated.

The ability to attach emotionally to others not only helps the infant develop trust in her world, but sets the tone for being able to give and receive love throughout life. John Bowlby put this matter succinctly: "Intimate attachments to other human beings are the hub around which a person's life revolves, not only when she is an infant or toddler, but throughout adolescence and the years of maturity as well as into old age."

So what happens when a child's parent or other primary caregiver dies? Most children undergo a period of protest, where they cry for their caregiver and don't want to be attended to by anyone else; then a period of despair, during which they may become withdrawn and apathetic; and finally a period of detachment, where they question their desire to trust anyone again. In other words, the detachment that occurs when a child is not reunited with a primary caregiver is a defense mechanism against the pain of separation.

The only children who, when separated from primary caregivers, do not protest in some way are those who have never had anyone to whom they can become attached. In addition, children who have had repeated separations (such as movement from one foster home to another) are also at risk for becoming permanently detached.

In my counseling experience, I would also suggest that children who experience bereavement overload (multiple deaths within a short period of time) are also at risk for becoming permanently detached. They tend not to trust people to care for them, so they may not learn to care for others. In sum, children who experience bereavement overload may decide in their subconscious that they cannot trust and then project this lack of trust into their outside world.

How do you know if a child is detached? Usually it is obvious that something is wrong. Yet, many caring adults find it difficult to admit that something is deeply disturbing about a child. In addition, many children, when taken to professionals for help, are misdiagnosed. Many mental health professionals have received little, if any, training in identifying and helping detached children.

For readers who would like an excellent summary of symptoms we see in detached children, I recommend the text *High Risk: Children Without a Conscience* (Bantam Books, 1987, New York, New York) by Dr. Ken Magid and Carole A. McKelvey. The authors provide an overview of the following symptoms:

1. Lack of ability to give and receive affection

2. Self-destructive behavior

3. Cruelty to others or to pets

4. Phoniness

5. Stealing, hoarding and gorging

6. Speech pathology

7. Extreme control problems

8. Lack of long-term childhood friends

9. Abnormalities in eye contact

10. Unreasonably angry parents

11. Preoccupation with blood, fire and gore

12. Superficial attractiveness and friendliness with strangers

13. Learning disorders

14. Crazy lying

Insufficient attention has been paid to the needs of children who experience bereavement overload and who subsequently may become detached children. While we don't yet know all there is to know about attachment disorders, we do know that if a child has become detached it is important to seek help as early as possible. The older the child becomes, the more difficult it is to help him reattach to those around him.

Children who experience bereavement overload are at risk for becoming permanently detached.

Prior experiences with death

A bereaved child's past experiences with death greatly affect the ways in which he will respond to the most recent loss. Children who have been taught, for example, to repress their grief will typically fall back on that impulse whenever someone loved dies. The more negative the prior experiences with death, the more complicated each new encounter.

The number of losses children have experienced also affects their grief responses. Some children grow up in environments that expose them to losses from the time they're born. Children who live in foster home after foster home, for example, confront loss every time they must leave a family. Inexplicably, other children encounter an inordinate number of losses early on. One eight-year-old boy I counseled, for instance, had already experienced the unrelated deaths of seven people he loved. (For more on multiple losses, see p. 49.)

Bereavement overload such as this can cause attachment disorders. Consciously or unconsciously, these children reason that bonding with others does no good and, in fact, can cause great pain. "If I don't love anyone," they think, "I won't get hurt again." In general, children with extensive loss histories are more prone to both attachment disorders and acting-out behavior. (For more on attachment disorders, see p. 50.)

On the other end of the spectrum are children who never encounter death in their young lives. Thanks to better nutrition and medical care, ours is the first death-free generation. It isn't unusual for today's children to reach early- or mid-adult-hood before someone close to them dies. As a result, some don't learn that death and loss are an integral part of life.

The child who hasn't been exposed to death may not know what to do with his grief when someone loved does die. In such cases, especially, it is important for adults to model healthy mourning because inexperienced grievers learn through imitation.

Questions to ask yourself as grief gardener:

- What has the child's history with death been?
- Has she experienced multiple losses in a short time span?
- How have the child's prior experiences with death influenced her attitudes about grief and mourning?

Notes _____

_____

_____

_____

_____

The child's ritual/funeral experiences

Most of the rituals in our society focus on children. What would birthdays or Christmas be without kids? Unfortunately, the funeral ritual, whose purpose is to help bereaved people begin to heal, is not seen as a ritual for children. Too often, children are not included in the funeral because adults want to protect them. The funeral is painful, they reason, so I will shelter the children from this pain.

Yes, funerals can be very painful, but children have the same right and privilege to participate in them as adults do. Funerals are important to survivors because they:

- help survivors acknowledge that someone has died.

- provide a structure to support and assist them through their initial period of mourning.

- provide a time to honor, remember and affirm the life of the person who died.

- allow for a "search for meaning" within the context of each person's religious or philosophical values.

Children have the same right and privilege to participate in funerals as adults do.

Thus, if a bereaved child has not been included in the funeral ritual, she may have a more difficult time acknowledging that someone loved has died and embarking on the grief journey. Moreover, if the child was allowed to attend the funeral but wasn't gently guided through the experience by caring adults, she may have questions or even fears about what happened. Asking bereaved children age-appropriate questions about their funeral experiences will help you better understand how this ritual has affected their grief journeys.

Questions to ask yourself as grief gardener:

- Was there a funeral for the person who died?
- If so, was the child allowed to be involved?
- Did the funeral help the child express his grief?
- Are there other rituals (like making a memory book or planting a tree) that will help this child express her grief?

Notes _____

_____

_____

_____

_____

When a Child's Pet Dies

The death of a pet is often a child's first introduction to death. Some of my happiest childhood memories were of time spent with my dog, Chico. But one day she ran out the door and was hit by a car. I'm not alone when I say that Chico was a member of my family. She slept with me, she played with me; she was not only by dog, but my loving friend. The dogs in my life right now are Tasha and Keesha—and they too are my friends and my children's friends.

No, our pets are not "just a dog" or "just a cat." With the death of a pet, children experience a significant loss. As caring adults, we have the opportunity and responsibility to respond in ways that empower children to grieve for their pets. Your response during this time can determine whether children's experience will be a positive or negative part of their personal growth and development.

- *Model your own feelings about the death of the pet.* If you do so, children will have a model for expressing their own feelings.

- *When appropriate, explain that the pet's illness and death was no one's fault.* Some children feel they are responsible because they forgot to feed the dog or pay attention to the cat.

- *Use simple and direct language in sharing facts about the death.* Do not make up stories or tell half-truths to protect children.

- *If euthanasia is used, do not describe it as "putting the pet to sleep."* Children need to understand that sleep and death are not the same thing. Instead, explain euthanasia as a quick, painless way to help a suffering pet die.

The death of a pet is a significant loss for children.

- *Encourage involvement in ritual.* Children use the funeral ceremony of a pet to help them understand the death and mourn the loss.

- *Encourage creative outlets for feelings*—writing a poem or a story about the pet, creating a memory book or planting a tree in the pet's memory are just a few of many ways to help children mourn the pet's death.

- *Openly discuss what will be done with the pet's body.* This helps children feel involved and they can often participate in the process.

- *Do not attempt to replace the dead pet before the child has an opportunity to mourn.* After time, it may be appropriate to suggest finding another pet—not to take to take the place of the previous pet but to enter the family as a new member.

Helping Children with Funerals

What follows is a brief guide for parents or other guardians who have the opportunity to include their children in a funeral ritual.

Unless they have attended one before, children don't know what to expect from a funeral. You can help by explaining what will happen before, during and after the ceremony. Let the child's questions and natural curiosity guide the discussion.

Give as many specifics as the child seems interested in hearing. You might tell her how the room will look, who will be coming and how long everyone will be there, for example. When possible, arrange for the child to visit the funeral home before the funeral. This allows her more freedom to react and talk openly about feelings and concerns.

If the body will be viewed either at a visitation or at the funeral itself, let the child know this in advance. Explain what the casket and the body will look like. If the body is to be cremated, explain what cremation means and what will happen to the ashes. Be sure the child understands that because the person is dead, he doesn't feel pain or anything at all during cremation.

Also help children anticipate that they will see people expressing a wide variety of emotions at the funeral. They will see tears, straight faces and laughter. If adults are able to openly show feelings, including crying, children will feel much more free to express a sense of loss at their own level.

Help children understand the why of funerals. Children need to know that the funeral is a time of sadness because someone has died, a time to honor the person who died, a time to help comfort and support each other and a time to affirm that life goes on.

One why children seem to embrace easily is that funerals are a time to say goodbye. And saying goodbye helps us all acknowledge that the person we loved is gone and cannot come back. If the body is to be viewed, tell the child that seeing the body helps people say goodbye and that he may touch the person he loved once last time.

Now is also a good time to explain to the child what spiritual significance the funeral has for you and your family. This can be difficult, for even adults have a hard time articulating their beliefs about life and death. One guideline: children have difficulty understanding abstractions, so it is best to use concrete terms when talking about religious concepts.

Include children in the ritual. When appropriate, you might invite children not only to attend the funeral but to take part in it. Bereaved children feel like their feelings "matter" when they can share a favorite memory or read a special poem as part of the funeral. Shyer children can participate by lighting a candle or placing something special (a momento or a photo, for example) in the casket. And many children feel more included when they are invited to help plan the funeral service.

Children should be encouraged to attend and participate in funerals, but never forced. When they are lovingly guided through the process, however, most children want to attend. Offer the reticent child options: "You can come to the visitation today with everyone else or if you want, I can take just you this morning so you can say goodbye in private."

Understand and accept the child's way of mourning. Do not prescribe to children what they should feel or for how long—particularly during the funeral. Remember that children often need to accept their grief in doses, and that outward signs of grief may come and go. It is not unusual, for example, for children to want to roughhouse with their cousins during the visitation or play video games right after the funeral. Instead of punishing this behavior, you should respect the child's need to be a child during this extraordinarily difficult time. If the child's behavior is disturbing others, explain that there are acceptable and unacceptable ways to act at funerals and that you expect the child to consider the feelings of other mourners—including yours.

The Language of Funerals

Remember to use simple, concrete language when talking to children about death. Here are some suggestions for explaining funeral terms:

Ashes (also "cremains")	What is left of a dead body after cremation. Looks like ashes from a fire.
Burial	Placing the body (which is inside a casket) into the ground.
Casket	A special box for burying a dead body.
Cemetery	A place where many dead bodies are buried.
Cremation	Reducing the body by heat to small pieces of bone.
Dead	When a person's body stops working. It doesn't see, hear, feel, eat, breathe, etc. anymore.
Funeral	A time when friends and families get together to say goodbye and remember the person who died.
Funeral home	A place where bodies are kept until they are buried.
Grave	The hole in the ground where the body is buried at the cemetery.
Hearse	The special car that takes the dead body in the casket to the grave at the cemetery.
Obituary	A short article in the paper that tells about the person who died.
Pallbearer	The people who help carry the casket at the funeral.
Viewing	The time when people can see the body of the person who died.

Additional influences

Physical health influences

A holistic understanding of the child requires awareness of the child's physical condition. An excellent standard of care is to have any child you counsel get a good general medical examination. Why? Just like adults, children's bodies respond to the stress of the death of someone loved. Actually, school nurses, pediatricians and family physicians are among those who most commonly refer children to me for help.

To experience bereavement on top of physical disability may be overwhelming for children.

In many situations, the physical "hurts" the child expresses are a form of emotional communication. After all, we often teach children that when you don't feel well (whether emotionally, spiritually or physically), the most immediate way to receive attention is to be "sick". Even very young children pick up on these cues. If the child is in a closed family system where open mourning is discouraged, this tendency is heightened. The child unconsciously reasons, "If I can't play it out, act it out or talk it out, I'll get sick—and then maybe I'll get nurtured." Aren't kids smart!

Learning and physical disabilities, injury, illness and hospitalization are obviously loss experiences for children. To experience bereavement on top of these types of losses may create normal feelings of physical vulnerability and, in general, unwellness. A child with concerns about his own physical well-being ("Will I die too?") will often express these concerns indirectly through a preoccupation with his health. Remember Veda, in the movie *My Girl*, and her frequent visits to the doctor? This represented a need to learn more about her mother's death, who died giving birth to her.

Questions to ask yourself as grief gardener:

- What is this child's current physical condition?

- What has been her medical history?

- Is this child attempting to communicate about underlying needs through the expression of physical symptoms?

- Do I need to refer this child for a complete physical exam to help me in my holistic, growth-oriented approach to caregiving?

Notes _____

_____

_____

_____

_____

School influences

Children spend much of their time in school. Consulting with school personnel about observations of a child, before and after a death in the child's life, can provide you with valuable information as you work to better understand the life of the child. Teachers are often very open to working collaboratively with counselors in efforts to help children impacted by grief.

Moreover, a compassionate teacher, school counselor or principal may be one of the bereaved child's major supporters. As grief gardener-advocates, we can help them know how to compassionately be present to the child. We can also sensitize school personnel to the importance of recognizing that grief is a process, not an event. Loss histories in the life of the child should be passed along as the child progresses through school.

When I was first getting started with my work in this area, one of my favorite things to do was go around to schools and invite myself to provide them with inservice trainings. While I was rejected by some (I shouldn't have expected any less in this mourning-avoiding culture), many schools received me with enthusiasm. (For more on grief in the school setting, see Chapter 10.)

Questions to ask yourself as grief gardener:

- How has this child historically done—emotionally, socially, behaviorally and academically—in the school setting?
- What can school personnel do in their efforts to help me help this child?
- Is a consultation in the school setting needed in this situation?
- What educational resources can I provide the school to help this child?

Notes _____

_____

_____

_____

_____

Peer Influences

Perhaps the most instinctive place children turn when in crisis is to their peers. The grief gardening approach to caregiving mandates us to work to determine who the bereaved child's friends are. After all, peers are often the ones who let us adults know when one of their friends is struggling in some way.

Children appear to have an almost intuitive sense of the emotional and spiritual well-being of their friends. Any concerns they express about a peer should be taken seriously.

Many bereaved children feel different than their peers who haven't been impacted by death. Some kids will move toward other children who have had similar losses, seeking support and understanding. Interestingly, other kids will try to ignore their new "difference" (being bereaved) and project a need to be just the same as everyone else. The problem is that everything isn't the same. They may project feeling ashamed that they are no longer a "family," for example.

As caregivers we can encourage peer play as the child doses herself with her grief.

As caregivers we can encourage supportive peer contact and play activities as the child doses herself in her grief journey. In the midst of change, the constant of peers is critically important in the life of the bereaved child.

Questions to ask yourself as grief gardener:

- Which peers have historically made up this child's support system?
- Are any of the child's peers expressing concern for the bereaved child?
- How have the child's peers been impacted by this death?

- Do I see any changes in peer relationships since this death occurred?
- How can I involve this child's peers in my helping efforts?

Notes _____

_____

_____

_____

Yes, many factors influence a bereaved child's mourning. Each child comes to grief with a different set of life experiences, and once she has begun to grieve, experiences a different set of thoughts and feelings.

What else have you seen influence a bereaved child's mourning?

_____

_____

_____

_____

_____

Grief Myth

Children only grieve for a short time.

If you're seeing mourning behaviors in a bereaved child, the child still needs your support.

When our gardens are shredded by a July hailstorm (an all-too-frequent happening in Colorado), we gardeners naturally want our plants to recover quickly. We pinch off damaged stalks, clear the debris and stand back, drumming our fingers impatiently. But gardens don't always bounce back right away. It may take a few weeks or even another whole season before our garden seems itself again.

Bereaved children don't bounce back right away, either. Still, many adults simply do not understand that grief and mourning are processes, not events. Those adults who want the bereaved child to "hurry up" and "get over it" usually project that the child needs to be strong and stoic. (Of course, who are these adults really protecting? Themselves. If adults can assume the child's grief and mourning are short in duration, then they don't have to walk with the child as he encounters the pain of loss.)

I continue to read in professional texts comments like, "If the child's symptoms persist past six months, he or she should be referred for professional assistance." Actually, nothing could be further from the truth. Around six months after a death, it is not unusual to see more, not fewer, visible signs of mourning in a child. This is largely because for children, grief gets intertwined with the developmental process. If I'm just five years old when I first come to grief, that grief will change for me as I mature and begin to understand it with more cognitive depth.

So how long should a child's grief last? If ideal conditions exist (which they rarely do) and the child is actively working on his six needs of mourning with the support of caring adults and family members, active mourning can still take three-four years. And even that lucky child will encounter intermittent mourning as he develops and reintegrates his grief experience.

My best advice is this: If you're seeing mourning behaviors in a bereaved child, the child still needs your support.

Have you seen this myth carried out? When and how?

_____

_____

_____

_____

3

Sad/Scared/Mad/ Tired/Glad: How a Grieving Child Thinks, Feels and Mourns

It is often easy to tell when flowers in the garden are under stress of some kind. Their leaves turn yellow, they droop, they fail to flower—all visible symptoms that let the gardener know something is wrong. Children, too, often express their underlying needs in ways we can see, typically through behaviors.

Grief gardeners spend time with the bereaved child to understand the ways she thinks, feels and mourns.

Bereaved children can and often do undergo major emotional, spiritual, physical, and behavioral changes. As grief gardeners we can learn to understand these changes as symptomatic of underlying grief needs. This understanding will in turn help us to help the bereaved child.

This chapter presents some of the most typical feelings and thoughts bereaved children experience—and the behavioral ways in which they express those feelings. Following a discussion of each grief dimension, I have included caregiving suggestions—things you as grief gardener can do to encourage the expression of each feeling.

*"Daddy is **not** dead. I'm going to go play now!"*

Shock/ apparent lack of feelings

As you might expect, children often initially feel a sense of emotional shock when someone they love dies. The child may say or think, "No, this didn't happen. Daddy's not dead. He'll come back," or, "If I pretend this isn't happening, then maybe it won't be." The mind blocks and at times is not connected to what the child hears. Actually, "shock" is a generic term that subsumes a variety of emotions, such as disbelief, numbness and denial, as well as physiological responses.

Sometimes outside observers jump to the conclusion that the

child's disbelief or apparent lack of feelings means a complete denial of, or even indifference to, the death. Parents often have difficulty understanding, for example, how Scott can be out in the backyard playing only an hour after learning of Grandpa's death. They frequently feel hurt and angry with a child's apparent lack of feelings, and as a result, sometimes end up distancing themselves from the child.

In fact, the bereaved child's apparent lack of feelings serves a very useful purpose. Often children dose their early grief by allowing just a little reality in at a time. In this way they move toward their grief—at their own pace—instead of away from it. When the full reality of the death seeps through, children may well do some "catch-up grieving" as previously blocked thoughts and feelings surface.

Often children "dose" their grief by allowing just a little reality in at a time.

Pay attention to the ways in which other adults respond to the child's apparent lack of feelings. Many will tacitly affirm this stoicism because our society advocates facing trauma without showing feeling. The person who doesn't cry when someone dies is most often the one whom others believe "took things so well." So, while the child receives this destructively affirmative message from some adults, others simply can't understand why the child is not grieving and ask themselves if the child really loved the person who died. The result is that the child is frequently stuck in the middle not knowing what to think, feel or do.

While it is critical to allow bereaved children this initial period of numbness, we must be careful never to inappropriately encourage a child to suppress other emotional responses. It is cruel to reinforce a child's belief that Dad will come home, for example, when we realize this is impossible. At times, adults' difficulty in explaining the finality of death to children makes them confused about what to think or feel. And admonishments like "Be strong," "You shouldn't cry," and "Well, now you will have to carry on" often encourage the suppression of emotions and as a result reinforce a prolonged sense of denial.

This experience of shock, denial, numbness and apparent lack of feelings is typically most intense during the first several months after the death. However, to see this dimension of the child's grief recur suddenly is not at all uncommon, particularly on the anniversary of the death or on other special occasions (birthday, Christmas, etc.). I also have witnessed this dimension when the child visits a place associated with a special memory of the dead person.

• Accept the child's apparent lack of feelings as a natural response. The major role of the grief gardener during this period of shock is to keep the grieving child in touch with a supportive, caring part of her world. You can also educate the child's parents or other caretakers about the naturalness of this response.

• Talk "with," not "at" the child about the death. The tendency to talk "at" instead of "with" a bereaved child is often a reflection of our frustration that the child isn't responding. It's OK to spend time just being with the child who isn't yet ready to embrace his pain; don't feel you need to make a counseling breakthrough at the first session.

• Respect the child's need to talk, or not to talk, about the death. Grief gardeners respect a child's need to move in and out of grief. Most bereaved children will provide cues when they feel comfortable and safe talking about the person who has died. Moreover, a child will often test adults to see if they feel comfortable communicating their own thoughts and feelings about the loss. As you build a relationship with the child based on sensitivity, warmth and understanding, the child will feel more comfortable sharing her grief with you.

"My stomach hurts!"
Physiological changes

At a time of acute grief, a child's body responds to what the mind has been told. Among the more common physical symptoms a grieving child exhibits are:

• Tiredness, lack of energy
• Difficulty in sleeping, or sometimes excessive sleeping
• Lack of appetite or excessive appetite
• Tightness in the throat
• Shortness of breath
• General nervousness, trembling
• Headaches
• Stomach pain
• Loss of muscular strength
• Skin rashes

Headaches, tiredness and lack of energy are some of the physical symptoms of grief a child may experience.

Do Children Grieve Differently Than Adults?

As I noted a number of year's ago, "Grief does not focus on one's ability to understand but instead on one's ability to feel. Therefore any child mature enough to love is mature enough to grieve." Still, while children are quite capable of mourning, there are some distinctions between child and adult grief:

- *A child's world is primarily a world of play.* Children will teach you more through their behaviors than through their words.

- *A child mourns in "doses"—or on an intermittent basis.* The apparent lack of feeling witnessed at times is a normal defense reflected in their inability to tolerate acute pain for long periods of time.

- *Cognitive development affects a child's capacity to integrate the finality, inevitability and irreversibility of death.* Children appear to proceed from little or no understanding of death to recognition of the concept in realistic form. While evidence does support age-level understanding of children's concepts of death, we need to keep in mind that development involves much more than simply growing older. Environmental support, behavior, attitudes, responsiveness of adults, self-concept, intelligence, previous experiences with death, and a number of other factors have an important role in the child's unique understanding of death.

- *Children are more at the mercy of those around them for help or hindrance.* They are at the mercy of the gardeners who care for them. Bereaved adults are able to seek support when it is not available, while children who don't have family or friends to support their need to mourn may be emotionally alone for years.

- *Children (particularly teens) don't want to be different from their peers.* Therefore they may resist open invitations to mourn if this makes them feel different than other children.

In most situations, adults can help the grieving child recognize that these physical "hurts" are quite normal and temporary, thereby lessening some of the child's concern. We also need to be aware that sometimes children unconsciously assume these "sick roles" in an effort to receive care for the emotional hurt. This happens most often in cases where the child isn't receiving adequate emotional support. In addition, it is not unusual for a child to identify with the physical symptoms that caused the death of the loved person. For example, if Dad died of a heart attack, the child may complain of chest pains.

The grief gardener's helping role

- *Remember that children's bodies respond to the stress of the death of someone loved.* The aches and pains the child may complain of are often very real and they do hurt. The physical hurts a child expresses are often a form of emotional communication.

- *Don't punish or shame kids for seemingly unfounded feelings of illness.* When children feel shut off from avenues of emotional expression of their fears, questions and concerns, the frequent consequence is that they become physically ill. The child unconsciously reasons, "If I can't play it out, act it out, or talk it out, I'll get sick—and then maybe I'll get nurtured!"

  Keep in mind that the child who is sick as a result of unexpressed thoughts and feelings does not consciously want to be sick—and certainly does not feel in control of her illness. We would not want to punish or shame a child for these physical expressions of grief.

- *Stay conscious of any pre-existing conditions (illness, injury, hospitalization) in the bereaved child.* To experience bereavement on top of these types of losses often creates normal feelings of physical vulnerability and malaise. A child with concerns about his own physical well-being ("Will I die, too?") will often express these concerns indirectly through preoccupation with the well-being of others, as well: "Mommy, are you sick?" can mean "Mommy, are you going to die, too?"

- *An excellent standard of care is to have any child you counsel get a good general medical examination.* This will often provide the child, other concerned adults and you with reassuring information about the child's physical health.

Occasionally, something that needs appropriate medical intervention will be found. A grief gardening approach to counseling bereaved children is a holistic one.

- *You will sometimes see transient forms of identification with the person who died through physical illness.* A child whose father died of cancer may complain of cancer "symptoms." A child whose sibling died of a brain tumor may complain of a headache. These are generally natural ways of identifying with and expressing longing for the person who died. Again, a physical exam is the best standard of care and often reassures the child as well as adults in the life of the child.

"Mommy, please don't go to work today."

Regression

When they're under the psychological stress of grief, children often want to return to the complete sense of protection and security they felt earlier in life. Among the more common regressive behaviors of childhood bereavement are the following:

- Over-dependence on a parent to the point of declining to go outside to play as they have done in the past.

- Desire to be nursed or rocked as they were at an earlier stage of development.

- Desire to sleep with parent.

- An unwillingness to separate from a parent for any length of time.

- Desire to have others perform tasks for them that they are able to do for themselves, such as tying shoes, getting dressed, being fed and so forth.

- Refusal to work independently in the school setting and/or demanding constant individual attention and demonstrating dependent behaviors to the teacher and peers.

- Taking on a "sick role" in an effort to avoid attending school.

- Regression to talking baby talk and in general presenting themselves in an infant-like manner.

- Breakdown in the ability to function adequately in peer relationships.

Typically, regressive behaviors in bereaved children are temporary (although they sometimes last for months, even years, after a death) and pass as the child receives support in the journey through grief. Unfortunately, our society often perceives regressive behaviors as a total lack of self-control and discourages (or even punishes) both adults and children for displaying them.

When regressive behaviors continue for long periods of time, however, other factors may have complicated the child's grief response. On occasion, parents or other significant adults in the child's life actually reinforce or encourage this dependence. Why? Because adults experiencing grief themselves often feel guilty about not providing enough support to their children. They may attempt to compensate for this (real or false) sense of neglect by overprotecting or overindulging the child. Consequently, the child is kept in a dependent position as a result of the adult's need to feel in control of both the child and the situation.

Regressive behaviors can surface at any time during the grief process; however, they tend to be demonstrated to a greater extent within the first one to two years after the death. Typically, I view continued regressive behaviors as a barometer of emotional needs that are either not being met in a healthy, loving manner or, on the other hand, as an indication that adults in the child's life are attempting to meet their own needs through their child's behaviors.

Typically, regressive behaviors in bereaved children are temporary and pass as the child receives support in the journey through grief.

The grief gardener's helping role

- *Allow the regressing bereaved child to retreat to this safer, less complex time; this behavior is natural after the death of someone loved.* Regressive behaviors in a bereaved child are usually temporary and pass as he is supported in his grief journey. Note, too, that though these behaviors tend to be most noticeable in the first year or two after a death, a return to prior developmental levels can take place at any time during the child's grief experience.

- *Remember that demonstrating regressive behaviors may fill a significant need in the bereaved child's life.* Be patient and understanding. Temporary, self-preserving regression undoubtedly serves a useful purpose for many bereaved children. It signals a need to be cared for, nurtured and loved. It may also represent an attempt to return to a time in life before the trauma of the loss. The child may even see it as a way to retrieve the person who died.

- *Try to understand the unmet need underlying the behavior.* If a bereaved nine-year-old tells you she's been staying home from school because she isn't ready to return to schoolwork yet, you might involve the girl's parents or guardians in several counseling sessions to sort out the causes of this behavior.

- *Provide a trusting, supportive presence for the child.* This suggestion stands no matter what the child's behavior. For children, to regress is simply to ask for care from the adults around them.

"What's happening to me?"

Disorganization and panic

A feeling bereaved children have that often occurs suddenly and unpredictably is a heightened sense of disorganization and panic. A wave of overwhelming thoughts and feelings makes the child wonder, "Who is going to take care of me now? Will our family survive? Will I survive?" At times children may feel as if they are out of touch with the ordinary proceedings of life, and many children become frightened by the duration and intensity of their feelings.

During this time the child often confronts both good and bad memories from the past. For example, while the child receives comfort from remembering the sound of Mom's voice, it is also painful. And then at other times the child may want to remember experiences and memories and finds doing so impossible. While this loss of memory is normal, it can be very scary to the child who doesn't understand it.

During this phase of grief the child may dream of the person who died, appear restless and irritable, seem unable to concentrate, or experience a disruption in normal eating and sleeping patterns. The child

The bereaved child may wonder, "Who is going to take care of me now? Will our family survive? Will I?"

may seem hypersensitive and cry over things that seem totally unrelated to the death.

The grief gardener's helping role

- *Remember that these thoughts and feelings of disorganization and panic may ebb and flow for months, even years after the death.* What children need most during this time is the constant physical presence of someone they trust. They also often need physical contact (hand-holding, hugging, caressing) to assure them of the caregiving that is and will continue to be extended to them. They need to be reassured about the naturalness of their feelings and behaviors, which in other circumstances would be considered highly unusual.

- *During this time the child may also have a real need to cry, talk or play out his grief.* The role of the adult caregiver is not to interrupt with false reassurances, but to let crying and talking take their natural course. (Most children don't cry for more than two-three minutes at a time, even though it seems longer to us adults.) At times the content of what the child says may make little sense, but that's OK—it will still help him feel better. In moving through and being supported during this frightening part of grief, children are capable of turning grief into growth and pain into gain.

- *Remember that disorientation in grief proceeds reorientation.* Practice being patient with the child and keep in mind you are a caregiver, not a curegiver. Be aware that many children work through disorientation and panic through repetitive play and activities. Watch for the symbolism in the play that often reflects needs for safety and security. Repetitive play is often a form of "telling the story" and is developmentally appropriate for children as they do the work of mourning.

- *The thoughts, feelings and behaviors of this dimension of grief do not come all at once and are often experienced in a wave-like fashion.* The child may one day appear to be "fine" and the next day experience disorientation or panic. Again, this is normal and remembering this will help the child to feel safe with you. The child may teach you and other adults that she doesn't need a lot of words from you, but instead non-verbal forms of support like eye contact, gestures of care and a willingness to play with her.

Attention
Deficit
Hyperactivity
Disorder or
Normal
Grief?

Each day in North America hundreds of children are diagnosed as suffering from Attention Deficit Hyperactivity Disorder (ADHD). The diagnosis of ADHD centers around three primary features: inattention, impulsivity, and hyperactivity.

As an advocate for the needs of bereaved children and adolescents, I am concerned that we counselors are sometimes too quick to label a bereaved child with this "disorder." My experience suggests that many bereaved children and adolescents naturally struggle with issues of distractibility, impulsivity and hyperactivity.

What is ADHD?

It surprises most people that ADHD is not an illness or a disease but rather a syndrome, or a cluster of symptoms. As a syndrome, ADHD can be a manifestation of any number of underlying causes. A good analogy is a fever, which is a single symptom caused by any number of problems.

Likewise, a child appropriately diagnosed with ADHD may suffer from a variety of underlying triggers, including, but not limited to, the following: thyroid dysfunction, food allergy, brain injury, disorganized or chaotic environments, child abuse or neglect, fetal alcohol syndrome, learning disability, depression, anxiety or post-traumatic stress disorder. These different causes often call for different helping responses. Obviously, a careful, well-thought-out assessment is critical to creating appropriate interventions.

The diagnosis of ADHD

Because there is no "test" for ADHD, the best approach to accurate diagnosis is a comprehensive assessment that explores the history, biology, psychology, and spirituality of the child. Because the disorder typically manifests itself in a variety of settings, behavioral observations in the home, the school as well as in the therapist's office are critical to accurate diagnosis. Moreover, some children with ADHD can appear fairly calm in a one-on-one situation. Thus, the observations of teachers in the classroom and adult caregivers at home are often the most critical tools in diagnosing ADHD.

Let's look at the formal diagnostic criteria for Attention-Deficit Hyperactivity Disorder used by mental health practitioners:

A. Either (1) or (2):

(1) six (or more) of the following symptoms of inattention have persisted for at least 6 months to a degree that is maladaptive and inconsistent with developmental level:

Inattention

(a) often fails to give close attention to details or makes careless mistakes in schoolwork, work or other activities

(b) often has difficulty sustaining attention in tasks or play activities

(c) often does not seem to listen when spoken to directly

(d) often does not follow through on instructions and fails to finish schoolwork, chores or duties in the workplace (not due to oppositional behavior or failure to understand instructions.)

(e) often has difficulty organizing tasks and activities

(f) often avoids, dislikes or is reluctant to engage in tasks that require sustained mental effort (such as schoolwork or homework)

(g) often loses things necessary for tasks or activities (e.g. toys, school assignments, pencils, books or tools)

(h) is often easily distracted by extraneous stimuli

(i) is often forgetful in daily activities

(2) six (or more) of the following symptoms of hyperactivity-impulsivity have persisted for at least 6 months to a degree that is maladaptive and inconsistent with developmental level:

Hyperactivity

(a) often fidgets with hands or feet or squirms in seat

(b) often leaves seat in classroom or in other situation in which remaining seated is expected

(c) often runs about or climbs excessively in situations in which it is inappropriate (in adolescents or adults, may be limited to subjective feelings of restlessness)

(d) often has difficulty playing or engaging in leisure activities quietly

(e) is often "on the go" or often acts as if "driven by a motor"

(f) often talks excessively

Impulsivity

(g) often blurts out answers before questions have been completed

(h) often has difficulty awaiting turn

(i) often interrupts or intrudes on others (e.g. butts into conversation or games)

B. Some hyperactive-impulsive or inattentive symptoms that caused impairment were present before age 7 years.

C. Some impairment from the symptoms is present in two or more settings.

D. There must be clear evidence of clinically significant impairment in social, academic or occupational functioning.

(Source—American Psychiatric Association. (1994). *Diagnostic and Statistical Manual of Mental Disorders* (4th Ed. Rev.). Washington, DC.)

Depression and anxiety: ADHD or normal grieving?

As noted above, potential triggers for ADHD are depression and anxiety.

The majority of bereaved children I see in my practice have components of both depression and anxiety brought about by the death of someone loved. Some of the children I see have been previously diagnosed with ADHD with little, if any, attention being paid to the normalcy of depressed mood and agitated behavior. The healthy work of mourning requires a respect for the "survival value" of depression and anxiety.

For example, a common reason that medication stimulants (Ritalin and Dexedrine are the most common) often fail to help bereaved children diagnosed with ADHD is that the components of "normal" depression and anxiety have been overlooked or misunderstood. Dramatic improvements often occur when the child is taken off stimulants (under medical supervision) and supportive counseling is initiated.

Acting-out: normal grieving or ADHD?

Normal bereavement and ADHD have yet another commonality: acting-out behaviors. Many bereaved children express the pain of grief by acting-out. The counselor who isn't sensitive to the normalcy of this behavior is often tempted to see distractibility, impulsivity and hyperactivity as reflecting full-blown ADHD. Careful attention to the history of symptom onset frequently demonstrates a relationship between the stress of the death (or coping with a chronic illness in the family) and the initiation of survival-driven acting-out behaviors. Some adults are still unaware that behaviors are the primary way children teach us they are embracing pain and loss.

What about those children with long histories of ADHD?

Some bereaved children bring an accurately diagnosed history of ADHD into their personal grief journeys. These children require special consideration in the development of caregiving strategies.

Education: Parents, teachers and the child need help in understanding the syndrome. Emphasis can be placed on the child's strengths and weaknesses, without perceiving them as "sick" or as "failures."

Support: The child and caregivers often benefit from help with self-esteem, anger management, social skills and grief counseling. The parents often need a safe place to express themselves and learn stress reduction skills. Effective parenting skills can be taught in a group setting with parents who struggle with similar problems. Ongoing support groups should always be considered for both caregivers and children.

Medication management: The wise use of medications is often a part of the comprehensive effort to help children with ADHD. The medication plan should always be carried out by well-trained persons who specialize in this area of work with children. All medications need to be carefully monitored based on individual responses, both biological and behavioral.

"I hate you!"

Explosive emotions

A child's explosive emotions—including not just anger but feelings of hate, blame, terror, resentment, rage and jealousy—can be upsetting and threatening to adults because they are often uncertain how to respond.

Explosive emotions often express a child's desire to restore things to the way they were before the death. Anger and other related emotions are a grieving child's natural, intelligent response to the death of someone loved and an effort to restore a valued relationship that has been lost.

Explosive emotions may also signal a bereaved child's anger at the person who died because, as the child views the situation, "If Daddy loved me enough, he wouldn't have died and left me." The child may then further reason, "If Dad doesn't love me, no one can love me. There must be something about me that makes me unlovable."

A bereaved child's rage may be directed toward anyone available: a surviving parent, a teacher, playmates, God or the world in general. Through this behavior, some bereaved children may even be testing the idea that they should never love again. The rationale: If they love anyone again, that person may die, too.

Behind a bereaved child's explosive emotions are the primary feelings of pain, helplessness, frustration and hurt.

The fact that the dead person does not come back, despite the child's explosive emotions, is actually a part of the reality testing necessary for eventual healing to occur. As the child gradually becomes aware that the person who died will not return, these explosive emotions will typically soften.

My grief gardening experiences with hundreds of bereaved children have taught me one final, fundamental lesson about explosive emotions: There is a healthy survival value in being able to temporarily protest the painful reality of the loss. Having the capacity to express anger gives a child the courage to survive during a difficult time. Children who do not receive permission to do so may slide into chronic depression. They are literally deprived of a means of psychological survival.

Adults tend to be intolerant of explosive emotions because we reason, "If the child is angry at me, something must be wrong with either him or me." And so we discourage the anger, the rage. The children in turn see how uncomfortable we are with their anger and they may begin to feel guilty about it.

Unfortunately, bereaved children who repress or deny their explosive feelings will turn their anger inward. The painful results are low self-esteem, depression, chronic feelings of guilt and physical complaints.

The grief gardener's helping role The major role of caring adults when a child demonstrates explosive emotions is to be a supportive stabilizer. Adults need to tolerate, encourage and validate explosive emotions without judging, retaliating or arguing.

A word of caution: Never attempt to prescribe what these emotions should be for a bereaved child. Simply be alert for them. Let the child teach you if explosive emotions are part of his grief experience. In some cases, such as when a death is anticipated due to terminal illness, the demonstration of explosive emotions may be mild or nonexistent.

- *Encourage the healthy expression of a child's explosive emotions so these feelings will be expressed, not repressed.* If you simply listen and watch as the child demonstrates her anger, she will come to understand that her feelings are accepted. When she has calmed down, you might also ask her why she thinks she is feeling so angry; if she can't offer an explanation that will help her understand her explosive emotions, perhaps you can.

- *Remember that explosive emotional behavior often signals the child's underlying feelings of pain, helplessness, frustration, fear and hurt.* During this difficult time, caring adults need to "be with" and support the grieving child as he does the painful work of mourning.

- *Provide alternate outlets for expression of anger.* During counseling sessions, you can encourage children to express their anger through shadow boxing, pillow fighting and other physical activities. You might also ask them to paint their anger or write about it. In using these techniques, you are not only learning about the child's anger, you are teaching her constructive ways to deal with her anger.

"I got in a fight at school today!"

Acting-Out

Many children express the pain of grief through acting-out. This behavior usually varies depending on the child's age and developmental level. The child may become unusually loud and noisy, have a temper outburst, start fights with other children, defy authority, or simply rebel against everything. Other examples of acting-out behavior include getting poor grades in school or assuming a general attitude that says, "I don't care about anything." Older children may even run away from home.

Understanding and appropriately responding to the bereaved child's acting out may seem a daunting task. But when broken down into its component parts, it is not so overwhelming. To begin, it is important to understand why bereaved children act out in the first place. A number of factors influence this behavior.

Feelings of insecurity—Bereaved children naturally experience a sense of insecurity following the death of someone loved. After all, when it is a family member who has died, the child's most stabilizing influence—the family—has been disturbed. Acted-out feelings unconsciously provide the child with a sense of control and power.

While temper outbursts don't resolve the child's anxiety, they do provide a way for the child to feel she has regained some control. Tantrums and fighting also frighten others around the child, adding to the bereaved child's feelings of power.

Feelings of abandonment—Bereaved children may feel as if their dead parent has abandoned or "died on them." Consequently, they sometimes feel unloved; their self-esteem is affected. As a result, some bereaved children will act out to create a self-fulfilling prophecy: "See, nobody loves me."

A desire to provoke punishment—Even though it is not rational to adults, some bereaved children reason that, "If I'm so bad that somebody I loved died, then I deserve to be punished." Again, this reasoning is usually an unconscious process.

When it is a parent who died—especially the parent who was the family's primary disciplinarian—the child may act out in an attempt to get the parent to "come back" and mete out punishment. The rationale: "If I'm bad, Dad will have to come back and make me behave."

Protection from future losses—Bereaved children sometimes initiate rejection in an effort to prevent feelings of "abandonment" in the future. Their acting-out behaviors serve to keep people at a distance. The result: They become the ones who control the situation rather than passively suffer the possibility of being left again.

Essentially, the bereaved child unconsciously reasons that it is better to be the abandoner than the abandoned. Acting-out behavior protects the child from intimate relationships and the additional hurt and pain of a future loss.

Bereaved children sometimes initiate rejection in an effort to prevent feelings of abandonment in the future.

Demonstration of internal feelings of grief—As I have said, many bereaved children grieve but do not mourn. When this happens, feelings build up inside the child with no way to be expressed outwardly. Ultimately, the stress erupts—often in the form of acting-out behaviors.

The grief gardener's helping role

• *Understand the needs that underlie the acting-out behaviors.* Acting-out in bereaved children is often an indirect, unconscious cry for help, so adults must work to understand what function the acting-out behavior serves. Caregivers should first ask themselves, "What are the genuine needs of a bereaved child who acts out?"

But being aware of this phenomenon does not mean you should ignore it. Caregivers must still set appropriate limits while at the same time recognizing the possible reasons for the child's actions. My experience as a grief counselor has shown me that the two greatest needs of a bereaved child are for affection and a sense of security. Appropriate limit-setting and discipline, then, should attempt to meet these essential needs. We must let bereaved children know that we love them despite their present behavior.

• *Set limits without demonstrating anger or using violence.* Too often, bereaved children are punished in ways that are counterproductive. Discipline and limit-setting must communicate to the child that adults accept and love the child despite the misbehavior. Unfortunately, some adults attempt to set limits on acting-out behavior while communicating to the child that he or she is a "bad boy" or "bad girl." The message often is, "You are being punished because you are bad." No distinction is made between inappropriate behavior and being a bad person.

- *Recognize that adult discipline will eventually lead to self-discipline.* Adult modeling and reasonable boundary-setting help bereaved children develop their internal controls while at the same time providing them the opportunity to make painful mistakes. As we all know, discovering we make mistakes as we grow up is an important lesson.

"I'm the man of the house now."

Hypermaturity

The opposite of regressive behavior on the part of the bereaved child is hypermaturity. This is when the child attempts to grow up very quickly and become the "man" or "woman" of the house, often in an effort to replace a dead parent. In my past writings I have referred to this tendency as the "Big Man" or "Big Woman" Syndrome.

An example: *Amy's mother died six months ago, and Amy and her father have been working through their grief.* However, Amy's father said to a friend, "My daughter Amy, who is only ten years old, tries to be just like her mother was. She has been trying to cook all of the meals and insists that she sit where her mother did at the kitchen table…She cleans the house in the same order and manner of my wife…She waits at the door when I return from work and asks me about my day in exactly the same words my wife used for years."

Our society often overburdens bereaved children through statements such as this: "John, you're the man of the house now."

Bereaved children act overmature for a variety of reasons. This girl's attempt to take on her mother's role may be a symbolic way of keeping Mom alive. Or, it could be another way for her to protect herself from a common sense of hopelessness and helplessness. She probably also thinks that filling in for Mom makes Dad feel better, too.

Many times, though, bereaved children don't dream up this behavior all by themselves. Adults encourage them by saying things like, "You're the oldest, John. You'll have to be the man of the house now" or "You'll need to take care of the other kids now that your mom is gone." Some adults also encourage this hypermature behavior because they simply feel more comfortable dealing with "adult-acting" kids. And a surviving parent may actually, consciously or unconsciously, attempt to have the child replace the dead parent.

Regardless of the cause, hypermaturity is dangerous for bereaved children because it doesn't allow them to deal with their grief at their own developmental levels. In fact, it tends to displace grief because the suddenly grown-up children focus on their difficult, new roles instead of on their normal thoughts and feelings.

The grief gardener's helping role

- *Remember that children in single parent families often naturally mature more quickly due to the economic and social realities of this lifestyle.* While we as caregivers need to understand this reality, we must also encourage same-age peer contact and help the family to understand the normalcy of this. Don't shame families in which the children are of necessity hypermature, but rather help them understand the behavior and respond appropriately to it.

- *Keep in mind that well-meaning adults sometimes encourage this forced sense of maturity on a bereaved child because they find it easier to respond to the child at this inappropriate level.* If this occurs, a systems approach to helping the family is often useful. Again, be conscious not to prematurely confront or shame families; join them before you move them. Often, this hypermaturity isn't something they have consciously set in motion. As a matter of fact, at a societal level, it is often a projection of messages to "put things behind you and go on" (in other words, "grow up"). Actually, the bereaved child and family need to go into neutral before they can get into gear. A grief gardener's task is often to help them compassionately slow down, not speed up!

- *Be aware of the potential negative impact that trite comments can have on a bereaved child.* As grief gardeners, we can help educate well-intentioned but misinformed adults about not handing out clichéd, damaging advice such as, "Now you have to be the man of the house." The goal should be to work to help bereaved children and their families experience as normal as possible maturational and development patterns following the death of someone loved. A difficult but achievable task!

"I'm so scared."

Fear

Grieving children often feel afraid. When the reality begins to set in that the parent or other significant person in the child's life will not be coming back, it is not unusual for the child to become frightened. During these times children may ask themselves, "If one parent dies, will the other?" or "Susie left us, will Ricky die, too?"

Grieving children often feel afraid.

Frequently, the underlying fear is that there will be no one left to take care of them. This fear often is increased when the child witnesses a surviving parent struggling with his or her own grief. The parent may seem detached from the child's world and appear incapable of caring for the child. Related to this experience is the child's fear of watching people whom they love mourn. Parents and other adults around the child must reassure her that she is loved and will be cared for.

Another common fear of the bereaved child is the fear of loving again. Children may reason that if they had not loved the dead person so much, they would not be experiencing the pain of this grief.

Helping children understand and accept these feelings will help them cope. Children can be helped to understand that giving and receiving love are two of the greatest gifts of life. Often children have difficulty understanding that the pain of grief is part of life, living and loving. However, the presence of caring adults can make a true difference in a child's ability to cope with many fears.

Another common fear that many bereaved children experience is the fear of their own death. They may be frightened at the slightest hint of illness or secretly feel that they too will soon die. Again, the child needs reassurance and the loving support of adult caregivers.

*The grief gardener's
helping role*

- *Grief gardeners must train themselves to be sensitive to a child's fears.* For example, children's questions related to an adult truly caring about them are frequently an attempt to determine if they can count on the adult not to leave or to die. Accepting children's questions and fears means you accept each child—critical because bereaved children can be extremely sensitive to the slightest hint of rejection. Also recognize that underneath expressions of fear is the emotional need for warmth, acceptance, and understanding.

- *A sometimes helpful approach to exploring potential unspoken fears is to use the "wishes and fears inventory" with the child.* This is where you ask the child to tell you three wishes and three fears. Having expressed some wishes (a task most children are used to), children often go right into fears they might be concealing. This is only one of many ways you might learn from a child about fears he might be experiencing. Be creative; do what seems to work for you.

- *Another potentially useful tool to learn about fears is to do what I call "going fishing."* With proper timing and pacing, you simply say to the child, "Some kids have taught me that when someone in their life dies it can be pretty scary. It there anything that's scary to you?" Sensing your desire to understand, they will often go on to teach you about their unique fears.

*"It's my fault
Uncle Jim died.."*

Guilt

It is very human for both adults and children to blame themselves when someone they love dies. For children this can be an especially tough struggle because they have particular difficulty understanding cause-effect relationships.

Young children are susceptible to magical thinking; they believe that by thinking about something they can make it happen. What child, for example, hasn't wished his parents would go away and leave him alone? So when a parent dies, the child may well assume blame and feel guilty for thinking these thoughts. The child may blame himself for any number of things, ranging from being bad to having had angry feelings toward the person who died. The child may even take total responsibility for the death, yet say nothing to anyone about this feeling. If adults are not perceptive and aware of this phenomenon, it may well go unnoticed.

The Dying Child's Grief

Terminally ill children naturally experience grief at the prospect of their own death. They will often have many of the same feelings—described throughout this chapter—that other bereaved children have. Following are some other special considerations for what I think of as the most poignant of all griefs:

Don't underestimate the child's capacity to understand

Children have the capacity to understand more than we often give them credit for. Like adults, they deserve our respect and compassion—and our honesty. Sometimes adults, in an effort to protect themselves, assume that children are incapable of understanding or should be protected from the truth. They don't talk directly to dying children about their prognoses, which can leave them feeling alone and isolated.

Children can cope with what they know. They can't cope with what they don't know. Dying children deserve an atmosphere that creates open, two-way communication. Many terminally ill children will go back and forth between wanting to know details about their illness and not wanting to acknowledge they are even sick. It is critical to follow the lead of the child. Always listen first as you support open dialogue about any feelings, concerns or questions they might have. If they ask something and you don't know the answer, simply say, "I don't know."

Be honest with the child about her coming death

As the child comes to comprehend her illness and its severity, a parent or other primary caregiver should explain to her that she will likely die—in language she will understand. This may be the hardest thing a parent ever has to do. But honest love is what the dying child needs most.

Depending on her age and developmental maturity, she may not immediately (or ever) fully understand what this means. But she will begin to incorporate the notion of death into her remaining life and will have the opportunity to think about it and ask questions. She will also have the privilege of saying goodbye.

Encourage parents not to lie to her about her condition. The dying child who is told she will get better will notice the disparity between this false hope and the way those around her are acting. She will be confused, frustrated and perhaps angry.

Encourage open communication, but do not force it

As caring adults we should encourage honest communication among the child, caregivers, family and friends. However, we should never force it. Children will naturally dose themselves as they encounter the reality of the illness in their life. They aren't able to take in all the information at once, nor will they want to.

Answer only what is asked in the child's terms. Don't over-respond out of your own anxiety. Remember—children will determine with whom they want to share their pain. Often, the child wants to protect his parents or other close adults and will adopt a "chin up" attitude around them. The child may share with you, the counselor, more intimate thoughts and feelings. This is a normal response and should be respected.

Helping the dying child live

Terminal illness presents human beings with an exceedingly difficult and contradictory challenge: you are dying, you know you are dying, yet it is your nature to want to live. Dying children often feel this tension, too. If the adults around them have been honest, they understand that they will soon die, but they still want to live and laugh and play as much and as often as they can.

Help the dying child live happily. Do what is in your power to make him comfortable. Help his family and friends create special, memorable moments for him. Let them know it is important to not completely abandon his normal routine (this may make him feel out-of-control and unprotected), but do encourage them to work to make each remaining day count. Above all, encourage them to spend time with him. See that the people who mean the most to him are around him as often as possible.

Peer relationships are very important to children, and the illness will likely create some social and physical barriers to these friendships. Adults can see that friendships continue to be nurtured when possible. Help arrange a special party for the dying child. Encourage parents to make play dates with the child's one or two best friends. Help the children write letters back and forth when personal contact isn't possible.

This dimension of guilt may be revealed when the child says things like, "If only I would have..." or "I wish I could have..." or "Why didn't I..." Self-defeating thoughts and behaviors often mount as the grieving child experiences feelings of guilt. Frequently, a guilt-wracked child feels helpless and worthless. The child may say to herself, "I am a bad person for what I have done (or not done)."

In fact, bereaved children who feel responsible for the death of someone loved often think that they will be punished in some way and may actually seek out forms of self-punishment. This sense that something bad will happen may become a self-fulfilling prophecy.

Moreover, when children feel helpless, they may attempt to gain some sense of control by thinking that if they would have done something differently, the person they loved would not have died. In other words, if they see themselves as being the cause of the death, they think there may well be something they could do to bring the person back to life. The child may say, "If you come back I'll be good; I'll never be noisy again or make you get up early with me." This kind of thinking is at times reinforced in those families where someone is always to blame for whatever happens.

It is very human for both adults and children to blame themselves when someone they love dies.

Survival guilt and relief—Surviving a person who has died, particularly a parent, brother or sister, can generate feelings of guilt in bereaved children. The child may observe the other parent's pain and reasons, "Maybe it should have been me instead of my father." What the child may not realize is that if she had died, the parent would be experiencing the same pain of grief.

Relief-guilt syndrome—Another type of guilt may evolve when a person's death brings a child some sense of relief or release. This situation often occurs when the person who died had been ill for a long time or the child's relationship with the person who died was in conflict.

After a long illness, a child may not miss the frequent trips to the hospital or the family's ongoing focus on the dying person. If the bereaved child is not able to acknowledge this sense of relief as natural and not equal to a lack of love, she may feel guilty for feeling relieved.

Personality factors and guilt—Another form of guilt evolves from long-standing personality factors within the bereaved child. Some children are taught early in life that when anything bad or unfortunate occurs, it is their fault. Consequently, when a death occurs, they look first within themselves to find blame. This kind of guilt becomes an ingrained part of their character development.

These children definitely need the context of a professional counseling relationship to make constructive changes. Unfortunately, these children often live in families where outside help is not made available.

Guilt and punishment—Some bereaved children anticipate that punishment (from outside or inside) should result from experiencing feelings of guilt. As a consequence, adults might see children attempting to lessen their guilt through punishment. They may directly or indirectly ask to be punished.

Obviously, seeking out punishment is self-destructive and only makes the child's situation worse. For caring adults, the task is to help the bereaved child feel less guilty and thus reduce his need to demonstrate self-destructive behaviors. These children are often also accident-prone and exhibit a high level of risk-taking behavior.

Joy-guilt syndrome—A bereaved child can also experience feelings of guilt when she begins to re-experience any kind of joy or happiness in life. These feelings often stem from a sense of loyalty to the person who died and a fear that being happy in some way betrays that relationship. Opportunities to explore these feelings are necessary as the child moves forward in her grief experience.

The grief gardener's helping role

- *Foremost, we must provide opportunities for the child to talk and play out the circumstances surrounding the death.* Try to prevent adults around the child from reinforcing the thought that death is a form of punishment. As the child recalls memories, either good or bad, talk about them openly and honestly.

Help the child understand that being angry or upset with a person does not cause the person to die. The child can be helped to understand that at times it is normal for people to get angry with people they care about. The bereaved child also can be helped to understand that we cannot control certain things in life.

- *In the case of the child who is too young to articulate thoughts and feelings, the sense of a trusting relationship with an adult figure is paramount.* Adults are capable of expressing a sense of warmth and acceptance through nonverbal as well as verbal means. Just as children learn to be able to give love by being loved, they learn self-acceptance by being accepted. For the verbal child the opportunity to participate in a permissive, patient, and non-judgmental conversation often allows for the opportunity to work through feelings of guilt.

- *Go slowly in working through guilt with children. First, work to enter into what they think and feel in an effort to understand.* What is their phenomenological reality? As adults, we are sometimes quick to want to take away a child's feelings in general, but particularly guilt. Yet, if children feel guilty, they feel guilty—we cannot and should not try to save them from this feeling.

- *Do be alert to some children's conscious or unconscious need to punish themselves because of feelings of guilt.* Self-punishment themes in children may be illustrated through inappropriate risk-taking, accident-proneness, chronic depression and general self-neglect. These types of behaviors demand immediate help from caring adults.

"*I'm glad Grandma died.*"

Relief

At times, a bereaved child very appropriately experiences a sense of relief when someone in her life dies. Death can bring relief from suffering, especially when due to a long and debilitating illness. The bereaved child's sense of relief is an emotion that is frequently overlooked, misunderstood or repressed by adults.

When adults do not allow (and therefore do not help the child understand) this emotion, the child may feel guilty. Children may think they are the only ones who feel relieved. The result is all too often a tremendous self-imposed attack on the child's self-esteem, potentially resulting in depression.

Bereaved children may also experience a sense of relief due to their developmental stage. Egocentrism is normal in childhood, and when someone is ill in the family, the focus of attention is usually diverted toward the sick person. After the death, many children are naturally relieved because they think that now they will receive some of the attention they crave. Of course, we as adults should never blame or shame a child for this normal feeling.

Feelings of relief also relate to the reality that we as humans, regardless of age, do not begin to grieve and mourn at the moment of a terminally ill person's death. The experience of grief may begin when the person we love begins the transition from being alive and well to becoming unwell and dying. Herein lies the source

The bereaved child's sense of relief is an emotion that is frequently overlooked or misunderstood by adults.

of another potential complication for children: When the child is deceived about an illness or, worse yet, flat out lied to, she may have no knowledge that the person has even been ill. So, when the death occurs, what others may perceive as an anticipated death actually becomes a sudden, unexpected death for the child. Therefore, some adults might assume the child is relieved when in reality she has come to grief before she is prepared to mourn! This often occurs in closed family systems in which children are isolated from events impacting the family.

In an open-family system, I often witness a natural progression of anticipatory mourning that includes the children. This progression may occur as follows: what starts out as sense of "he is sick" becomes "he is very sick" becomes "he may die" becomes "he is going to die" becomes "he is suffering so much" becomes "I'll be glad when he is out of pain" toward "he is dead," which in turn opens the doorway to many other thoughts and feelings. Obviously, the child who is openly involved in this progression is more likely to express some aspects of relief when the death does come.

Death can also be experienced as relief when the child has been the victim of physical, emotional or sexual abuse by the person who died. The child may teach you she feels safe for this first time in her life. I also frequently witness relief in children when someone has died due to chemical abuse or dependence. They may have loved the person but not liked the fall-out consequences from the chemical abuse or dependence.

Regardless of the death circumstances it's caused by, relief is experienced not in isolation, but in tandem with a number of other emotions. Many children will be confronted with mourning not only what they lost, but what they wish they could have had in a relationship with this person. They may do more work on this as they grow into adulthood and do some catch-up mourning.

The grief gardener's helping role

- *Remember that relief is often a normal response for the bereaved child.* Listen to or observe acceptingly the child's sense of relief without projecting shame or guilt.

- *Keep in mind that relief does not necessarily equal a lack of love for the person who died.* Actually, being relieved that someone is no longer suffering is a natural element of love.

- *Do not prescribe relief, particularly in the period of time shortly after the death.* The child and family are rarely, if ever, fully prepared for the moment of the death, even when the terminally ill person has been near death for some time. If the child should teach you that he feels immediate relief, so be it. However, grief gardeners do not prescribe feelings. They allow bereaved children to teach them what feelings are present and then respond to them.

"There's a big hole in my heart."
Sadness

This dimension of grief is often the most difficult for bereaved children. The full sense of loss and emptiness never takes place all at once, and as it begins to set in, sadness, emptiness, and feelings of depression often follow. These feelings often surface when the child really realizes that the dead person will not be coming back.

One difficulty with this sense of loss and emptiness is that it may take place long after adults in the child's life think grief support is necessary—typically months following the death. Children may wonder why they are crying more at this time than they did just after the death occurred.

As children struggle to come to terms with the finality and reality of the death, they very naturally become depressed.

As children struggle to come to terms with the finality and reality of the death, they very naturally become depressed. Of course, the death of a significant person in their life is something about which to be depressed. During this time the child may demonstrate:

- A lack of interest in self and others
- Change of appetite and sleeping patterns
- Prolonged withdrawal
- Nervousness
- Inability to experience pleasure
- Low self-esteem

The children may feel totally alone and empty, usually resulting in a heightening of these feelings. These characteristics of their mourning should change very slowly over time, assuming they have a safe place to mourn.

The child who is not in an environment conducive to recognizing and encouraging loss, emptiness, and sadness will sometimes feel unable to express these feelings. Suppressed feelings often push for release, while the child is encouraged to repress them. The frequent result is increased anxiety, agitation, and a sense of being emotionally and physically drained.

Obviously, the bereaved child is particularly vulnerable during this period. The child may actively seek a substitute for the person who died. Feelings of attachment can be displaced to the extent that a strong dependency upon another person occurs. The person to whom the child attaches often reminds the child—and us—of the person who died.

The grief gardener's helping role

- *Encourage the child to talk about his intense feelings of sadness.* The regular presence of a supportive and stabilizing adult caregiver is helpful when the bereaved child is feeling sad. While strong new attachments may appear to be helpful to the child at this time, continuing the work of grief is really the task at hand. The child should be encouraged to talk about and/or play out intense feelings. An important person in the child's life has died, but that person still exists in the child's memory. The child should not be denied the opportunity to express these feelings and work them through.

- *Find creative ways for the child to express her sadness.* At times, bereaved children find it easier to express such intense feelings through play, artwork or writing. Whatever helps the child to express and explore feelings should be respected. Don't be surprised that if during this dimension of grief the child wants to review the events preceding the death and the death itself. It is as if each time the child talks about the death it becomes a little more bearable.

- *Teach bereaved children about "griefbursts" so when they experience one, they'll be less frightened.* "Griefbursts"—sudden, unexpected and strong feelings of sadness— can be extremely frightening to children . For grief gardeners, helping means not allowing children to feel alone as they struggle with these feelings. Many children will not initiate talking about their grief attacks. They often, however, give indirect cues. When these urgent cues are not heard or are misunderstood, the result is often another experience of loss for the bereaved child.

"I miss Mom, but I'm going to be OK."

Reconciliation

In many grief models, the final "stage" of bereavement is referred to as resolution. Other paradigms use the terms recovery, re-establishment or reorganization. The problem with these definitions is that people— children and adults alike—do not "get over" grief. My personal and professional experience tells me that a total return to "normalcy" after the death of someone loved is not possible; everyone is changed by the experience of grief. Recovery, as it is often understood by mourners and caregivers, is erroneously seen as an absolute, a perfect state of re-establishment.

We as human beings never "get over" grief, but instead become reconciled to it.

Reconciliation is a term I find more appropriate for what occurs as the bereaved person works to integrate the new reality of moving forward in life without the physical presence of the person who has died. With reconciliation comes a renewed sense of energy and confidence, an ability to fully acknowledge the reality of the death, and a capacity to become reinvolved in the activities of living. There is also an acknowledgment that pain and grief are difficult, yet necessary parts of life.

How Parents Can Tell If Their Grieving Child Needs Counseling

(and how counselors can tell if a child's grief is complicated)

Bereavement counselors are often approached by parents who want to know if their bereaved child's mourning behaviors are "normal" or if the child might need counseling. What follows is a list caregivers can photocopy for such parents in helping them make this decision.

As I've said throughout this chapter, many of the behaviors listed below are normal grief responses (with the exception of those that might harm the child or others.) What makes these "red flags" is a matter of degree. Panic and fear, for example, are normal. Persistent panic and fear, on the other hand, are symptomatic of unmet mourning needs. Mourning behaviors should soften in intensity and duration over time if the child is making progress in her grief journey.

On a similar note: We counselors often use the word "pathological" in describing unreconciled grief. We also use terms like "atypical," "abnormal" and "unresolved." I prefer the word "complicated." For one, pathological is a medical term implying a "disturbed" state of mind; bereaved children who are persistently angry or excessively sad are typically not disturbed. And for another, the word pathology connotes something irreversible. We cannot depathologize a disease. We can, however, help children uncomplicate their mourning.

Here are some signs of complicated mourning:

- total denial of the reality of the death

- persistent panic, fear

- prolonged physical complaints without organic findings

- prolonged feelings of guilt or responsibility for the death when the child obviously isn't responsible. (Children who feel guilt because they are responsible for the death often benefit from individual counseling as well.)

- *chronic* patterns of apathy and/or depression

- *chronic* hostility, acting-out toward others or self

- prolonged change in typical behavior patterns or personality (e.g. the amiable child who now gets in fights all the time or the normally outgoing child who becomes introverted and withdrawn.)

- consistent withdrawal from friends and family members

- dramatic, ongoing changes in sleeping and eating patterns

- drug or alcohol abuse

- suicidal thoughts or actions

Also, don't discount your own feelings of discomfort about a child's mourning progress. If your gut feeling tells you a bereaved child needs special help, work to get that help for him.

So once you've determined a bereaved child could benefit from counseling, how do you tell the child? With compassion and understanding. The last thing a bereaved child needs is to feel something is "wrong" with her. You might say to the child, "The painful feelings you have about the death are just as real as the pain you experience when you fall off your bike. Just like there are doctors and nurses to help you with a broken arm, there are people who can help you with the pain of your grief."

Normal Grief or Clinical Depression?

- In normal grief, children respond to comfort and support; clinically depressed children often reject support.

- The bereaved child is often able to use play to work out feelings of grief; the depressed child is more often resistant to the use of play.

- The bereaved child is often openly angry; the depressed child may complain and be irritable, but may not directly express anger.

- Bereaved children will usually connect depressed feelings to the death; depressed children often do not relate their feelings to any life event.

- In normal grief, bereaved children can still experience moments of enjoyment in life; depressed children often project a pervasive sense of doom.

- Caring adults around the bereaved child can sense feelings of sadness and emptiness; the depressed child often projects a sense of hopelessness and chronic emptiness.

- While the bereaved child is more likely to have transient physical complaints, the depressed child may have chronic physical complaints.

- Bereaved children may express guilt over some aspect of the loss; depressed children often have generalized feelings of guilt.

- While the self-esteem of bereaved children is temporarily impacted, it is usually not the deep loss of esteem typically seen in clinically depressed children.

The bereaved child's reconciliation after a death is a process, not an event. Adults should avoid using specific timetables with specific points at which a child should "be over" grief. Human beings never get over our grief, but instead become reconciled to it. Caregivers who allow and encourage children to move toward their grief, instead of away from it, aid in this reconciliation process.

Among the changes often noted during the child's reconciliation process are:

- A return to stable eating and sleeping patterns
- A renewed sense of energy and well-being
- A subjective sense of release from the person who has died
- Increased thinking and judgment-making capabilities
- The capacity to enjoy life experiences
- A recognition of the reality and finality of the death
- The establishment of new and healthy relationships

Perhaps the most important gain for the child in this reconciliation process is the discovery of the ability to cope successfully with the loss. This coping is achieved only with the assistance of caring adults.

The grief gardener's helping role

- *If we are able to recognize that grief is a complex emotion that varies from child to child, we can be more open and honest in helping young people cope with death and achieve reconciliation.* Grief is not something a child should be ashamed of or try to hide. Only because children give and receive love are they able to grieve and grow. As caregivers, we must model the giving and receiving of love as we interact with the child.

- *In a very real sense, grief is a privilege for both children and adults.* We have a capacity for deep feelings that lower life forms are not able to experience and appreciate. Only because we have the capacity to love do we grieve. When children are born into this world, they do not have the choice of feeling or not feeling. The capacity to feel is innate. However, we do have the choice as to how open and honest we will be about our feelings and how committed we will be to helping both ourselves and our children in working through these feelings in a healthy, life-affirming manner.

- *The child's grief gardener must understand grief as an integral part of life and living and must work to reverse the trend toward protecting children from grief.* Therefore, if the material shared in this chapter stimulates discussion, raises questions, and increases one's sense of hope, it will have served a most useful purpose.

Grief Myth

A child's grief proceeds in predictable, orderly stages.

We should never prescribe what a child's grief and mourning experiences should be.

Have you ever heard a well-meaning but misinformed person say of a bereaved child, "He's in stage two"? If only it were that simple! People use the "stages of grief" to try to make sense of an experience that isn't as orderly and predictable as we would like it to be.

The concept of "stages" was popularized in 1969 with the publication of Elizabeth Kubler-Ross' landmark text *On Death and Dying*. Kubler-Ross never intended that people should interpret her "five stages of dying" literally. However, many people have done just that, not only with the process of dying, but with the processes of bereavement, grief, and mourning as well.

No two children are alike. No two children will grieve in the same way. As caring adults, we only get ourselves in trouble when we try to prescribe what a child's grief and mourning experiences should be.

A good gardener doesn't approach his garden with textbook in hand and say, "Well, today I must water thoroughly and thin the new seedlings." Instead, he examines the garden on hands and knees and only then decides what is needed that day. Likewise, the grief gardener encourages the bereaved child to teach her about the child's needs: "Teach me about your grief, and I will be with you. As you teach me, I will follow the lead you provide and attempt to be a stabilizing and empathetic presence."

To think that one's goal is to move children through the stages of grief would be a misuse of counsel. Children experience a variety of unique thoughts, feelings and behaviors as part of the healing process. We must remind ourselves not to prescribe how and when they should mourn, but allow them to teach us where they are in the process.

Have you seen this myth carried out? When and how?

_____

_____

_____

_____

4

How the Bereaved Child Heals: The Six Reconciliation Needs of Mourning

Thus far in this text we have examined several aspects of childhood grief. We have reviewed the influences on a child's mourning (what I've also called "mourning styles") and the ways in which those mourning styles are manifested through a child's behaviors, thoughts and feelings. In Chapter 1, we also explored my grief gardening model and what it can mean for a child to grow through grief.

But how does a bereaved child mourn his way from the starting point of his grief—which is largely a factor of mourning style influences—through his many thoughts and feelings to the destination of reconciliation and growth? Asked more simply, how does the bereaved child heal?

I believe the bereaved child heals, over time, when her mourning needs are consistently met. For a flower to grow, the plant must receive adequate nutrients from the soil, adequate water and sufficient sun. It also needs protection from pests, disease and invasive weeds. The gardener who understands and helps his plants meet these needs will be rewarded with a lush, healthy garden.

Bereaved children have equally fundamental needs that must be met if they are to heal and grow. This chapter defines what I term "the six reconciliation needs of mourning." Others have labeled these the tasks of childhood mourning. As a grief gardener, you probably know intuitively what a child's mourning needs are, but you may never have analyzed and articulated them in this manner. I find that doing so helps me better understand each child's grief journey and my role as her companion.

Following a discussion of each need are questions for you, the grief gardener, to ask yourself as you work to understand the child's progress toward reconciliation and healing.

"O Lord, grant that in some way it may rain every day, say from about midnight until three o-clock in the morning, but, you see, it must be gentle and warm so that it can soak in; grant that at the same time it would not rain on campion,… lavender, and the others which you in your infinite wisdom know are drought-loving plants …and grant that the sun may shine the whole day long, but not everywhere…and not too much; that there may be plenty of dew and little wind, enough worms …no mildew, and that once a week a thin liquid manure… may fall from heaven. Amen."

Karel Capek,
The Gardener's Year (1929)

Need 1

Acknowledge the reality of the death

Before he can move on in his grief journey, the bereaved child must be helped to gently confront the reality that someone he loves has died and will not return.

Of course, children must be provided with an open and honest explanation (at their level of developmental understanding) about the nature and cause of the death if they are to meet this mourning need. As caring adults, we must openly share clear information about the death with the affected children. Remember, kids can cope with what they know. They cannot cope with what they don't know.

We as a society must work to overcome our instinct to protect children from sad news. We must also refrain from thinking that children are "too young to understand." Perhaps they are too young to fully understand everything about the death, but they are never too young to feel.

The news of a death is best conveyed by someone close to the child. When possible, it shouldn't come from someone who doesn't have a pre-existing, stabilizing relationship with the child. Keep in mind the importance of eye contact, a comforting tone of voice and appropriate physical comfort that conveys security. Be certain to avoid euphemisms such as, "sleep" and "passed away" that will only confuse the child.

Kids can cope with what they know. They cannot cope with what they don't know.

As a counselor, of course, you more often see children who have already been told about a death. So, while at times you may not be able to influence the way in which children first hear about the death of someone loved, you can help explain what death means. If a child teaches you that she doesn't understand what death is all about, explain that the dead person's body has stopped working and it will never again work the way it used to. The person's body will not see or hear and won't talk, move or breathe anymore. The body won't feel cold or hot or be happy or sad. When a person's body dies, the person doesn't feel anything anymore. These kinds of explanations help the child understand that the person who died cannot come back. Being supportive of the child as she gently confronts this new reality is a vital part of helping with this reconciliation need of mourning.

Remember, do not expect that the child's acknowledgment of the reality will be similar to an adult's response. Many children naturally respond to news of death with indifference or an apparent lack of feelings. This is the child's natural way of protecting herself; she will embrace the full reality of the death only intermittently, in doses. A lack of outward mourning does not mean that children are not moving toward the reality—they are just doing it in their own way and time.

Many times a bereaved child asks questions that are prompted by this need to acknowledge the reality of the death. Do not try to attach adult meanings to the child's questions, which are usually quite simple and factual. The questions they ask and re-ask are one of the central ways in which they embrace the full reality of death.

A lack of outward mourning does not mean that children are not moving toward acknowledging the reality of the death.

The ability to acknowledge the reality of the death only comes about after the child is provided with opportunities to talk out, play-out and even act-out the circumstances of the death. Typically, the child does not embrace the full sense of loss until several months after the death. (Meeting this need can take years if the child has been told half-truths or even out-and-out lied to about the reality of the death.) Prior to that, the child will likely, consciously and unconsciously, work to distance himself from the pain that is part and parcel of meeting this critical first mourning need.

For the adult caregiver, the art of helping meet this need lies in balancing the child's need to acknowledge this new reality with the child's normal desire to push the reality away. As we learn to companion children in grief—and not to push or pull them through the experience—we become capable of being true grief gardeners. We become available to the child not only with our heads, but with our hearts.

Grief gardening questions:

- Where is the child in confronting the reality that someone in her life has died?
- What is the child's developmental level of understanding about death?
- Is anyone in the child's environment withholding information, being dishonest or distorting the facts about the death?
- Are the adults in the child's environment aware that children often respond to death news with an apparent lack of feelings?

- Does the child ask questions indicating that she needs help in continuing to embrace the reality of the death?
- Are there any adults in the child's environment who are inappropriately pushing the child to "be strong" and "get on with life"?

Notes _____

_____

_____

_____

_____

Need 2

Move toward the pain of the loss while being nurtured physically, emotionally, and spiritually

To heal, the bereaved child must be not just allowed but encouraged to embrace the wide range of thoughts and feelings that result from the death.

This task is often complicated by adults who want to protect the child from the impact of the death. This tendency is understandable, but in prematurely moving the child away from the hurts of grief, well-intentioned but misinformed adults can interfere with the child's healing and may even cause long-term harm.

The desire of many adults to "spare children" is often caused by their own feelings of discomfort, fear or anxiety. The reasoning? If adults can get the child to avoid feelings of pain and hurt, they won't have to "be with" the child in the grief journey. The sad reality is that many adults will try to protect themselves from pain by protecting children from pain.

As grief gardeners, we must be careful not to blame or shame those adults who have adopted this overprotective stance. After all, they have grown up in a culture in which the role of pain is misunderstood. In our society, to feel and express thoughts and feelings (or in a child's situation, to play or act out these feelings) connected to loss is often considered unnecessary and inappropriate. Mourning makes us uncomfortable. Yet, in reality, it is in moving toward our hurts that we ultimately heal.

So, to heal from losses in our culture takes tremendous courage, particularly for children. Why? Because many children must overcome adult behaviors such as isolation, deception and overprotection from the events surrounding death.

The art of helping bereaved children with this need is to allow them to teach you how they feel. You cannot prod children into this, but you can work to create a safe, nurturing environment where they sense your desire to understand.

Bereaved children need permission to mourn.

Bereaved children need permission to mourn. Sometimes what they need most from adults is an awareness that it is OK to talk out and play out their many thoughts and feelings. If the suffering is avoided, denied or repressed by adults surrounding bereaved children, those very children will be abandoned at a time when they most need the presence of loving adults. Actually, it's not really a question of, "Will the child feel or not feel?" It is a question of, "When he feels, will he be able to express himself in the companionship of loving adults?"

If we are to be those loving adults, we must also be careful not to project to bereaved children that they will (or should) feel exactly as we do about death. So, while the child must move toward whatever feelings he experiences, keep in mind that these feelings can be, and often are, very different from our own grief feelings.

We must also remember that children mourn intermittently, moving at times toward and then away from the depth of the loss. Respecting children means understanding this wave-like quality in their capacity to mourn. This also means remaining available as a stabilizing presence long after the event of the death.

Note, too, that moving toward the pain of the loss is just one facet of this reconciliation need. The child's simultaneous need to be nurtured physically, emotionally and spiritually is the other facet. Physically, the child needs adequate nutrition and hydration, daily rest and regular physical activity. Her emotional needs are many, but at bottom what she needs is a safe psychological environment and a nurturing support system that assures her she is loved and cared for. And the bereaved child's spiritual needs include such things as embracing "meaning of life" issues in the face of death.

Grief gardening questions:

- Has the child been allowed and encouraged to experience the pain of grief? Do adults around the child understand that many bereaved children play-out and act-out their painful thoughts and feelings? What behaviors does the child demonstrate that indicates he is trying to do some of the work of mourning?

- Was the child provided with a sense of feeling understood in the expression of grief? Are there adults in the child's environment who are trying to protect the child from experiencing painful feelings? In what ways has the child received permission to mourn?

- Are there any adults around the child who are projecting the notion that the child should feel the same as they do? Does the child ask questions or demonstrate behaviors that teach you she needs help in moving toward the hurt?

- Does this child live in an environment where physical, emotional and spiritual needs are being met? What can I as grief gardener do or be to help this child work on this task?

Children mourn intermittently, moving at times toward and then away from the depth of the loss.

Notes _____

_____

_____

_____

_____

Need 3

Convert the relationship with the person who has died from one of presence to one of memory

This reconciliation need involves allowing and encouraging the child to move from the "here and now" of his relationship with the person who died to the "what was." Though the bereaved child should not be expected to give up all ties to the person who died (actually it is unwise and often damaging to communicate to the child that any and all relationships with the person who died are over), there must be an alteration of the relationship from one of presence to one of memory.

Precious memories, occasional dreams reflecting the significance of the relationship and living legacies are among the manifestations of this different form of a continued relationship.

The process of beginning to embrace memories often begins with the funeral. Unfortunately, there are some adults who prevent children from this vital part of the work of mourning by excluding them from the funeral. Remembering the person who has died through the funeral helps affirm the value of the life that was lived. In fact, the memories that families share during this time often set the tone for the changed nature of the relationship. The ritual encourages the expression of cherished memories and allows for both tears and laughter. Memories that were made in love can be gently embraced in the companionship of loving adults.

Memories that were made in love can be gently embraced in the companionship of loving adults.

Remembering can be a very slow, painful and incremental process. When children are particularly hurting from the sting of grief, nonjudgmental support and understanding may be what is most needed. However, sometimes as grief gardeners we must encourage the gentle encountering of memories. Stimulating the child to keep memories alive rather than blocking them out helps affirm the value of the relationship. In a culture where many people do not understand the value and function of memories, most bereaved children will need help meeting this important mourning need. There are many ways you can help bereaved children with memory work. A few examples are noted below:

- Modeling the expression of your own feelings and memories.
- Encouraging the child to teach you about some of her own memories.
- Providing the child with keepsakes that belonged to the person who died.
- Allowing the child to be involved in the funeral ritual.
- Talking about experiences the child had with the person who died.
- Displaying photos of the person who died.
- Visiting places of special significance that stimulate memories.
- Naturally bringing up the person who died in conversations with the child.
- Reviewing photo albums together at special times like holidays, birthdays and anniversaries.
- Keeping in mind any major milestones that might create occasions for reminiscing, e.g., graduating from grade school to middle school, the child's own birthday, etc.

Perhaps one of the best ways to embrace memories is through the creation of a "memory book"—a scrapbook containing photos, momentos, letters, reflective writings, etc. that commemorate the person who died. This scrapbook will often become a valued collection of memories that the child will call upon often during her grief journey.

The process of beginning to embrace memories often begins with the funeral.

Special mention should be made of children with ambivalent memories, particularly those children whose memories are marked by emotional, physical or sexual abuse. These kinds of experiences make it naturally difficult to openly embrace memories. These children need nonjudgmental adults they trust enough to explore these painful memories with. Obviously, these kinds of memories complicate the task of mourning and require your special professional attention. Children who are not helped to place these memories in perspective (and helped to understand that they were victims) may carry an underlying sadness or anger into their adult lives.

My experience in learning from thousands of bereaved children is that remembering makes hoping possible. Bereaved children's futures become open to new experiences and relationships to the extent that past memories have been embraced.

Grief gardening questions:

- Where is the child in the process of converting the relationship from one of presence to one of memory?

- Are there any misinformed adults around the child who are discouraging memory work? Is the child being given the perception that he must give up all forms of bonding to the person who died?

- Was the child allowed and encouraged to be a part of the funeral ritual?

- What can I do to help the child embrace a new type of relationship rooted in memory (e.g., stimulation of memories, modeling the expression of my own memories, the creation of living legacies)?

- Has there been any history of emotional, physical or sexual abuse? What is my understanding of how these memories complicate the child's mourning process? What can I do or be for this child that will help him work on this task?

Need 4

Develop a new self-identity based on a life without the person who died

Among the most difficult changes the bereaved child encounters are those that reflect her personal identity. Personal identity or self-perception comes from the ongoing process of establishing a sense of who one is. The death of someone loved can, and often does, permanently change the child's self-perception.

The death of someone loved can permanently change the child's self-perception.

To experience the death of a parent, grandparent, brother or sister or best friend is among life's most stressful encounters for children. The specific roles the person who has died played in the child's life are critical to the child's self-definition. As ten-year-old Katie said after the death of her mother, "I used to have a mommy who loved me and took care of me. Now, I don't have a mommy here for me anymore." Obviously Katie was confronted with the difficult task of redefining herself without the presence of her loving mother.

As children work on this central need of mourning, every aspect of their capacity to cope is tested. The bereaved child often finds herself thinking, feeling and acting in ways that seem totally foreign. This process appears to be an inherent part of the search for a new identity in the absence of the person who died.

Social and functional role changes must be integrated into the bereaved child's new identity. For example, having a mother or father is typically a vital part of a child's self-concept. To go from having a mother or father to not having one is a process, not an event. Beyond the change in self-identity, there is also the loss of the "old" part of one's self—the significant part attached to one's parent. The child is mourning the loss not only on the outside, but on the inside.

The death of someone in the family also requires family members, children included, to take on new roles. For example, if Dad had always taken the garbage out and then he dies, someone still has to take out the garbage. If Mom always made breakfast and she dies, someone still has to make breakfast. The changed identity is confronted every time the child does something that the person who died used to do. Many outside observers are not aware of how difficult this can be for the child.

Adults sometimes reinforce a new "hyper-mature" identity on the bereaved child.

Well-intended yet misinformed adults sometimes reinforce a new "hypermature" identity on the part of the bereaved child. This happens when comments such as this are made: "Now you have to be the man of the house." While everyone in the family will have new roles and responsibilities when a death occurs, we should never assign inappropriate role responsibilities to children. To encourage a boy or girl to be the "man" or "woman" of the house can damage his or her capacity to mourn and heal.

The trauma of grief for bereaved children can also result in what I would term a "regressive self-identity." Early on in grief there are often some regressive expressions of self-identity. You might observe the child teaching you that she has a temporary heightened dependence on others, feelings of helplessness, frustration, inadequacy and fearfulness, as well as a generalized feeling of loss of control of her environment. These feelings usually hearken back to earlier developmental periods in which these self-images were a part of the child's learning experiences. These feelings can be frightening to the child, but they are actually a natural response to this reconciliation need of mourning.

During the early days of their grief journey, bereaved children typically call on any and all of their resources just to survive. Their "regressive" thoughts, feelings and behaviors are a natural and appropriate means of trying to survive the trauma to their self-identity. As they begin to heal in grief, their need to regress typically lessens. If these regressive self-reflections do not change over time, the child is simply attempting to teach you about her need for support and understanding.

The bereaved child's identity is also impacted in that she becomes aware that she and others around her are mortal. She learns that she is not immune from the potential of experiencing losses in life. Some of these children develop a more serious or cautious view of themselves that reflects this sense of vulnerability. As caring adults, we must be watchful that this potential seriousness does not hinder the child's long-term capacity to play and have fun. Sometimes bereaved children who haven't been helped to work through such feelings grow to become chronically depressed adults. This is a reminder that working with bereaved children is an excellent way of practicing preventive, proactive mental health care.

On the brighter side, I have also seen many bereaved children evolve more compassionate self-identities. They often develop a special sensitivity to the needs of others, demonstrate patience and have a gift for being nurturing. Essentially, their experience of personal suffering can enhance their ability to be sensitive, compassionate and aware of the needs of others who have losses in life. A way I like to say it is that the bereaved child's gift in helping others often comes from embracing and learning from the pain of his own loss.

Each year thousands of bereaved children begin their encounter with this reconciliation need of mourning. Unfortunately, many of them will struggle with their changed identity alone and in isolation. As grief gardeners we have a responsibility to companion bereaved children as they struggle with many of these self-identity issues. Your desire to understand coupled with consistency, trust and security in the child's environment during this time are critically important!

Grief gardening questions:

- Where is the child in the process of forming a new self-identity? How do I see the relationship this child had with the person who died impacting this child's self-identity? What roles did the person who died play in this child's life?

- What behavior am I seeing in the child that reflects a changing self-identity? What are the social and functional role changes that this child is experiencing as a result of the death? Is the child performing any roles that were previously filled by the person who died? Is anyone around the child reinforcing a hypermature identity on the child?

- Am I seeing any forms of regressive self-identity? Does the child's changing self-identity include a lack of ability to play and have fun? Is time a factor in influencing where the child is in working on this reconciliation need?

- Is there consistency and stability in the child's environment as he encounters this reconciliation need? What can I as a caring adult do or be for this child, that will help him work on this task?

Need 5

Relate the experience of the death to a context of meaning

This reconciliation need involves allowing the child to search for and restore a sense of meaning in life after the death. After the death of someone loved, the child's perception of the meaning and purpose of life is naturally changed. Many adults are surprised to learn that even young children search for meaning when they are bereaved.

In the process of working on this reconciliation need of mourning, meaning is usually searched for through "How?" and "Why?" questions. The bereaved child will only verbalize these to adults whom he trusts. When these conditions are met, the child will teach you about his search for meaning not only in words, but more frequently through play and acting-out behaviors.

A few examples of questions the child might naturally be exploring are: "How could a drunk driver crash and kill my mommy?", "Why didn't my daddy's body work right?" or "How can my sister die when she is younger than me?"

It is interesting to note that many adults make the mistake of thinking they must always have answers to the bereaved child's cosmic questions. An essential component of truly helping bereaved children is to know we don't have all the answers. In acknowledging our "not knowing," we ultimately become more helpful to the child who is searching for meaning. This may seem paradoxical, yet it appears to hold true in my work with thousands of bereaved children.

Inherent to the child's work on this reconciliation need is suffering. As caring adults, we naturally feel uncomfortable when we see a child who is hurting physically, emotionally or spiritually. Yet, suffering is a painful yet natural part of the work of mourning.

So, perhaps it will be helpful to explore the role of suffering in the context of this central reconciliation need of childhood mourning. I do not mean to suggest that suffering is a naturally desirable event. However, suffering is as much a part of life as is happiness, and the way that we respond (regardless of chronological age) to unavoidable suffering will in many ways determine the meaning we give to life. Actually, we all in part heal through embracing hurt.

We all heal in part through embracing hurt.

Our present western culture does not appear to understand the role of hurt, pain and suffering in the healing process. We have to remind ourselves of the collective wisdom of the ages that says people reflect on the true meaning of life when they experience loss. Through the search for meaning many bereaved children have taught me that they have grown in ways that, without knowing the pain of human loss, they otherwise might not have grown.

I would be remiss here if I did not note that the many children subject to great hunger, poverty and deprivation are not experiencing growth through such suffering. As a matter of fact, premature death is usually the consequence of this kind of suffering. This teaches us that basic security needs must be fulfilled before a bereaved child can do work related to the search for meaning.

However, when these basic needs are met, hundreds of bereaved children have helped me understand that they can and do respond to death with an amazing capacity to search for and find continued meaning in their lives:

Six-year-old Charles taught me, "Ghosts have learned goodness from the people in my life that have died."

Eight-year-old Diane taught me, "The people in Heaven have my grandma to watch over them now."

Ten-year-old James taught me, "When I feel sad I think of all the fun times we had."

With support and understanding, bereaved children learn a true appreciation for life and what it has to offer.

Sixteen-year-old Shawn taught me "Since my mom's death I'm very aware of other teenagers who I can help with their losses."

These are but a few examples of how children can and will teach you that if you allow them to ask how and why questions, they will search for—and find—continued meaning in life. If you disallow their mourning in general or project that you have all the answers, odds are that you will complicate this important task of mourning.

With support and understanding, bereaved children usually learn early in life that human beings cannot have complete control over themselves and their world. They learn that faith and hope are central to finding meaning in whatever one does in this short life. They learn a true appreciation for life and what it has to offer. They learn that it's the little things that sometimes matter the most. They learn a growing sense of gratefulness for all that life has to offer. They learn to look for the goodness in others. They learn an empathetic appreciation for the suffering of others. And, perhaps most of all, they learn to meet not only their own needs, but to help others meet theirs.

Grief gardening questions:

- Where is the child in the process of relating the death to a context of meaning? What kind of "How?" and "Why?" questions might this child have? Are there any well-meaning adults prematurely trying to provide pat answers to such questions?

- Do the adults around the child understand the role of suffering in the healing process? How does this child find meaning in the death? What religions or philosophical belief systems exist in this child's family? How has the death impacted these belief systems?

- Do the child and his family give themselves permission to question previously held beliefs? What new beliefs provide this child with a sense of meaning? What can I as grief gardener do or be for this child that will help her work on this task?

Notes _____

_____

_____

Need 6

Experience a continued supportive adult presence in future years

We have come to understand that grief is a process, not an event. The long-term nature of grief means that bereaved children will need adult "stabilizers" in their lives long after the event of the death. Unfortunately, because our society places so much value on the ability to "carry on," "keep your chin up" and "keep busy," many bereaved children are abandoned shortly after the event of the death.

Adult caregivers must view grief not as an enemy, but as a necessary consequence of having loved.

In spite of our awareness that children mourn long after the death occurs, attitudes are slow to change. "It will be best not to talk about it," "It's over and done with" and "It's time to get on with life" still dominate the messages that many bereaved children are greeted with. Obviously, these kinds of messages inhibit grief rather than allow for its expression. Those persons who see children's grief as something that must be overcome or simply endured typically do not remain available to the child very long after the event of the death. In my observation, these adults encourage children to go around their grief, instead of toward or through it.

Even those children who actively participate in the work of mourning will need stabilizing adults in their lives long after the event of the death. As the child grows into adulthood, she will mourn the loss in different ways at various developmental phases.

To be truly helpful, adult caregivers must appreciate the impact of loss on children. They must understand that to heal, the child must be allowed and encouraged to mourn long after the event of the death. They must view grief not as an enemy to be overcome, but as a necessary consequence of having loved.

Stabilizing adults must also be aware that a child's griefbursts—heightened periods of loss and sadness—demand understanding, not judgment. Griefbursts often occur during pivotal life moments: birthdays (the child's own or the person's who died); starting or getting out of school for the year; a change of seasons; receiving a report card; holidays; vacations; weekends; the child's first date; graduating from school; achieving a major goal; getting married; the birth of children; any kind of anniversary. These unsuspecting waves may come out of nowhere through a sight, a sound or a smell. Unless the child (or adult who is reflecting on childhood loss) shares this experience with someone, he can and often does suffer in silence. As caring adults, we must stay alert for these griefbursts.

The "bereaved" label is an attempt on the part of society to identify a group of people with special needs. The bereaved child does have special needs. One of the most important is the need to be companioned long after the event of the death. As grief gardeners we have a responsibility to remain available to these children long into the future.

Grief gardening questions:

- Does the child have the availability of adult "stabilizers" long after the event of the death?

- How do societal expectations about grief recovery timetables influence the availability and understanding of adults around the child?

- When griefbursts occur, are the adults understanding of this phenomenon?

As grief gardeners, we have a responsibility to remain available to bereaved children long into the future.

- Does the bereaved child understand that it is natural to live with grief as opposed to resolving it?

- What can I as grief gardener do or be for this child that will help him continue to have long-term stabilizers in his life?

Notes _____

_____

_____

_____

_____

I hope this outline of reconciliation needs will assist you in companioning the bereaved children in your care. The responsibilities of adult caregivers are complex and ever-changing as the bereaved child participates in the work of mourning. Helping the child meet these reconciliation needs demands your emotional as well as your intellectual involvement. You must connect on not just a professional level, but a personal level as well.

Each of the six reconciliation needs I have outlined is accompanied by its own challenges and stresses to both the mourner and the helper. To be of true help, you as grief gardener must:

1. Have a desire to have the child be your teacher;

2. Understand how your own experiences with loss influence your capacity to be emotionally, physically and spiritually available to the child;

3. Allow yourself to empathetically enter into the pain of the child;

4. Work to understand the challenges being presented to the child in the work of mourning; and

5. Develop a wide range of helpful skills that assist the child in reconciling the loss.

I hope that like me, you are excited by the prospect of such challenging, rewarding, valuable work.

Grief Myth

Infants and toddlers are too young to grieve and mourn.

Good gardeners know that young gardens can need the most attention.

In my experience, any child old enough to love is old enough to grieve and mourn. In fact, I see children as young as 18-months-old in my counseling center.

Infants and toddlers are certainly capable of giving and receiving love.

While they cannot verbally teach us about their grief, they protest their losses in a variety of ways. A few practical examples are regressive behaviors, sleep disturbances and explosive emotions. John Bowlby's research has shown us that even babies will protest when threatened with separation, death or abandonment.

Good gardeners know that very young gardens can need the most attention. Preparing a new perennial bed means tilling the soil, adding manure and taking steps to prevent weeds. Forego these steps and the garden will never be as healthy as it might have been.

Unless we support and nurture infants and toddlers when they are confronted with the loss of a primary relationship, they can develop a lack of trust in the world around them. Holding, hugging and playing with them are the primary ways in which we can attempt to help these young children. We can also teach the parents of bereaved infants and toddlers how best to care for them.

(For more on infant and toddler grief, see p. 36.)

Have you seen this myth carried out? When and how?

_____

_____

_____

_____

_____

_____

_____

One spring morning a gardener noticed an unfamiliar seedling poking through the ground near the rocky, untended edge of his garden . . .

The gardener trusted in the seedling's natural capacity to adapt and survive.

The Gardener and the Seedling: A Parable

One warm June afternoon the tightly wrapped, purple-blue petals unfurled. A columbine—the gentle wildflower whose name means "dovelike."

Soon a flower bud appeared atop the young plant's stem.

"Congratulations," the gardener whispered to the columbine. "You have not only survived, you have grown beautiful and strong."

A

My Guiding Model: Growth-Oriented Grief Gardening

Grief gardeners believe that grief is organic—as natural as the setting of the sun and as elemental as gravity.

Grief gardeners provide a nurturing environment in which bereaved children can not only heal, but grow. We do not cure the grieving child; instead we create conditions that allow her to mourn.

Growth through grief means change. Mourning is not an end, but a beginning.

Growth through grief means encountering pain. Ultimately, not learning to mourn well results in not loving or living well.

Growth through grief is a lifelong process of exploring how death challenges us to examine our assumptions about life.

Growth through grief means actualizing our losses, awakening us to the importance of utilizing our potentials.

C

Mourning Styles: What Makes Each Child's Grief Unique

The child's relationship with the person who died has a fundamental influence on her grief.

The nature of the death, including such factors as the age of the person who died and the suddenness of the death, greatly influences a child's grief.

The unique characteristics of the person who died certainly affect the child's unique feelings for him, both before and after the death.

The child's age and unique personality help determine his grief response. Remember—any child old enough to love is old enough to mourn.

The child's gender—and the social expectations tied to that gender—influence her mourning.

The child's support systems (or lack thereof) influence her mourning, either helping her or hindering her.

The child's prior experiences with death as well as her funeral experiences affect her current grief journey.

The child's cultural and spiritual backgrounds bring with them norms and values that influence his mourning.

How a Grieving Child Thinks, Feels and Mourns

The grieving young person often initially feels a sense of shock or numbness.

Bereaved children often feel afraid—of not being taken care of, of loving again, of dying themselves.

A feeling bereaved children have that often occurs suddenly and unpredictably is a heightened sense of disorganization and panic.

The full sense of loss and emptiness never takes place all at once, and as it begins to set in, sadness, emptiness and feelings of depression often follow.

When adults do not allow (and therefore do not help the child understand) her feelings of relief, the bereaved child may feel guilty.

With reconciliation comes a renewed sense of energy and confidence, an ability to fully acknowledge the reality of the death, and a capacity to become reinvolved in the activities of living.

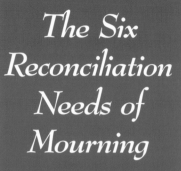

The Six Reconciliation Needs of Mourning

Need 1: Acknowledge the reality of the death.

Need 2: Move toward the pain of the loss.

Need 3: Remember the person who died.

Need 5: Search for meaning.

Need 6: Continue to receive support from adults.

Need 4: Develop a new self-identity.

GREENHOUSE

PERSONALITY

NATURE OF DEATH

4. DEVELOP NEW SELF-IDENTITY

3. CONVERT THE RELATIONSHIP

RELATIONSHIP WITH DEAD PERSON

FAMILY GARDEN

2. MOVE TOWARDS PAIN OF LOSS

1. ACKNOWLEDGE REALITY

SELF-CARE GAZEBO

SEEDLING

SPIRITUALITY

WEED PATCH

DRAWING: SJ SCHLICHT
COLOR: W GOODALE

RECONCILIATION GARDEN

ACTUALIZING OUR LOSSES

EXPLORING LIFE ASSUMPTIONS

NEW INNER BALANCE

ENCOUNTERING PAIN

CHANGE

SUPPORT SYSTEMS

5. SEARCH FOR MEANING

6. RECEIVE ONGOING SUPPORT

OTHER INFLUENCES

TOOLSHED

COMPOST

Wolfelt's Grief Gardening Model

See p. 315 for a written guide to this garden.

Foundations of Counseling Bereaved Children

The foundation upon which helping bereaved children takes place is the empathetic relationship between the counselor and the child.

A trusting counseling relationship can become a bridge to the world at large for the bereaved child.

When you accept the bereaved child, you consider him a unique, worthwhile person.

Because children are so very perceptive, they can easily detect when adults around them are not genuine.

The grief gardener thinks, believes and behaves as though healing can and will occur.

The gift of spontaneity is that it creates a dynamic "here and now" experience for both the child and the counselor.

For bereaved children, "playing out" their grief thoughts and feelings is a natural and self-healing process.

Art therapy, like all types of play therapy, provides a natural avenue for children to express their thoughts and feelings.

Techniques for Counseling Bereaved Children

To deny play to a bereaved child is to deny her the right to mourn and heal.

Play, for a child in pain, is necessary to affirm that life will continue in the absence of someone loved.

The great outdoors is a naturally healing place for children.

As the paint flows, feelings often get expressed, directly and indirectly.

A Systems Approach to Healing the Bereaved Child

To understand a particular bereaved child's needs we must understand the systems in which the bereaved child operates: the culture, the community, the classroom and most importantly, the family.

The good grief gardener helps families understand the "pressure cooker" phenomenon. When death impacts a family, everyone has a high need to feel understood yet a natural incapacity to be understanding.

A view of the counseling relationship between the counselor and bereaved child can be referred to as "the illusion of the dyad in grief counseling."

While most counselor-child interactions take place on a one-to-one basis, the therapeutic environment includes not only the child's family, but other influences such as peers, school, media and society in general.

L

Support Groups for Bereaved Children

Support groups provide a warm, sheltered environment in which bereaved children can safely mourn.

Support groups help bereaved kids by countering the sense of isolation many bereaved children experience in our shame-based, mourning-avoiding culture.

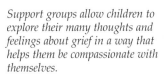

Support groups offer new ways of approaching problems

Support groups allow children to explore their many thoughts and feelings about grief in a way that helps them be compassionate with themselves.

As bereaved children give and receive help, they feel less helpless and are able to discover continued meaning in life.

Helping Grieving Children at School

Schools are an important source of support and affirmation for grieving kids.

School isn't just a place for book learning. It's a home away from home, a place for students to share their lives with others.

If, through a combination of education, modeling and open communication, you can make your classroom a safe place for mourning, your bereaved students are more likely to share their grief with you and their classmates.

Remember the concepts of the "teachable moment," the "nurturing moment" and the "created moment." (See p. 256)

N

The Grieving Adolescent

Bereaved teens need our time, attention and vigilant understanding if they are to heal and grow.

The teen may think, "If I mourn, that means I need you. But my stronger need right now is for autonomy so I don't want to mourn."

Friends, including love interests, are often the teen's most important source of affirmation and acceptance.

Most of the deaths that teens experience are sudden or untimely. The very nature of these deaths often causes the teen to feel a prolonged, heightened sense of unreality.

Many people assume that the grieving adolescent's friends and family members will support them in their grief journeys. In reality, this may not be true at all.

For the grief gardener, good self-care is critical.

The Importance of Self-Care

As caregivers to bereaved children, we need to remind ourselves that we are our own most important counseling instrument; what we know about ourselves makes a tremendous difference in our capacity to assist mourners. •

Assisting bereaved children in movement toward reconciliation is a demanding interpersonal process that requires much energy and focus.

Spiritual being time helps combat fatigue, frustration and life's disappointments.

Listen carefully to your inner voice and heed its whispers—before they become screams.

We cannot draw close to others without beginning to affect and be affected by them. We cannot help others from a protective position.

P

5

Grief Gardening Basics: Foundations of Counseling Bereaved Children

"Take it from us, it is utterly forbidden to be half-hearted about Gardening. You have to LOVE your garden, whether you like it or not."

W. C. Sellar and R.J. Yeatman, *Garden Rubbish* (1936)

Though I am a fledgling gardener, I have learned—through books and, more importantly, through digging in the dirt and seeing what happens—that soil quality has the most fundamental influence on the life of a garden. In Indiana, where I grew up, the soil is a fertile, black loam that easily nourishes the thousands of acres of corn and other crops grown there. As a kid I planted sunflower seeds in early spring in my backyard and watched with wonder as the tiny seedlings grew into towering, benevolent giants virtually overnight. I barely tended to them, but because of the soil's magical richness and the ample rainfall, my sunflowers grew and thrived.

Here in the foothills of northern Colorado, the soil is a heavy, red clay that inhibits root growth and tends to dry hard as cement in the summer. This soil (which in my yard is extraordinarily rocky, as well) must be amended with lots of organic matter—manure, compost, peat—before it will support most plants.

The soil of grief gardening—the foundation upon which the grief garden is built—is the relationship established between the grief gardener and the child. And it is the grief gardener's "ways of being," or essential qualities, that most strongly influence this relationship.

This chapter explores the core qualities and basic counseling skills every grief gardener must have—and work to improve. Because while many grief gardeners naturally possess the interpersonal skills to work effectively with bereaved children (that's why we were drawn to counseling in the first place), all of us have room for improvement. Yes, most of us enter this field (pardon the pun) with a generous portion of fertile, black loam. But most of us have stubborn deposits of hard, dry clay that need amending as well.

In addition to reviewing essential qualities and skills for the child's grief gardener, this chapter invites you to explore your own childhood losses and consider the ways in which those losses impact your work. Finally, a self-evaluation tying together the qualities and skills discussed here wraps up the chapter.

Essential qualities for the child's grief gardener

You are probably aware of what we as counselors have come to refer to as the core conditions or qualities of helping behaviors. I believe the key core condition of grief gardening with bereaved children is the following:

The foundation upon which helping bereaved children takes place is the empathetic relationship between the counselor and the child.

How do you create and maintain an empathetic, hope-filled relationship with bereaved children? If you have worked with children for a long time, you've probably already honed most of these fundamental skills. But even if you are a seasoned child counselor, please take the time to review the qualities outlined below. They are the foundation upon which you build the knowledge and skills to help children reconcile their grief.

Empathy

Perhaps the most essential helping skill is the ability to communicate empathy to the grieving child. To communicate empathy we must recognize and understand the inner experiences and feelings of the child as the child experiences them. This means we must develop the capacity to project ourselves into the child's world, to view the situation through the child's eyes—to understand the meaning of the child's experience instead of imposing meaning on that experience from the outside.

Empathy does not mean that you experience the same emotions as the child. To attempt to do that would be over-involvement, and (fortunately) it is not necessary to personally experience the child's feelings to be helpful. Where sympathy involves the expression of compassion and care for the child, empathy does not involve the direct expression of one's own feelings, but instead focuses on the feelings expressed by the child, and as a result communicates an understanding of these feelings. Moreover, empathy picks up where sympathy leaves off. If you are sympathetic to someone's feelings, you may feel concern for that person, but you do not necessarily form a close, meaningful, empathetic relationship with him.

Another caregiver attitude that is even more destructive than sympathy is identification. This attitude is conveyed by those who merge themselves with bereaved children and try to take on their feelings for them. These are people who make comments like, "I know just how you feel." When identification occurs, caregivers lose themselves in the helping relationship and actually become destructive to the healing process. The last person a bereaved child will do the work of mourning with is the adult who conveys this attitude of over-identification.

Empathy involves expansion of one's boundaries to include the child.

On the other hand, don't think that empathy means passively waiting for the bereaved child to say something and then simply repeating what the child has just said. Active empathy means the caregiver is actively and attentively involved in a process of exploration. The helper tries to grasp what the bereaved child feels inside. What is the inner flavor of this child's grief? What are the unique meanings of the death to that child? What is it that she is trying to express and can't quite say?

Empathy involves expansion of one's boundaries to include the child. It is not identifying or losing oneself, but coming to know the child's experiences. To achieve this requires a here-and-now awareness of the thinking and feeling world of the child. It means being open not only to the content of what the child says, but also to nonverbal cues such as facial expression, tone of voice, gesture and posture that reinforce (or at times contradict) the verbal messages.

While empathetic understanding is difficult in and of itself, it is not enough. We must also be able to communicate this sense of understanding to the child. The ability to communicate understanding helps children feel secure, trusting, warm and affirmed. This quality of empathy frees children to explore any and all memories, both happy and sad. It is the essence of a grief gardening counseling relationship.

Training Requirements for the Child's Grief Gardener

I'm often asked what the educational or training requirements should be for children's bereavement counselors. It doesn't always take a master gardener to have the flowers flourish. On the other hand, this doesn't mean that there isn't a role for the master gardener.

Some professional caregivers I have met believe only they can help bereaved children. This kind of thinking is so self-limiting. There are many gifted adults who help children heal naturally. Many of the gifted caregivers I observe do not have Ph.D.s or extensive formal clinical training. At the Center for Loss seminars on this topic, I would be excluding many natural healers if I only admitted caregivers based on years of education.

Perhaps a more useful way of responding to this question is to talk about some areas of training one could seek out to become an even better grief gardener:

- knowledge of developmental issues in children and teens

- knowledge and skill in using play as a primary medium of communication with the child

- knowledge of responses the bereaved have and appropriate adult helping responses

- knowledge of "red flag" behaviors indicating potential referral to someone more qualified to assist with the unique needs of a particular child

- the ability to explore influences surrounding the child that might help or hinder the healing journey

- knowledge of family systems influences on the bereaved child

- knowledge of the six central needs of mourning

Empathy means not trying to "fix things"

Let me interject another central learning I have come to understand related to empathy: The more I allow the child to teach me, the less I find myself wanting to "fix things." Allowing myself to be taught seems to take the burden off me to get children where I would like them to go. As I listen to and observe children teaching me, I seem much more content to just be myself and let children be themselves.

But, you might ask, how can a grief gardener have what might seem to be such an inactive philosophy? After all, aren't counselors supposed to have therapeutic goals to get the child where she needs to be? No, not if those goals place bereaved children where you would like them to be instead of where they are at this moment.

The more I can accept children where they are, the more movement toward healing takes place.

The paradoxical aspect of this attitude is that the more I allow myself to be taught and follow the lead of the child, the more change and growth seems to occur. The more I can accept children where they are (join them) and learn from them, the more movement toward healing takes place. This is a very real part of my experience and one of the greatest gifts I have discovered in my life's work.

Empathy means creating a relationship

Empathizing with a child also means making an effort to create a cooperative, hope-filled relationship in which there is a sense of working together toward mutual goals of healing grief's hurts.

My editor tells me that as she was running the contents of this book through her computer's spell-checker, the software flagged the word "empathetically." Apparently the word wasn't in the software's dictionary, so instead it tried to split the word into two words it did understand: empathetic ally. Creating a relationship with the bereaved child means just that—being an empathetic ally.

The opposite of the empathetic ally is the helper who presumptuously believes that his superior knowledge of grief qualifies him to project what is best for the child to think, feel and do.

126

Empathy means being personally affected

If you think you will be unaffected by empathizing and learning from bereaved children, you are only fooling yourself. If you work to empathize with the mourner you, too, will be open to the intense pain, fear, and deep sadness that is shared with you. The ability to empathize means a willingness to be involved in the emotional suffering that is inherent in the work of grief. So empathize, but take excellent care of yourself as you do so.

What is the effect on the grieving child when you respond with empathy? First of all, empathetic communication allows for the establishment of a relationship with the child. The child who feels understood is more likely to share personal thoughts and feelings, sometimes verbally but more often through the safer medium of play. Children will also recognize that you are listening, and that you understand what they wish you to understand.

Before responding to the child's feelings, caregivers must realize that recognizing their own feelings is an important first step toward making healthy contact with the child.

An example:

> Twelve-year-old Bobby, whose grandfather had died recently, began having temper tantrums at school and failed to complete his work. None of his teacher's attempts to reach him had been successful. Bobby's teacher began to realize she got frustrated and angry when she wanted to relate to Bobby and was unable to do so. In consultation, the teacher was able to realize that she had been attempting to make contact with Bobby by asking a number of "why" questions. "Why don't you want to do your work? Why won't you talk to me? Why are you being so difficult?" By becoming aware of how unproductive this kind of approach was, the teacher was able to shift to responses more descriptive of his behavior (without blame) and attempted to produce more interaction and less guilt. In doing so the teacher expressed her own feelings while at the same time sharing her awareness that Bobby's change in behavior could have been, and probably was, related to his grandfather's recent death:

> "Bobby, I want to understand what you are feeling. When I can't, I feel angry and frustrated at both myself and you. I know your Grandpa just died and that you miss him very much. I hope that you and I can talk about what you're feeling. I guess I need you to help me help you."

The ability of caring adults to communicate empathy has a number of benefits for the child whose life has been touched by death. Among them are the following:

- A truly helping relationship can only be built on the foundation of empathetic communication with the child.

- The child who feels empathetically understood is more likely to share deep and personal feelings.

- An adult's genuine commitment to understanding creates a trusting, low-threat environment for the child, which obviates the need for self-protection or isolation.

- When a child has been made to feel safe in exploring her own feelings, the first step has been taken toward self-understanding and reconciliation of grief.

- Empathy makes it possible for children to clearly understand thoughts and feelings that may have been puzzling before.

Teach me about your grief and I will be with you.

While counselors may possess tremendous knowledge about grief, without empathy there is no basis for healing to occur. It is the foundation upon which other helping qualities are built. Adults who care about helping bereaved children will continually work toward bettering their capacity to respond with empathetic understanding.

Of course, adopting an empathetic attitude of "teach me about your grief and I will be with you" means we may well have to give up some of the status and power of being the all-knowing "professional." However, I suspect that in giving up or letting go of some of this ego-based identity, we may well discover the unfolding of our natural compassion.

Exploring Your Own Personal Childhood Experiences with Death

My experience as a grief counselor has taught me that all too often caregivers-in-training want to rush into learning "techniques" to help children before they have even explored their own personal encounters with grief.

The purpose of this activity is to help you recall and explore your own early experiences with death. To help bereaved children, we as adults will find it invaluable to embrace our personal losses (not only death, but other life losses and transitions as well) and discuss how our grief has changed our lives. In doing so, we can become more available to the children we want to help. In addition, we can remain conscious of not projecting our own "unfinished business" onto the children with whom we work.

To help bereaved children, we as adults must embrace our personal losses.

If you allow this activity some time and reflection, you may find it helps you determine the unwritten rules about death that your family abided by, as well as recognize that the anxiety you may feel in the loss situations of others (including the children you help) is often a reflection of your own loss fears.

So that you have an opportunity to process your findings and feelings about this exercise, I encourage you to discuss your responses with others—perhaps a trusted friend or a small group of colleagues. I have found that such discussions open all kinds of doors to understanding that the exercise in and of itself cannot.

Please complete each of the following sentences. Be honest and thorough. Remember, there are no good or bad, right or wrong answers.

1. My first experience with death was _____

_____

_____.

2. Right after this first experience, I felt _____

_____

_____.

3. My primary source of emotional support during childhood was _____

_____

_____.

4. When death occurred in my family, my parents _____

_____

_____.

5. The biggest rule my family had about death was _____

_____

_____.

6. When I was a child, the worst thing about death was _____

_____

_____.

7. When I think about my childhood experiences with death, I realize ___

_____

_____.

8. As a child, I had these needs when someone (or something) close to me died: _____

_____

_____.

9. Talking to children about death is _____

_____

_____.

10. When I think about children and funerals, I _____

_____

_____.

11. When people talk about children and death 50 years from now, _____

_____

_____.

12. As a society, we teach children that death is _____

_____

_____.

We have all heard the statement, "If you want to help someone else, you've first got to help yourself." I hope that by completing the activity above, you will better understand how your own childhood experiences with death have influenced (and continue to influence) your life as well as your work with bereaved children.

A desire to understand Closely related to active empathy is the desire to understand. To be effective in helping children cope with loss, grief gardeners must convey a commitment to understand. Communication—the sending and receiving of both overt and highly subtle messages—must occur between the adult and the child in order for understanding to take place. While we will not always understand the child's messages completely, the child will usually sense our desire and effort to understand.

Nonverbal communication—the primary way that feelings and attitudes are transmitted, particularly at times of distress—is critical to the helping relationship. Children are frequently confused by what Virginia Satir referred to as double-level messages. This is when we give one message verbally and a totally different message nonverbally. For example, telling children that you want to talk about their feelings about or memories of the loved person but moving quickly away and avoiding eye contact as you speak sends a double-level message. The nonverbal message that is communicated is, "I'm tired of talking about this," or "I don't have time to talk to you about the person you loved."

Grief gardeners must convey a commitment to understand.

Situations like this convey a basic rejection of the child's needs and when they occur, children are perplexed because they do not know which communication is real. This kind of interaction is confusing and often proves destructive to vulnerable children.

Communication can also look different from the bereaved child's perspective. For her, communication may well involve simply sending thoughts, feelings, and perceptions either by talking about them or by exhibiting behaviors. But as adults, we know that sending a message does not ensure it will be received. We can assist this communication process by confirming the messages we receive.

Communication, then, involves both the child and the adult—the sender and the receiver. With young children, the lack of language ability often results in an emphasis on nonverbal or behavioral methods of communication. As I've said, expressions of grief in children are frequently seen in actions, not words. This highlights the need for a commitment on the counselor's part to understand and search for the meanings attached to a child's efforts to communicate.

Sensitivity and warmth

Grief gardeners convey sensitivity and warmth on many different levels. First, we physically demonstrate sensitivity by monitoring tone of voice, maintaining good eye contact, and being continually aware of what is being communicated, both verbally and nonverbally.

We also convey sensitivity by putting ourselves in the bereaved child's place. A counselor who is clearly sensitive to the bereaved child's unique perspective can help ease the child's natural anxieties. This "self" theory of helping is based on the belief that children respond in relationship to their self-concept and that their self-concept is for the most part influenced by their experiences with others. In other words, we should concern ourselves with the child's perception of self and of the situation, not the adults' or the community's perception of the child. An example: If a father loved his son, but the child perceives his father's suicide as dislike and rejection, then for the child, the reality at that moment is that his father disliked him. The caregiver's understanding of this concept is vital to creating a caring relationship with the child.

Perhaps sensitivity is best described as an ability to sense what the child is thinking and feeling. Above all, sensitivity implies love, patience, and the ability to hear and respond to the child's needs.

Acceptance

When you accept the bereaved child, you consider him a unique, worthwhile person. To assist children at the time of a loss, counselors should remember that the goal is to understand the child's feelings and to help, not to judge the child or the child's behavior. This means that even the child's defenses and normal resistances to the work of mourning are met with patience and a desire to understand the function these behaviors are serving for the child.

To communicate acceptance, we must also remember that while children often ask questions that seem shocking or seem irrelevant to adults, we must respond to such questions without shock or embarrassment so that the child will feel loved and respected. Acceptance is also about never purposely damaging or hurting a child's self-esteem. Finally, we must also accept children not only for what they are, but also for what they are capable of becoming.

Genuineness

The child's grief gardener must be truly herself—non-phony and non-defensive. Her words and behaviors should match her inner feelings. To be genuine in the relationship with bereaved children is essentially about being sincere in one's helping efforts.

Because children are so very perceptive, they can easily detect when adults around them are not genuine. If they sense a lack of sincerity they will pull in emotionally and withhold their innermost thoughts and feelings. Genuineness creates safety for the child to do the work of mourning.

Trust Obviously, trust is an integral component of most of the qualities I'm reviewing here. However, I would like to reinforce its importance in the counseling relationship.

Children learn about trust by experiencing relationships with people who are trustworthy. Conversely, they learn to be fearful, suspicious and lacking in trust through unhealthy, untrusting relationships.

Bereaved children often feel a lack of trust in their world because of the death of someone loved. They often wonder if they should risk trusting or loving again.

The bereaved child must learn, slowly and over time, that she can trust again.

The bereaved child must learn, slowly and over time, that she can trust again. In fact, a trusting counseling relationship can become a bridge to the world at large for the bereaved child. She may reason, "If I can learn to trust you (e.g. to not leave me or abandon me emotionally), perhaps I can learn to trust in the world again."

When sad, sometimes tragic experiences with death have influenced the child's view of the world, trust may be difficult for the counselor to achieve. The child will often act out to test trust issues. The child's behavior might be saying, "OK, counselor, I'm going to keep you distant for awhile and see what you do with me. I need to know if I can trust you to hang in here with me." To earn the child's trust, grief gardeners work to stay consistent in both words and behaviors. Even little things like being on time for your counseling appointments and following-up on promises are very important to the bereaved child.

In large part, trust is about consistency and safety. Can you help the child feel consistently safe with you?

Spontaneity

You may have rarely, if ever, seen this characteristic noted in descriptions of core conditions of effective helping relationships. However, in working with children, I see this as vital!

The always successful "lesson plan" for counseling bereaved children does not exist, nor can it exist. The grief gardener must learn to respond to the ever-changing, moment-to-moment situation as she sees it. As opposed to responding to the child in any kind of rehearsed way, the counselor responds with spontaneity based on the unique needs of the moment.

You might think of spontaneity as a facet of intuition. I find that the more I work with bereaved kids, the more I rely on my intuition as I respond to their words and behaviors instead of any set-in-stone clinical approach. I do and say what "feels right" rather than overanalyzing my every move.

The gift of spontaneity is that it creates a dynamic "here and now" experience for both the child and the counselor. Spontaneous ways of being in the relationship allow the child to use unique and creative ways

Spontaneity creates a dynamic "here and now" experience for both the child and the counselor.

of doing the work of mourning. In other words, the counselor's spontaneity can encourage the bereaved child to make use of helping resources that evolve from within rather than prescriptions laid down from outside. My experience suggests that spontaneity can inspire children to have the courage to mourn in ways that are inner-directed, not outer-imposed.

Fundamental Counseling Skills for the Child's Grief Gardener

There are certain essential helping skills every child's grief gardener needs. You may have already been trained in these in your preparation as a counselor. If so, great! If not, you will be well served to attend training seminars or child counseling classes that would help you integrate the skills outlined below into your "way of being."

It is beyond the scope of this book to teach these fundamentals in depth. However, I hope that your awareness of their importance will inspire you to continue your own growth as a counselor by learning them from a trusted teacher.

Please note: Chapter 6 of this book describes various techniques you can use in working with bereaved children. I cannot emphasize enough that a prerequisite to the use of any technique is the mastery of the counseling skills reviewed below. If you are a novice counselor, be patient with yourself as you work to build your knowledge and skills over time.

Attending behaviors: Appropriate eye contact, tone of voice, rate of speech, posture of involvement, facial expression.

Listening, observing and the capacity to be taught: Sensitivity to and understanding of the child's nonverbal communication; the capacity to listen intently and purposefully; and the ability to communicate your willingness to be taught by the child.

The ability to follow the child's lead: Helping bereaved children demands "joining them" where they are. This requires the awareness of the counseling skill of leading, which, in fact, is really learning how to follow! We invite the child to teach us what is most important to him at this "here and now" moment in time. If my agenda is more important than the child's, I'm probably trying to treat her instead of companioning her. I invite the child to the dance, but I always allow her to lead.

Empathetic responsiveness: This crucial skill is discussed in depth earlier in this chapter.

Clarification: The skill of being able to tell the child when you are lost and uncertain of what he is trying to teach you; as grief gardeners to bereaved children we would never want to assume we understand when we in fact don't. To be able to clarify when necessary helps communicate our desire to be taught by the child.

Perception checking: When you use this skill, you invite the bereaved child to confirm your perceptions of what he is teaching you. You solicit feedback about the accuracy of your responsiveness to him. This skill helps you guard against assuming that mutual understanding is taking place.

Questioning: The skill of gaining information in an effort to assist the bereaved child in the healing journey. It's critically important to learn to gain information from children without getting into a question-answer pattern that creates a defensive interaction. It's also vital to learn the art of asking gentle, compassionate, open-ended questions that invite the child to teach you in a way that is non-demanding and non-threatening. Poor questioning skills prevent many child counselors from being as effective as they could be.

Confronting: The skill of being able to gently confront observed behaviors in the child and compassionately challenge the child to explore areas she teaches you she may need to explore yet naturally resists. (Timing and pacing are critical to this skill.)

As grief gardeners to bereaved children, we would never want to assume we understand when in fact we don't.

By no means is the above summary list all-inclusive. However, it will allow you to be aware of my perception of some of the most essential, fundamental helping skills important to companioning bereaved children. You may want to list below additional skills you find important in your work with children:

_____

_____

_____

_____

_____

_____

_____

_____

Flexibility

Flexibility is a close cousin to spontaneity (and to intuition). This relates to how there is no "one way" for a counselor to counsel bereaved children. I also want to reinforce that there is no right way for a specific counselor to work with all children, nor is there a fixed or static way for a counselor to work with a particular child.

Flexibility means a willingness to change, to modify, to switch courses when such moments become appropriate. For example, you may be trying to engage the child in play, only to discover the child has never learned to play (which often happens when a chronic illness has consumed the family). Therefore, you switch gears and quit trying (for now, at least) to engage the child in play. Flexibility, in part, means going on a mutual search to discover safe ways for the child to mourn in her own unique style, thereby honoring the individual personality of the child.

There is no "one way" for a counselor to counsel bereaved children.

A belief in the child's capacity to heal

It seems logical that anyone companioning bereaved children would be undergirded by a belief in the capacity of children to heal from the wounds of grief. After all, if children did not have the ability to heal, we would have squandered vast amounts of time and resources in our effort to help them. The beauty of it is that bereaved children can and do heal, or as I refer to it, come to reconciliation. (See p. 94 for a detailed discussion of reconciliation.)

This healing is, however, very much influenced by the expectations and beliefs held by those around bereaved children. If adults in a child's life lack a secure hope and belief in the child's capacity to heal, I truly believe the child's grief journey will be hindered.

Moreover, an intellectual belief in children's capacity to heal is not enough. It's one thing for the counselor to say "bereaved children can heal," but it's totally another thing to incorporate this belief into your way of being. The grief gardener thinks, believes and behaves as though healing can and will occur. In my expe-

The grief gardener thinks, believes and behaves as though healing can and will occur.

rience, when this belief is well communicated (primarily non-verbally) in the helping relationship, it gives children the courage to actively participate in the hard work of mourning.

In a grief gardening relationship, the counselor communicates her desire to "hang in there" with the child, to walk with her through her time of need, and to care beyond the confines of the professional work role. In other words, the counselor's attitude about the desire to understand and belief in the capacity to heal is demonstrated in word and deed—regardless of the setting. This kind of counselor commitment helps instill trust, self-respect and hope for healing in the bereaved child.

The desire to be a "responsible rebel" and come from the heart

You are probably asking, "What in the world is this?" Well, bear with me and let's explore this strange-sounding but desirable quality in a grief gardener.

I believe truly helpful counselors to children in pain are responsible rebels: They facilitate creative healing as they become fellow travelers in the child's journey. They do not function as agents of conformity to "get the child over" grief, but instead foster growth in the bereaved child. They stay in touch with their hearts without becoming contaminated by the formality of professional training.

The grief gardener opens her heart to the bereaved child and witnesses the need for a safe place to mourn.

Grief gardeners listen and learn from the bereaved child with their hearts as opposed to their brains. They are relaxed, naturally caring and innately nonjudgmental. They continue to learn and grow themselves each and every day and are open to embracing their own life pains. They do not think of themselves as experts, but as companions. They have moved beyond the mechanical use of counseling techniques and learned to accept their God-given gifts as human beings capable of being with and learning from children in grief.

In sum, the grief gardener follows her heart, not her head. She opens her heart to the bereaved child and witnesses the need for a safe place to mourn. She remembers the words of Saint Exupéry, who in his book *The Little Prince* wrote, "It is only with the heart that one can see rightly; what is essential is invisible to the eye." Oh, what a joyous discovery!

Twelve

Important

Characteristics

of the

Counselor to

Bereaved

Children

Rate Yourself

What do we as caring adults bring to the grieving child? When we enter the world of the child, we bring, among other things, our personal characteristics or "ways of being". This self-evaluation sums up many of the basic teachings found in this chapter and throughout this book.

Obviously, no counselor is likely to have all the characteristics outlined below. I wouldn't want to suggest that being a helpful counselor to a bereaved child means being perfect! However, those counselors who are willing to look within themselves and continue to aspire to these qualities are, in my experience, the ones most likely to help children reconcile their grief.

The characteristics outlined here are also applicable to parents of bereaved children and other concerned adults. Indeed, anyone who wants to help grieving children would be well served to develop these qualities.

As you explore the following list, ask yourself whether or not you agree that these are important characteristics of an effective helper to bereaved children. Also see if you can come up with additional qualities you find important. To help you identify those areas you might want to work on, I have included a spot for you to rate yourself on each characteristic. Be honest as you assess your strengths and weaknesses.

Helpful counselors to bereaved children stay in contact with their own children within.

1. *The ability to keep one's own "child within" alive and nurtured.* Helpful counselors to bereaved children stay in contact with their own children within. I frequently read the words I have posted in my office: "To be truly helpful to children, I must return to the beginning as I become a child again." The capacity to play, for example, is a natural method of self-expression and communication that doesn't have to end when you get to be 21. Embrace your own childhood memories of play and fantasy. Observe children at play and learn to use these observations as therapeutic tools in your work. Most importantly, enter the world of the child within as you work with and learn from bereaved children.

Low		Average		High
1	2	3	4	5

2. *The capacity to be empathetic.* Effective child counselors perceive the child's experience and communicate that perception back to the child. This means we must develop the capacity to project ourselves into the child's world, to view the situation through the child's eyes. We must understand the meaning of the child's experience instead of imposing meaning on that experience from the outside.

Low		Average		High
1	2	3	4	5

3. *The willingness to adopt a "teach me" attitude.* Creative child counselors are always learning from those they help. In fact, we must realize that bereaved children are our teachers about their unique experiences. To achieve this, we must be open and even vulnerable. Counselors with a "teach me" attitude trust in the child's innate capacity to heal and see themselves more as gardeners than as doctors.

Low		Average		High
1	2	3	4	5

4. *The ability to achieve immediacy in the helping relationship.* The effective child counselor connects to the "here and now" of what is happening in the counseling process. This means not being distracted, but at this moment merging with the child's world. By being physically, emotionally and spiritually present, we enhance our empathy and can be more intuitive in our attempts to understand the child. Interestingly enough, achieving "immediacy" also requires self-awareness; we must recognize our own emotions as being separate from and different than those of the children we are helping.

Counselors with a "teach me" attitude trust in the child's capacity to heal.

Low		Average		High
1	2	3	4	5

5. *The willingness to develop a personal theory of helping bereaved children.* Developing a theory of helping bereaved children challenges the counselor to explain what she is doing in the helping relationship and why. The grief gardening model embraced in this book reflects my

most recent attempt to articulate what I mean by effective child counseling. While we can borrow and build on the ideas of others, there is tremendous value in challenging ourselves to articulate our own key assumptions about the helping process with bereaved children.

Low		Average		High
1	2	3	4	5

While you're thinking about it, take a moment to jot down some ideas about your own personal theory of helping bereaved children: _____

_____

_____

_____

_____

6. *The desire to seek new knowledge about childhood grief and mourning.* To be effective, the grief gardener must be committed to continued education. We must take advantage of new resources and training opportunities as they become available. The key, of course, is then to take our new insights and learn to apply them as we work with bereaved children.

Another part of learning about grief involves exploring our assumptions about life and death. Think about your own personal losses. Who close to you has died? What did their deaths mean to you? Were you a child when someone you loved died? If so, how did you feel? How did the important adults in your life help you with your feelings of grief? Thinking about these issues will help you better help children.

Low		Average		High
1	2	3	4	5

7. *The capacity to feel personally adequate and to have self-respect.* Helpful counselors feel good about themselves. They feel good about their ability to relate to the child's world. Their sense of self-value invites the same "self-comfortableness" in the children they help.

Low		Average		High
1	2	3	4	5

8. *The ability to recognize and accept one's personal power in the helping relationship with the bereaved child.* Tremendous responsibility comes with the helping relationship that the counselor has been entrusted with. Effective counselors acknowledge the personal power of the relationship, but do not misuse it. We should not feel superior to the children we work with but instead realize that our helping role is to empower them by encouraging their own autonomy and discovery of strengths. Paradoxically, keeping our own personal power under control stimulates the personal power of the child.

Low		Average		High
1	2	3	4	5

9. *The willingness to express a sense of humor.* Effective counselors to bereaved children know that even in the midst of pain there is humor. Children appreciate and seek out adults who laugh, play and have fun with them. As grief gardeners, we should appreciate this way of being with the child.

Low		Average		High
1	2	3	4	5

10. *The desire for continued growth, both personally and professionally.* Effective counselors know their strengths and weaknesses. They stay in touch with their own losses and the ways in which those losses influence and change their lives. In the same way that they encourage the children they work with to grow, they strive to clarify their own values and live by them rather than by the expectations of those around them. They yearn to continue to live and grow each day.

Effective counselors yearn to continue to live and grow each day.

Low		Average		High
1	2	3	4	5

11. *The ability to stay contemporary.* To be able to "connect" with children we must know what's "in" and what's "out." If Power Rangers are all the rage and you don't know it, children may perceive you as unable to understand their world. The space you use for counseling should reflect your awareness of what is popular at

this time. The beauty of it is, children are more than happy to keep us abreast of what is "in" and "out"—if we only ask them.

Low		Average		High
1	2	3	4	5

12. *The capacity to be patient.* Some of the deepest communication you may have with a bereaved child comes during silences. We must remember to go slow and allow children to teach us about their experiences at a pace comfortable for them. Being patient is a way to build trust and enhance the child's awareness that we are there to learn from him about his unique experiences.

Low		Average		High
1	2	3	4	5

So, how did you do? While there is no acceptable or unacceptable overall "score", I suggest that you examine those areas for which you circled a 1, 2 or 3. Do you agree that these are important characteristics for counselors to bereaved children to have? If so, what can you do to improve your counseling "readiness" in these areas?

Helping children cope with grief is never easy. But as many of you know, it can offer unparalleled satisfaction. It follows, then, that while becoming a better helper to bereaved children is hard work, it, too, is well worth the effort. I challenge you to challenge yourselves and to hone those qualities that make you a better grief gardener.

Grief Myth

Parents don't have to mourn for their children to mourn.

Parents should not conceal their own grief and mourning from their children.

My experience has taught me that parents and other significant adults in a child's life have the biggest influence on the child's own grief experiences. I may be the master gardener for the bereaved children in my care, but their parents are the real gardeners. It is they who day in and day out water, weed, hoe and stake.

The problem comes when these parents, however loving and well-intentioned, try to conceal their own grief and mourning from their children in an attempt to protect them from more pain. This is a mistake. Modeling is a primary way in which children learn.

Children instinctively love and try to emulate their parents. So when the parents deny their own grief, they teach their children to do the very same thing. When Mom or Dad is openly sad, children learn that mourning is OK and that the sadness everyone is feeling is not their fault. Children who haven't been taught these things will often assume they are responsible for the emotional environment of the household.

One of the most loving things we can do as bereaved adults is allow ourselves to mourn; the first step in helping bereaved children is to help ourselves. In fact, our ongoing ability to give and receive love depends on our willingness to mourn in healthy ways.

Have you seen this myth carried out? When and how?

_____

_____

_____

_____

_____

_____

_____

6

The Grief Gardener's Tools: Techniques for Counseling Bereaved Children

The grief gardener's tools are the counseling techniques he calls upon as he companions the bereaved child. Just as the gardener learns to use different tools for different tasks—spades for digging, rakes for grading, hoes for weeding—the grief gardener uses different techniques as he helps each unique child meet the six reconciliation needs of mourning.

So the more tools the better, then? Yes and no. Many gardeners plant and tend lovely gardens with just the most basic tools. The trick is learning to use a spade, rake and hoe well in many different situations. The same can be said for grief counseling: You must master the use of fundamental relationship skills (described in the previous chapter) before you pull any shiny new counseling techniques out of your toolshed. The bereaved child will probably not be helped by the Tell-A-Story technique (p. 178), for example, if your attending and empathy skills are not razor sharp.

"Just as an un-assorted assemblage of mere words, though they may be the best words in the language, will express no thought, or as the purest colours on an artist's palette...do not form a picture, so our garden plants, placed without due consideration or definite intention, cannot show what they can best do for us."

Gertrude Jekyll,
"A Definite Purpose in Gardening,"
The World,
15 August 1905

The grief gardener's tools are the counseling techniques he calls upon as he companions the bereaved child.

If you have mastered your "grief gardening basics," then yes, having many counseling tools at your disposal will help you help the bereaved child heal. The next trick is knowing when and how to use a particular technique with a particular child. As I perused Smith & Hawken's (a great gardening retailer) latest catalog today, I marveled at the variety of pruning tools they sell. They offer small and large hand pruners, left- and right-handed. They sell ratchet pruners, pole pruners and pruning knives. And for those times when pruners of any ilk won't do, they also sell an assortment of loppers and shears.

Now a master gardener could probably tell me which cutting tool would work best for which gardening challenge, but I don't have a master gardener at my side as I garden my way through the seasons. Over time and through trial and error, I will learn myself. With experience and the supervision of mentor counselors, you, too, will grow confident in the selection and use of bereavement counseling techniques.

What you will find in this chapter is a multitude of such tools to choose from as you grief garden with bereaved children. Pick and choose these selectively based on the needs of the child you are companioning. While it is beyond the scope of this text to train you in the use of each technique, where possible I have provided recommended resources for you to pursue more insight and training.

The following categories of counseling techniques are described in this chapter: play therapy, art therapy, "word" therapy, music therapy and a catch-all category I've called "potpourri." Under each of these broad headings are therapeutic rationales and, in many cases, a number of specific techniques that you can try straight off the page.

Play Therapy

It is not by chance alone that the first technique I will explore here is play. Actually, most of the techniques described in this chapter are forms of play therapy, for there are elements of play in all creative interactions with children. So here I dedicate a great deal of space to a rationale for play therapy because this rationale undergirds the entire chapter.

Play is the bereaved child's natural method of self-expression and communication.

I believe that play is the bereaved child's natural method of self-expression and communication. Play allows the child to embody the "teach me" principle that is the theme of this text. As. F. Froebel noted, "Children's play is not mere sport. If is full of meaning and import."

I believe that children often use play in response to losses because they are trying to learn about what no one can teach them. It is through their play that they have taught me about the meaning of death in their lives. For bereaved children, "playing out" their grief thoughts and feelings is a natural and self-healing process.

Play is a child's natural method of self-expression and communication. It helps children relate to the world around them and gives them the freedom to explore and express their feelings when they may be developmentally unable to do so verbally. When a child's world is impacted by death, his pain and loss are often expressed through the use of play. Compassionate parents, teachers, and counselors can and should be familiar with how play can act as an important tool to aid in the healing of the bereaved child.

A very wise person once said, "Play is the child's response to life." In my experience, I think we could also add that play is often the child's response to death.

Play: misunderstood and minimized

To deny play to a bereaved child is to deny her the right to mourn and heal. Children are sometimes denied play when the adults around them consider play non-essential or trivial. In fact, many adults perceive play as self-indulgent and think children are being spoiled if there aren't efforts made to restrict and inhibit their activities.

The messages surrounding bereaved children often deny them the right to mourn, and as a result, the right to play. How can a hurting child feel that it's OK to play when he hears messages like, "You need to take care of your Mom now" or "Be the big man of the house now"? These kinds of messages emphasize that this is no time for play, but instead a time for a child to be serious.

In their text *Healing the Hurt Child*, Donovan and McIntyre voice their concerns about the medical model of mental health care, particularly as it relates to children:

> *We live in an era which is witnessing the rapid remedicalization of psychiatry and in which "mere psychotherapy" is increasingly viewed with disdain as unscientific, unsophisticated, and "just talking." Psychotherapy with children, especially very young children, appears even less scientific and sophisticated. For many it is "just playing."*

On the contrary, helping bereaved children live again is far from "just playing." It requires some sound knowledge, a desire to be taught by each child, and an intuitive heart that invites the child to the dance, but allows her to lead.

Why is it that our culture generally doesn't value play as a natural right and feels it must "earn it" after the work gets done? There are probably a multitude of reasons for this, but several themes come to mind for me as I contemplate this question.

Our contemporary society places a high value on achievement, or on doing, not being. We have a high product orientation. If we can see it, measure it, control it, then we can prove it, according to a rational, scientific point of view. Because play has no end result (as perceived from the rational, logical perspec-

Play is especially helpful in providing children a way to bring their feelings out safely and at their own pace.

tive) that can be seen as materially valuable or productive, it is seen as a "waste of time." Play can be, in fact, very productive in helping children process unexpressed feelings of grief. Play is especially helpful in providing children a way to bring their feelings out safely and at their own pace. The results may be hard to measure, but are very productive for a child's ultimate healing.

Along with our achievement orientation comes a reinforced need to be serious. To "be serious" and "to play" are often seen as opposites. Children are taught to be serious about behaving properly, performing in school and getting into the right college. Actually, there is even a current trend in our culture that teaches parents about the seriousness of getting our children into the right preschool!

To "be serious" implies in our culture that there is a "right" way and a "wrong" way to do things, and that we should make no mistakes along the way. If we are not "serious" about it, we might not do it "right." Play, on the other hand, is equated with frivolity, irresponsibility and explosive emotions. Play is regarded as something we "treat ourselves to when the work is done." Both concepts of being serious and of play are severely limited. If play is seen as the serious or necessary work of mourning for children, then it will help them move through their grief more effectively.

We, as adults, have learned to aspire to have material goods and high standards of living in this country. Elegant schools with orderly children symbolize a "prosperous and advanced culture." Acting-out behavior is punished and noise is often not allowed. We communicate to our children that it is better to look good than to feel good. Yes, the children may look good, but inside feel restricted and confined with few ways to express their inner turmoil, energetic bodies, thoughtful minds and spontaneous feelings. Speed, efficiency, and a high-intensity lifestyle are not only valued, but prized. The complexities of society urge parents to prepare children to meet the demands they will face in today's world. We are taught to equip children with the intellectual skills to enable them to survive in a "competitive marketplace."

Play encourages development of the emotional skills children need as they grow to adulthood.

But many children are not taught the emotional skills they need to survive the universal experiences of life, love and loss. Play encourages development of the emotional skills that children need as they grow to adulthood. Play provides a safe and creative place to express their innermost feelings.

A few years ago, I watched the Disney classic *Mary Poppins* with my then three-year-old daughter. You may remember that in that movie there are two young children who have a banker-father. Mary Poppins is the children's nanny. In one particular scene, the banker-father is chastising Mary Poppins for allowing and encouraging the children to play. Essentially he says, "There isn't time to play … be serious … turn the children into little adults for me … I can't wait until they grow up." Ironically, he didn't have time to work with the children on these goals himself, for he was too busy working somewhere else.

Play Therapy: My Philosophy

Prior to entering the playroom, counselors who work with bereaved children should know why they will do what they're about to do. In other words, counselors must already have in hand their own personal theory of the ways in which play therapy works (and doesn't work.) Theory helps create a framework for how the counselor works to help bereaved children.

Without asking the following questions, a counselor who works with bereaved children is not likely to continue to grow as a helper: What is happening here? Why am I using play to assist this bereaved child in the healing process? What are my assumptions about the child's need to mourn? What accounts for the observations I am making? Asking yourself these questions encourages you to articulate your assumptions about counseling bereaved children and can also help you generate new ideas about how to be helpful.

In an attempt to encourage you to write down your own thoughts about bereaved children and play, I will express my own set of guiding principles. The following observations are reasons I believe play therapy to be invaluable in helping bereaved children do the work of mourning:

1. *Play is the child's natural method of self-expression and communication.* It is in this context of play that children learn that feelings, whatever they might be, can be safely expressed.

2. *Play permits and encourages the child to express difficult, painful emotions in ways she can't verbally.* To limit the child strictly to speaking is to make unrealistic demands.

3. *Play is often the child's natural response to the death of someone loved.* Play for the bereaved child is as necessary as the air she breathes or the food she eats. Play is connected to the whole of the child's being.

4. *Play is an essential ingredient in establishing a therapeutic relationship with a bereaved child.* The ability to let children know that their feelings are understood helps them feel secure, trusting, warm and affirmed. The creation of an empathetic relationship through the use of play makes it possible for bereaved children to more clearly understand thoughts and feelings that may have been puzzling before.

5. *Play assists the counselor in understanding the inner world of the bereaved child.* Play is one way in which bereaved children teach us what they think and feel on the inside. To be effective in helping a bereaved child, the counselor must work to understand what this inner world of the child's experience is like.

6. *Play increases the child's involvement and interest in the helping process.* Play helps relax children and allows them to experience "time outs" from the tragedy of the death. Play respects the fact that developmentally, children often have short attention spans and can't sit and do traditional talk therapy.

7. *Play allows for the use of fantasy.* Fantasy is an integral part of the inner world of the child. Fantasy play can allow a child to feel control or power he feels he doesn't have otherwise. Fantasy and imagination appear to be innate processes through which the child attempts to make sense of the world outside himself.

8. *Play allows the child to teach the counselor.* If the counselor can create a context where the play is free of judgment and constant evaluation, the child can feel free to teach the counselor about whatever she thinks or feels.

9. *Play is energizing and refreshing.* It creates a safe place to "be" while you are "doing." Play combats some of the inner turmoil and loneliness often experienced by many bereaved children.

10. *Play is a loving, compassionate way to help bereaved children heal.* Bereaved children do not play out of an "outer compulsion", but from an "inner necessity". (See Gessall quote, p. 156.) To respect that reality means we as counselors are respecting the child's right to mourn.

Right now, while you're thinking about it, make a few notes about your own personal beliefs about play therapy:

_____

_____

_____

_____

_____

_____

_____

Play affirms life If our society in general doesn't understand the value and need for inventive, creative, and at times, therapeutic play, odds are that many bereaved children are being discouraged from doing their healing through play. Play, for a child in pain, is necessary to affirm that life will continue in the absence of someone loved. Play has been part of the child's world prior to the death. Now, turning to play as he confronts the death allows the child to confirm his own continued living. Play provides a place to transcend ordinary levels of being and experience an inner world of peace, love and safety. Play is the part of the world that is safe in an otherwise scary and uncertain world following the death.

Play allows the bereaved child to be accepted for where she is in her emotional state at any given moment in time. Play is where she lives while she mourns. In instinctively moving toward play, she creates a personal experience where she can "let go" and respond to herself, to others and to her world. If she is discouraged from play, she moves into regimentation and loses her confidence and ability for self-expression. She may look good, but she certainly doesn't feel good! She may not feel at all.

A naive counselor may ask a young bereaved child, "What brings you here today?" A shrug of the shoulder or a blank stare would be the likely response. Few children in our mourning-avoiding culture will talk about struggling with their grief, even when adults around them see their calls for help, such as regressive and acting-out behaviors. Once in a counselor's office, few children will spontaneously talk out the pain of their grief. Fortunately, the tools of play therapy can be used to create an environment where the counselor can compassionately accompany the child on his journey into grief.

Parents and other helping-healing adults can learn to value the use of play with bereaved children even in moments of ordinary living; getting dressed, bathing, going to bed or getting up can be natural moments for playful interactions between adults and children. We can and should consciously create imaginative, constructive and creative play environments for children.

Important to mention is that some children may have had a special play object throughout their young lives. Perhaps it is a blanket, a teddy bear, or (as in my own daughter's case, a bunny rabbit) to which they cling. Their chosen object gives them comfort in times of stress and helps them feel safe. It gives them something to hold on to—to love and feel loved in return. This "linking object" usually goes everywhere they go. They touch it, they caress it, they play with it. The object symbolizes a connection to all they hold dear and from which they do not wish to be apart. For bereaved children, these objects take on even more significance. Adults can help by encouraging these children to embrace and play with these objects as they continue to mourn and heal.

Children reveal themselves most transparently in their play lives.

As caring adults, we can learn so much from bereaved children through their use of play. As Arnold Gessall, a leading child development specialist, has written, "Children reveal themselves most transparently in their play life. They play not from outer compulsion, but from inner necessity." Perhaps we adults can re-learn to play to help ourselves connect with our own inner worlds. In playing with or observing children in play, we can remember that place of safety for our own emotions to be expressed.

If you do use play therapy with children, there are many considerations you must take into account. Among them are playroom size and location and toy selection. You will also need to consider more theoretical questions, such as how parents or adult guardians fit into the play therapy process and how you as counselor can gauge therapeutic healing in the context of play. While these questions are beyond the scope of this book, I urge you to pursue the training and information listed in the Resources section on p. 160.

Here are a few of the types of play I've used successfully with bereaved children:

Physical self-expression

As you undoubtedly know, children are full of energy. Their idea of a counseling relationship is not to sit quietly and talk with a counselor who sits across from them.

A child who has a lot of internalized grief will naturally want to engage in physical activities that allow for release. Again, a child's feelings will likely be expressed more through behaviors than through words. Therefore, as a companion to the bereaved child I don't want to limit her ability to express herself behaviorally.

Because protest (explosive emotions) is often part of the child's grief journey, have available means to allow for its expression. Get creative; offer punching bags, boxing gloves, soccer balls, footballs or basketballs. (I have an indoor basketball hoop and it's used frequently.) You can also help the child know that when she feels things are all bottled up, there are appropriate ways to express herself—running around the house ten times, hitting the punching bag, playing soccer—whatever works for her. You can also help the child make a connection between her feelings and actions—"Sometimes when I get mad, I run around. I guess that's better than hitting somebody and hurting them."

A child who has a lot of internalized grief will want to engage in physical activities that allow for release.

One of your biggest tasks here is to educate the adults around the child that this expressive behavior is necessary, appropriate and survival-driven! (This often goes back to our own capacity to stay in touch with our inner children. Have you been out to play lately?)

Tape recorders and play telephones

Kids have taught me that they enjoy the play aspect of using these tools. They often say things into a recorder or telephone they won't otherwise say.

I suggest you have these toys available and allow the child to teach you if they work for her. Some kids don't want to write in a journal but will keep a talking journal on a recorder. They can take this home with them and record thoughts and feelings that come up. They also learn they can say things into the recorder and once the recording has served its purpose, they can erase it as they wish.

Play telephones (walkie-talkies work, too) often encourage the child to chat with you about whatever he wants to. I invite children to go into a separate room as we talk on the phone. The distance sometimes help them feel safe to teach me in ways they might otherwise not. Again, be creative in how you might use these tools.

Stuffed animals

My Center is full of stuffed animals. Have you ever noticed there is a sense of safety and comfort they provide? Just having them present is a counseling technique in and of itself. It's always enlightening to see which stuffed animals the children (and adults) are drawn to. They often begin spontaneous play activity with the stuffed animals.

Stuffed animals provide children a sense of safety and comfort.

Children have also taught me they like to take one home with them sometimes. I invite them to pick out which one they will watch over for me and ask them to bring it back the next time. They are usually happy to tell me what they did with the animal at home; I learn some interesting things from them this way.

Puppets

Puppets offer a certain anonymity and distance that often frees the bereaved child. I usually offer the child a box of many different puppets and ask him to choose one. I often learn a lot just from the child's choice of puppet.

John, age six, whose brother died at birth, picked up the lion puppet and roared, "I'm strong and I can get you!" This led us into a nice play therapy interaction whereby John was a great teacher about his innermost feelings.

Variations on the use of puppets include:

- Asking the child to teach you what the puppet likes and doesn't like about the child who picked him.
- Inviting the child to be the voice of the puppet in portraying different feelings, i.e. a sad puppet, a happy puppet, a mad puppet, etc.
- Joining the child in a dialogue with your own puppet. This often works with shy, timid kids who have a hard time talking to you otherwise.
- Creating a puppet show with a story theme. I often start this out by simply saying, "Once upon a time . . ." and let the child take it from there. All sorts of amazing things come from the story that is created.

Use puppets to fit the needs of the unique child. Some kids even enjoy making puppets; lots of resources are now available on the construction and use of puppets.

Dollhouses

Wow! I've learned a lot from kids playing with a dollhouse. They will often assign roles to the different dolls and play out scenes that are rich with meaning. They often openly express feelings and teach about fears and needs.

The jeep technique

When I need a special, safe yet fun place for bereaved kids to share their thoughts and feelings with me, I take them out to my jeep. The child sits in the driver's seat (which puts him in control) and I sit in the back (which means he doesn't have to look directly at me while we talk), and we pretend to go on a picnic.

Children often assign roles to different dolls and play out scenes rich with meaning.

We often break into song ("Chitty-Chitty-Bang-Bang" works well) or get a little silly. There is never a set direction for the journey to take; we "go" wherever the child drives us. But during our journey, the child often spontaneously expresses thoughts and feelings about the death as well. One little girl turned to me right in the middle of our drive and asked, "Am I still a big sister?" She went on to teach me about her need to explore this question.

The paradox of the jeep technique is this: The pretend trip seems to create enough distance from the pain of the grief that the child feels safe in approaching that pain.

Recommended resources

Organizations

Association for Play Therapy
California School of Professional Psychology
1350 "M" Street
Fresno, CA 93721
The Association publishes a quarterly newsletter and sponsors a conference each year in a different region of North America.

Center for Play Therapy
University of North Texas
P.O. Box 13857
Penton, TX 76203
The Center serves as a clearinghouse for information regarding play therapy literature, training and research as well as a site for ongoing play therapy training and research. Maintains a comprehensive bibliography of play therapy literature.

Journals

Journal of Play Therapy
Association for Play Therapy
540 Scarsdale Road, Yonkers, NY 10707

Play material suppliers

School Specialty
New England Division
P.O. Box 3004
Agawam, MA 01001-8004
1-800-628-8608

Childswork Childsplay
Center for Applied Psychology,
P.O. Box 61586
King of Prussia, PA 19406
1-800-962-1141

Kidsrights
10100 Park Cedar Dr.
Charlotte, NC 28210
1-800-892-KIDS

Learn & Play
Troll Associates
P.O. Box 1811
Peoria, IL 61656
1-800-367-3255

Play Therapy Associates
1750 25th Ave., #200
Greeley, CO 80631
1-800-542-9723

Toys to Grow On
P.O. Box 17
Long Beach, CA 90801
1-800-542-8338

Western Psychological Services
12031 Wilshire Blvd.
Los Angeles, CA 90025-1251
1-800-648-8857

Selected Readings

Axline, V. *Play Therapy*. New York: Ballantine Books, 1947.

Axline, V. Dibs: *In Search of Self*. New York: Ballantine Books, 1964.

Caplan, F. & Caplan, T. *The Power of Play*.
New York: Anchor Books, 1974.

Ginott, H. "A Rationale for Selecting Toys in Play Therapy",
Journal of Counseling Psychology, Vo. 24, pp. 243-246, 1960.

Landreth, G. *Play Therapy: The Art of the Relationship*.
Muncie, Indiana: Accelerated Development, 1991.

Monstakas, C. *Children in Play Therapy*. New York: McGraw-Hill, 1953.

Schaefer, C. & O'Connor K. *Handbook of Play Therapy*.
New York: Wiley, 1983.

Webb, N.B. *Play Therapy with Children in Crisis*.
New York: Guilford Press, 1991.

Art Therapy

Art therapy, like all types of play therapy, provides a natural avenue for children to express their thoughts and feelings. I have learned so much from bereaved

children by simply having colored pencils, crayons, felt-tipped markers and lots of paper available.

I'll never forget the three-year-old boy who picked up a pencil and paper from my floor and spontaneously drew a mommy whale, a daddy whale and a baby whale. (His father had recently died in an airplane crash.) He said (pointing to his picture), "The whales are a family. Do I still have a family?" Yes, children are our teachers!

Art therapy provides a natural avenue for children to express their thoughts and feelings.

Not all but most children will teach you that they enjoy some form of art. While participating in art may be threatening to some children, once they learn that their work is appreciated and not evaluated, they often become willing to participate. In general, art in grief counseling with children is beneficial in some of the following ways:

- Art media provide a means of establishing a helping alliance with reluctant or non-verbal bereaved children.

- Bereaved children can express their thoughts and feelings related to an illness, circumstance of death, nature of relationship with the person who died and present worries and fears in the context of art. As a result, the counselor can learn from the child in ways that are otherwise unobservable.

- Art allows for expression of explosive emotions, sadness and pain in an acceptable framework. While the bereaved child may be hesitant to "talk out" these emotions, they are often spontaneously expressed through forms of art.

- The creation of art is self-controlled. A bereaved child has experienced a loss of control, yet art allows for self-initiation and self-control. The finished expression of art often provides a sense of satisfaction, builds self-esteem and allows for this personal sense of control over the outside environment.

- Art provides counselors access to unconscious thoughts and feelings that the bereaved child's defense mechanisms may not otherwise allow access to.

Selecting art materials

Obviously, there are a variety of art materials to choose from. The bereaved child will often gravitate toward the medium that he is comfortable expressing himself through. Art supplies can be arranged so the child can select from many.

Do keep in mind that very young children lack fine motor coordination and may get frustrated with drawing or painting with small pencils or brushes; select art materials for young children that are simple and easy to use. As children get older, you can have more flexibility with your selection of art materials. Again, the key seems to be to provide a variety of choices that encourage spontaneity and creativity in the child.

Before we explore the different art media and their uses, I'd like to offer this caution: Offering your interpretation of the child's art to the child has limited value. You may develop some fairly good hypotheses about what the child is teaching you, but even if you're correct, your out-loud analysis may not help the child. So, I suggest you avoid direct interpretations such as, "Oh, I see you have unresolved feelings about . . ." Keep your hypotheses to yourself and let the child just keep on teaching you.

Drawing

I have found free drawing to be very helpful in having bereaved children teach me about their unique grief journeys. They seem to enjoy the freedom to draw whatever they want to instead of being told what to do. The supportive space of an empathetic, nonjudgmental counselor is vital to establishing the helping relationship and maintaining the healing process. Verbal support provided at appropriate times ("Casey, it is fun watching you draw") can also help build the child's self esteem.

Mary, age nine, whose father died suddenly of a heart attack, drew a large black bear that "would eat anything that got in its way." She spontaneously talked about how she was the bear and how strong she was. Of course this was very much in contrast to her own feelings of powerlessness.

Five-year-old Charles, whose little brother died from heart disease, drew a house.

Free drawing can be very helpful as a way for bereaved children to teach you about their unique grief journeys.

He told a story about the house and a boy who lived there. Then he drew the little boy trying to lift the house up off the ground. Bereaved children have taught me through their art how they often try to compensate for their feelings of helplessness.

Eric, also age five, whose mother died from cancer, drew a figure he described as Batman. He told a story about how Batman gets bad people. This resulted in him questioning me about whether his mom was bad because someone got her. He taught me that somewhere, somehow, he had internalized the belief that "only bad people die." I was then able to slowly help him understand that his mom wasn't bad and that people don't have to be bad to die. Through this drawing and the ensuing discussion, I also learned that he needed more information, at his level of understanding, about his mother's illness and cause of death. He also had some fears that if he was bad, he too might die.

Five faces technique

With this technique, you simply have the child draw five faces depicting various feelings, such as sadness, anger and happiness. From the interaction that evolves the child teaches you about her feelings. In addition, the child learns that feelings can be explored without being judged. Think about how you might creatively use this technique as you companion bereaved children.

The Artwork of Bereaved Children

Submitted by Lori Stahl, a registered music therapist and certified bereavement counselor, and Lois Pearson, a certified child life specialist and facilitator of children's grief support groups, these drawings represent intimate glimpses into the hearts of children whose worlds have been forever changed by the death of someone loved. Both women work with bereaved children under the auspices of the Family Services Department of Children's Hospital of Wisconsin.

You'll note that each drawing is accompanied by Lori's and Lois' insightful interpretation. Remember — such interpretations can indeed be useful for you as grief gardener, but generally it is not useful for you to share these types of interpretations directly with bereaved children.

Why can't we drive to heaven?

Amanda, age six, drew this picture following the death and ceremonious burial of her favorite pet. In the Jewish faith every mourner who visits the grave of someone loved places a small stone on top of the grave marker in remembrance of the person who died. Amanda expresses her question in words, but also by picturing the various modes of possible transportation—walking, bicycling or traveling to heaven by car.

Sad—A flood of tears

Throughout the first months of support group participation, five-year-old Krissy refused to talk, but her drawing speaks overwhelmingly of her pain in the months following the sudden death of her father.

School bus

Seven-year-old Tony drew this picture almost two years after the death of his father. When asked to draw where he was when he first heard of the death, he vividly recalls that he had just come home from school when his mom told him the sad news. He teaches us that a child's feelings are often projected on all who are part of the young child's world. All of the children and even the bus driver are visibly saddened by the news of the death.

The Dad angel

Four-year-old David drew this picture of his dad as an angel in heaven. It teaches us of the concrete thinking of preschoolers: The traditional angel wings are added to the person of his big, strong father.

The visitation

A ten-year-old member of a children's grief support group drew this picture to suggest ways that we might help someone whose loved one has died. His depiction of the open casket during the viewing is clear and accurate, as is his description of tears that "dropped and formed a puddle." He goes on to draw an extended hand offering the gift of flowers to the person standing near the casket—a gesture of sympathy likely offered his family upon the death of his parent.

The cemetery

Six-year-old Nick drew this picture in response to the question, "Where is your parent who died?" It is a well known cemetery in our city. He details the brook that runs through the grounds as well as the benches where mourners may sit and rest. He explains that his mother's grave is on the right nearest the bench. He goes on to explain that the brown graves are "the fresh ones that don't have any grass over them yet."

The grave as viewed from under the ground

Five-year-old Samantha's father died suddenly just five months before this picture was drawn. When asked where the dead person is now, she verbalizes that her daddy is in heaven and has included him as an angel, yet the graphic visualization of his body under the ground is most vivid. When her mother saw the drawing she explained that a three-dimensional cross was placed in her father's hand for the visitation at the funeral home.

The urn

This drawing by Kristen, age six, reveals a school-aged child's preoccupation with the physical details of her father's accidental death. While she has been told that he is in heaven, evidenced by the angel, she illustrates considerable confusion about the disposition of her father's body, which has been cremated. In the nine months since his death, the family has not been able to decide what to do with the ashes. She calls the urn a "canister" and while she explains that it contains his ashes, she draws it as life-sized.

Painting   Painting is another excellent avenue for working with bereaved children. (Do keep in mind that it requires more preparation and clean-up time than other art mediums.) As the paint flows, feelings often get expressed, directly and indirectly.

Painting has been particularly useful in my work with preschool through second grade children. They really enjoy the colors and the freedom painting encourages. My own preference is to use free painting, where they paint whatever they want. Just stand back and see what flows onto the paper. Sometimes I do suggest to the child that she paints what she is feeling right now. Children seem to be more naturally expressive of feeling with paints than with colored pencils or crayons.

The very act of painting helps the child with self-esteem and expression of feelings.

I once asked seven-year-old Jason, whose grandparents had been killed in a drunk-driving car crash, how he felt when he was sad and how he felt when he was happy. On one side of the paper he painted a little black ball and later said, "I feel really little when I am sad." On the other side of the paper he painted an abstract that filled the paper with reds, oranges and blues; he later said of that drawing, "When I'm happy I feel full of fun." I didn't interpret this to him, but just expressed interest and let him stay in the teacher role.

Becky, age nine, whose father died of a heart attack, painted a funny looking clown and then told an elaborate, detailed story of why the clown was happy. She was absorbed in the story when she just stopped, looked down and began to cry. She then talked to me about her underlying feelings of sadness, and how she didn't know if she would ever be happy again. She taught me how she had heard her mother say many times, "We will never be happy again." She then went on to tell me she was mad at her dad for leaving them. Many of Becky's feelings turned out to be internalized messages from a very depressed mother who needed support in her own grief work. Amazingly enough, children often teach you through art who else needs help in the family.

The very act of painting or drawing, with no counselor involvement, helps the child with self-esteem and expression of feelings. From this as a starting place, a variety of options evolve:

- Inviting the child to describe the picture as if it were the child, i.e. "Pretend you are the dinosaur and help me learn about you."

- Inviting the child to tell a story about the drawing or painting.

- Inviting the child to have a dialogue between two parts of the picture, i.e., "Can you have the sad part talk to the happy part?"

- While the child draws or paints, watching for changes in his body posture, facial expression, tone of voice and use of silence. If you remember there is no such thing as noncommunication, the child who is "doing art" can teach you much nonverbally.

Clay

For many bereaved children, clay is an excellent art form that encourages expression of thoughts and feelings. I like it because it's messy! It appeals across age groups; I've even used it with us play-avoiding adults.

Clay can be formed into a variety of shapes, pounded, cut and thrown (although preferably not at the counselor). Children who have explosive emotions can express their feelings in a variety of ways through the use of clay. The timid, withdrawn child often feels a sense of mastery with clay. Children who need large doses of self-esteem building may teach you they experience a real, satisfying sense of self when using clay.

The collaborative participation in working with clay is an excellent relationship builder.

When I use clay with a bereaved child (or in a group) I spread lots of newspaper out on the floor (I prefer the floor to a small table), then I have small pans of water available to help in molding and smoothing. I would also suggest you have something like a pencil for poking, a rubber mallet or any other items that allow you and the child to express yourselves. That's right—you should get involved, too. The collaborative participation in working with clay is an excellent relationship builder.

Jim, age eight, whose brother died from a brain tumor, used clay to mold the doctor who took care of his little brother. He then used a pencil to poke holes in this effigy. Obviously, he was using clay to express anger at the doctor. Not all children are as direct as Jim in their use of clay, but in my experience, they will invariably teach you something about their unique grief journeys.

Collages of feelings

Many children have previously been introduced to making collages. You can make available old magazines that portray a wide variety of feelings.

Invite the child to pick and choose different feelings that she has had or is now experiencing. She can cut them out and paste them on a piece of cardboard. Many an enlightening discussion can be had through the simple use of a collage of feelings.

Photography

My favorite use of photography with bereaved children is as follows: The child has a camera and I have a camera. We invite each other to take pictures of anything at first. Then I say, "How about if we make some faces of different feelings. Can you make a face like when you are happy, sad, mad, etc.?" We take turns shooting each other's faces as we portray these different feelings. At the next session the photos have been developed and can then be put up on the wall and we can talk about them (if we want to!). Or, you can use a Polaroid for instant use. Interestingly enough, many children will ask to take the camera home with them. The new disposable cameras are ideal for this kind of fun.

I always invite kids to bring in photos of the person in their life who has died. I learn more in a few minutes of photo sharing than I might in a day of just talking.

Recommended resources

Organizations

American Art Therapy Association
428 E. Preston St.
Baltimore, MD 21202
The Association publishes a journal and provides a professional forum to those who specialize in art therapy.

Journals

American Journal of Art Therapy
American Art Therapy Association
428 E. Preston St.
Baltimore, MD 21202

The Arts in Psychotherapy: An International Journal
Ankho International, Inc.
7374 Highbridge Terrace
P.O. Box 426
Fayetteville, NY 13066

Selected readings

Alliger, B. "Painting with Clay," *Instructor*. Vol. 79, No. 46, April 1970.

Cole, N. *Children's Art from Deep Down Inside.*
New York: John Day Co., 1966.

Dileo, J. *Young Children and Their Drawings.*
New York: Bruner/Mazel, 1970.

Furth, G. *The Secret World of Drawings.* Boston, MA: Sigo Press, 1988.

Kramer, E. *Childhood and Art Therapy.*
New York: Schoken Books, 1979.

Oaklander, V. *Window To Our Children.*
New York: Center for Gestalt Development, 1988.

Music Therapy

While I am certainly not (by any stretch of the imagination) a music therapist, I have come to appreciate how music can be used in grief gardening with bereaved children. The therapeutic value of musical expression has long been known in almost every culture in the world. While there are others who are more qualified to teach about this topic than I, I do think I should introduce this topic as a valuable technique in working with bereaved children.

Most of my involvement with music and bereaved children has had to do with a guitar I keep in my office. I'm amazed how kids seem drawn to it and often want to strum on it. So, following their lead, I've found it to be a valuable tool in my helping efforts.

Music can be used in a variety of ways. I've often had kids invite me to teach them a few chords on the guitar. This may evolve into wanting to make up songs, some just for fun, others reflecting feelings and experiences. I've found my guitar to be a great relationship-builder—now if only I could know it's OK to not be very good at it!

The use of music in counseling bereaved children is limited only by the counselor's and the child's imagination and available resources. Many children enjoy using rhythm, like tambourines, bells and drums. Even children with little or no real musical training or talent can use these instruments to express their feelings: "Show me what kind of drum beat you would use to show you are sad, happy, mad, etc." Each child has a unique "music personality" to teach you about.

The kinds of music to be sung, listened to, played or created will vary from child to child. Music can be used well in group work with children and usually results in a feeling of togetherness. After all, music often speaks when words alone fail. Drop me a note and let me know how you have used music with bereaved children.

Recommended resources

Organizations

American Association for Music Therapy
35 W. Fourth St.
777 Education Building
New York, New York 10003

Canadian Association for Music Therapy
6 Drayton Road
Point Claire, Quebec H9S 4V2
Canada

National Association for Music Therapy
P.O. Box 610
Lawrence, KS 66044

Selected readings

Benezon, R. *Music Therapy Manual.*
Springfield, IL: Charles C. Thomas, 1981.

Gaston, E. *Music in Therapy.* New York: Macmillan, 1968.

Nash, G. *Creative Approaches to Child Development with Music, Language and Movement.* New York: Alfred Publishing Co., Inc. 1974.

"Word" Therapy: Writing, Reading, Storytelling & Talking

While sometimes words are inadequate in the face of grief, at other times language—in all its various forms—can be healing for bereaved children. One teenager said it this way:

Expressions
by Nicole Cruson

TALKING,
   WRITING,
      LISTENING,
         FACES,

Are all ways to express feelings.
   But what way works best for you?
      Maybe it is not the same way your friend does.
But it is your way and you should feel good about that.
     WHY? You may ask do your ways of expressing your
       feelings differ from those of your friends?
Maybe it is because you are two totally different people, in some
   ways. But in others you are very much alike.
     But nobody is exactly the same.
All four of these play a major part in your attitude toward
   life and your view you have of other people.
     There is though an important thing to remember
when you are expressing your feelings, this is whatever
   way you use as your way of expression, make sure you
     use the way that you enjoy the most.
The way I find most helpful to me is WRITING.
   This is the easiest way I have found to show how I am
     feeling. If I am sad I will write something that
is going to touch the heart of those who read it.
   If I am happy then I will write something that is less
     touchy and more humorous.
It is the way I feel the most comfortable expressing my
   feelings.
     So realize that if it is your way you will always
have something to say.

Thanks to Carl Edwards, Fredonia Middle School, Fredonia, Kansas, for this submission.

This techniques section describes several forms of "word" therapy, including writing, reading, storytelling and talking.

Journals

A feelings journal is a tablet in which a child is encouraged to record her thoughts and feelings during her grief journey. The journal is just for her and is only shared with the counselor or others if the child chooses to. This is a particularly appropriate technique for use with a quiet, introspective child who may not be naturally verbal.

Letters

Letters to the person who died or to oneself can be invaluable in having the child teach you about thoughts and feelings. Writing the letter is a form of mourning because the child takes what is on the inside and expresses it on the outside. Be prepared to be startled by some of the content in these letters.

I have found it particularly useful to invite children to write a letter to themselves. In this way they often help me understand needs, fears and hopes that they might not otherwise express.

Feelings journals are particularly appropriate for quiet, introspective children.

Poetry

Poetry often comes from deep in the hearts of children. Poetry frees them to express what they really, truly feel. Even very brief poems reveal a lot about children's innermost feelings.

An eight-year-old boy whose father died in a car accident wrote the following and simply titled it "Dads."

Dads

Dads are for laughing with.

Dads are for playing with.

Dads are for making you feel safe.

My dad is dead and I miss him.

Thirteen-year-old Jessica wrote a poignant poem of her own after her father's death from cancer:

Fathers

My life has always been quite nice,
Until my father died.
But now my dreams are broken
And all I do is cry.

My mother says it will be all right,
As soon as it goes by.
But I am sure it will be with me
Until I go and die.

This poem should have some meaning,
A meaning tried and true,
You should always love your father,
Because he won't always be with you.

No the poems don't have to rhyme! You can often inspire the child to come up with a poem by modeling one of your own bad poems. You can then laugh together and learn together.

Essays

Essays are more for bereaved teens than for younger children. If the child has had a decent relationship with the person who died, I often suggest the following: "How about writing an essay, a story that you title 'A Tribute to (Name of Person Who Died)'?" This is very open-ended and allows the teen to go wherever he wants with it.

One sixteen-year-old, Matt, wrote the following:

My mom wasn't the most beautiful person in the world, at least not on the outside. Her real beauty was inside, in her heart. She was loving, caring, kind, friendly and much more. She would help any person who needed a hand, whether she knew them or not. She was a very strong person who took on any challenge given to her. She was always calm and almost never lost her temper. She stayed strong and calm until the end.

One of my last memories of her is her loss of hair (due to chemotherapy) and her wig.

I remember her looking weak and helpless. She just lay in her hospital bed, unable to move because the cancer took everything out of her. She had a strong will to live and fought as long as she could.

The lessons my mom taught me about life are more important than any schoolwork I will ever do. She taught me to help others and not expect a favor in return. "The pleasure you get from knowing you helped someone in need is greater than anything they can give you," she said. She showed me the value of being kind to others, taking care not to hurt them in any situation. She used to say, "If you are kind to everyone, more people will like you and respect you." From her, I realized that in order to judge a person, I needed to know them.

The last time I saw my mom alive, she told me the most important thing I've ever heard. She pulled me close to her bed and said, "Matthew, you know how much I love you, and I know how much you love me. You and Aaron are the best things that ever happened to your father and me. I don't ever want you to forget what I've taught you. Always be nice to everyone, help people when you can and most importantly, keep on living after I'm gone."

I started crying and said, "But Mom, I don't want you to go. All I want is for you to get better and come home. Please say you'll come home."

She just looked at me and said, "Matthew, I wish I could say that, but it's not possible. I want to see you grow up and have kids, and it makes me sad that I won't be able to do that. However, I know your father will be able to see you grow up and have a family and that makes me very happy. I want you to remember what I said and keep on living. This is what I want for you: to have your life go on and be full of happiness and love. I love you so much." She hugged me and started crying. I tried to comfort her because it hurt me to see her cry. It worked a little and she stopped crying. My dad came in and got me and we left. She died two days later, and I never talked to her again.

In my opinion, my mom was the greatest person I ever knew. Maybe my view of her is biased because she was my mom, but I know she was truly a great person who should have lived longer. She loved her family completely and didn't want to leave it. In the end, though, she knew it had to happen sometime and was ready. I wish I could be as strong as she was, but sometimes I sit down and cry because I miss her so much.

The world lost a great person when my mom died in February of 1986.

A Poem and Short Essay by Jessie White

A poem and a short essay by eight-year-old Jessie White following the deaths of her newborn baby brother, Sam, and her grandfather:

When a loved one dies your heart is taken.
When someone you love is sick your heart is broken.
When you're never going to see someone again your heart is gone.
That's what my heart is like.

I loved my brother and my grandfather very much. I missed them alot. A whole lot. I couldn't let them go. I didn't even get to hold my little brother. It's so hard to say goodbye to loved ones.

When a loved one dies your heart is taken.

Two more essays written by sixth graders when asked to describe their first experiences with death:

My Grandma Betty was my Dad's mom. She died in 1987. It was hard when she died. When she died, she was in her room. My mom, dad and his brother and sister were there. They only let us see her for a minute because I was only 7 or 8 years old and I probably didn't understand why. I didn't see my dad cry when I was around.

I bet it was hard for him. When my dad was 12 or 13 years old his dad had a heart attack. When we went to the funeral to see Grandma Betty for the last time, there were flowers and my relatives were there. Everyone cried and cried. It was a hard experience for all of us, even my dad.

I think death is just a thing that happens in life. Yes, death is sad but you live and get through it.

I have known a lot of people that have died, but here is one that hurt. My uncle Ben, he was my great great uncle. I was named after him. When I was a baby he loved to hold me. In one of our pictures he is holding me and has a cigar in his mouth, sometimes he smoked a pipe instead of a cigar.

Whenever we got together like at a fishfry, the second I see him I run to him like I haven't seen him in a year. Sometimes he would tell stories about when he was young or when he first drove a car. I wish he was still around to tell those funny stories.

He was always gentle and loving. He never wanted to hurt you or anyone. If you fell and got dirty he would clean you off. If you asked him to do something like kick a ball or fix something he would try his hardest to do it.

He wanted to go many places I'm sure, even if he was here today I could take him anywhere he wanted.

Thanks to teacher Dave Harris, St. John's School, Newburgh, Indiana, for these submissions.

Bibliotherapy

This formal-sounding term, simply defined, means helping through books. Carefully selected books, specific to the unique needs of a particular child, can help children with a variety of life difficulties. Because loss is a part of all phases of life, it is natural that loss is a common theme in books for both children and adults. The last 20 years has seen a plethora of books on death, dying and grief. A number of death-related bibliographies have even become available.

For bereaved children, written words can be less intrusive and demanding than spoken words.

In her text *Books to Help Children Cope with Separation and Loss,* Joanne Berstein outlines some of the benefits of using bibliotherapy with children:

- Reading offers an opportunity to identify with others.
- Reading helps children realize they are not alone.
- Reading can expand horizons.
- Reading can help children express feelings, aiding the catharsis process.
- Reading can lead to insight.
- Reading can facilitate the sharing of problems.

A number of questions need to be asked when you are considering a particular book for use with bereaved kids. How does the book present the material, language, text, illustrations, etc.? What kind of message would the child get from the book? How are feelings dealt with in the book? Are the content and language in the book appropriate for the developmental level of the child? How does the book define death? Does this book represent a general humanistic approach to death or a particular religious point of view? You can probably think of additional questions to consider when choosing books for bereaved children you have the honor of companioning.

In my experience with thousands of bereaved children, written words are less intrusive and demanding than spoken words. As with play, art and music, children approach books with a minimum of defensive posturing. Obviously, I am an advocate of helping bereaved children through the use of books.

Storytelling

Storytelling is a familiar and well-liked technique for working with children. While the formal study of storytelling as a helping medium is in its infancy, making use of stories to learn from and help children has been with us for some time.

In an excellent resource entitled *Therapeutic Metaphors for Children and the Child Within*, authors Mills and Crowley explore how storytelling can have therapeutic benefits. They note that through identification with the story or elements in the story, the child's sense of isolation about her situation dissolves when she hears that her experience is shared by others.

Mills and Crowley have created a series of stories that a counselor can tell the bereaved child. They also suggest that while the child listens to the story, he may want to relax and visualize some of the characters. Their stories are short and some are applicable to death losses. If you are interested in learning to use this technique, I would highly recommend this book.

The way in which I have more commonly used storytelling with children is through the Tell-a-Story technique. This is where you invite the child to create a story with you. I have found this method invaluable in having the child teach me about what might be going on inside him. Obviously, the story becomes a metaphor for aspects of the child's real life experiences.

Let's look at one of my favorite examples of how Tell-a-Story can be a useful technique:

Sara Smith, nearly six years old, was referred for evaluation by her mother after Sara's father, Larry, died by suicide. Sally Smith reported Sara had appeared sad and withdrawn during the past three- to four-week period. Mrs. Smith also reported that Sara recently attempted to nurse and is asking to be carried frequently, among other regressive behaviors. Mrs. Smith also described some recent difficulties with Sara's lack of feeling accepted and liked by peers.

The following is a verbatim excerpt from a tape recording made during my interaction with Sara during one phase of my initial evaluation process.

Alan Wolfelt:	*Once there was a girl who liked to...*
Sara:	Play.
A.W.:	*What did she like to play?*
Sara:	—play with books—play with toys—sometimes her

	mother put up her ponytails—she likes to put on her mother's shoes—she likes to turn on the lamp for her mommy.
A.W.:	*Who did she like to play with?*
Sara:	With a boy. They play hide-and-seek in the backyard.
A.W.:	*And what is the boy's name?*
Sara:	Tommy.
A.W.:	*Who did she not like to play with?*
Sara:	Her sister.
A.W.:	*Why was that?*
Sara:	Because she is big and she wants to be just like her sister.
A.W.:	*One day this girl went out with her mother and father, and they got cross with her. What about?*
Sara:	'Cause she didn't look both ways. She got hit and she got killed. She went in the graveyard.
A.W.:	*Did anyone come to see her?*
Sara:	Her daughter did.
A.W.:	*What did her daughter say at the graveyard.*
Sara:	(paused, got quiet) She said I love her and I don't want her to leave me.
A.W.:	*What would the girl wish?*
Sara:	I wish I had my Mommy back.
A.W.:	*What happened then?*
Sara:	Then she'd go away.
A.W.:	*This girl had a fried she liked very much. One day she said, "You come with me and I'll show you something, but you can't tell anyone, because it is a secret." What did she show him?*
Sara:	A cake.
A.W.:	*What was the cake for?*
Sara:	Her mother.
A.W.:	*And why was that?*
Sara:	Because she loved her mother very much.
A.W.:	*When this girl went to bed, what did she think about?*
Sara:	Her mother and the cake.
A.W.:	*Why was that?*
Sara:	Because she loved her mother and didn't want her to leave her.
A.W.:	*One night she cried. What was the matter?*
Sara:	(long pause) Because her daddy died.
A.W.:	*When she fell asleep, what did she dream about?*
Sara:	Outer space people coming down.
A.W.:	*What did the outer space people say?*
Sara:	I want your lamp (looking at the lamp in the room).

A.W.:	*And what did the little girl say?*
Sara:	No, you can't have it.
A.W.:	*The girl woke up in the night. What made her wake up?*
Sara:	The outer space people, the lamp, and her mommy and daddy.
A.W.:	*One night she had a nice dream. A fairy came to her and said, "If you say what you really want, it will come true." What did she say she wanted?*
Sara:	A baby doll. No, a real baby.
A.W.:	*What is going to happen after the baby comes?*
Sara:	Going to have to get rid of the boy baby.
A.W.:	*Anything else?*
Sara:	We'd have to get rid of the big girl.
A.W.:	*The fairy gave the girl a lot of money—$1,000. What did she do with it?*
Sara:	Bought a lot of stuff.
A.W.:	*What did she buy?*
Sara:	Some watermelon and a cherry tree.
A.W.:	*Before she went away, the fairy said, "You are growing up. Did you want to grow up?" What did she say?*
Sara:	No.
A.W.:	*Did she want things to stay just as they were or did she want anything different?*
Sara:	The house we used to live in.
A.W.:	*What did she want different?*
Sara:	Nothing.
A.W.:	*Did she want anything the same?*
Sara:	Everything the same as it was in the house we used to live in.
A.W.:	*What kind of end do we want to put on our story?*
Sara:	The girl's name is Cinderella and her last name is Snow White. I turn off the light and I go to bed. I go upstairs, and I go to sleep.
A.W.:	*What did you like about the girl in the story?*
Sara:	All of it.
A.W.:	*Is the girl like you in any way?*
Sara:	No.
A.W.:	*How are you different?*
Sara:	The little girl is a bat.
A.W.:	*And what are you?*
Sara:	I'm a person (smiles).

Sara's story illustrates her strong identification with her mother, as well as a fear of her mother's dying and leaving her. There was a hint at the sadness connected to her father's death; however, there also was a sense that this was something which was not to be talked about. There are also some significant fears about the birth of the expected child in September. Most notable is Sara's fear that she will not be needed once the new baby is born. This in addition to her grief response (note that the evaluation was done shortly after the one-year anniversary of her father's suicide) helps explain the regressive tendencies observed and reported by her mother.

Sara's regressive behaviors appear to be related to a fear of growing up and a desire for her life to return to the way it was prior to her father's death. While she has not really changed residences, she spoke of wanting to live in the house she used to live in. This, of course, was the home where her father was present. Sara's generalized fears and anxieties are portrayed in her references to her dreams of outer space people coming down. She also was able to communicate her sense of wanting everything to be all right, as indicated in her identification with Cinderella and Snow White.

The Jimmy Green technique

I have had success in drawing bereaved children out with the Jimmy Green technique. This is when you as counselor describe the child's fears as being similar to the fears of a hypothetical child, whom I call Jimmy Green. In doing this you indirectly give the child permission to feel feelings and to recognize the naturalness of these feelings. I find that children are much more receptive of this type of approach than when they are confronted directly about their fears.

For example, I might say to the child, "You know, Gary, I knew a boy not very long ago who had a fear a lot like yours. His name was Jimmy Green. His dad died too and he really got scared about going to school. Sometimes he would get a stomachache or a headache and would tell his mom, and she really didn't know what to do. Well, after Jimmy and I talked for a while, we got an idea about what was bothering him. He was afraid that if he went to school and left his mom alone that something might happen to her. He was so scared that he thought he better just stay at home with his mom because he loved her very much and didn't want anything to happen to her. You know, Gary, it sounds like you might have some feelings like Jimmy Green did. Jimmy and I talked about his feelings when we met together, and after a while it wasn't so scary for him to go to school. Do you think maybe you and I could talk like Jimmy and I did? I think we probably can."

In approaching the child in this way, you as a counselor can gain the child's attention and often encourage the child to share fears with you. This kind of technique can be used to test for a wide range of thoughts and feelings that you are aware the child is experiencing but is having difficulty expressing.

Sentence completion inventories One of the most valuable techniques I have ever used with bereaved children is sentence completion inventories. This is simply where you provide the beginning of sentences and then invite the child to complete them. This can be done out loud with the child or she can (if willing and able) write down her responses.

Pick and choose appropriate lead-ins for the sentences given the unique situation. An example of a sentence completion inventory follows:

1. Sometimes I wish that _____

    _____

2. If I could only _____

    _____

3. Sometimes I pretend that_____

    _____

4. I can't understand _____

    _____

5. My friends are_____

    _____

6. I get mad when _____

    _____

7. Since my (dad) died, I _____

_____

8. I worry that _____

_____

9. I'm happy when _____

_____

10. At home things are _____

_____

Wishes and fears inventory

This technique simply involves asking the child to teach you about some wishes and fears. I often say, "If you could have two or three wishes, what would they be? If you have two or three fears, what might those be?" Again, the hope is that the child will share some of his experiences through the use of this tool. Sometimes you can learn a lot, other times little if anything.

Five feelings technique

While children will often teach you more through their behaviors than through their words, the five feelings technique is sometimes very useful. This is where you attempt to make talking about feelings easier for the bereaved child by asking, "Did you know there are five common feelings that both adults and children have: sad, glad, mad, scared and lonely? Let's see if you ever have any of these feelings. Since your dad died, have you had some sad feelings?" Some children like to respond non-verbally by spreading their hands apart relating how much, if any, they have experienced or are experiencing these particular feelings.

Recommended Readings

Abbott, Sara. *The Old Dog.* Howard-McCann and Geoghegan, 1972. A boy's **dog dies**, leaving him feeling empty. Ages 5-9.

Bartoli, Jennifer. *Nanna.* Harvey, 1975. Children take part in the funeral ritual and estate decisions after their **grandmother's death**. Ages 4-8.

Bernstein, Joanne, and Gullo, Stephen. *When People Die*. Dutton, 1976. Life, death and loss are investigated from the perspective of one **woman's death**. Ages 5-9.

Braza, Kathleen. *Memory Book: For Bereaved Children*. Salt Lake City, UT: Healing Resources, 1988. This **workbook** encourages children to draw and write about their grief. Ages 5-11.

Brooks, Jerome. *Uncle Mike's Boy*. Harper and Row, 1965. A boy copes with the accidental **death of his younger sister**. Ages 8-11.

Brown, Margaret Wise. *The Dead Bird*. New York, NY: Dell Publishing, 1989. This classic tells of four children who find a **dead bird** and then bury it and hold their own special funeral service for it. Ages 4-8.

Buck, Pearl. *The Beech Tree*. John day, 1958. The metaphor of a beech tree is used by an **old man to explain his impending death**. Ages 3-7.

Buscaglia, Leo. *The Fall of Freddie the Leaf*. Thorofare, NJ: Charles B. Slack Co., 1982. In this tender text, the changing seasons act as a metaphor for death and the **natural lifecycles of all living things**. Ages 4-8.

Cleaver, Vera and Cleaver, Bill. *Grover*. Lippincott, 1970. The process of accepting a **mother's suicide**, a death she chose over her impending death from cancer. Ages 10-14.

Coburn, John. *Anne and the Sand Dobbies*. Seabury, 1964. A **religious account of death** as seen through the eyes of a young boy who loses his infant sister and dog. Ages 8-12.

Cohen, Barbara. *Thank You, Jackie Robinson*. Lathrop, 1974. The story of a relationship between a 12-year-old boy and an elderly black cook who suffers a **fatal heart attack**. Ages 8-11.

Cohen, Janice. *I Had a Friend Named Peter*. New York, NY: William Morrow and Co., 1987. When Betsy's **friend Peter dies** suddenly, she learns that he can live on through memory. Ages 5-10.

Coutant, Helen. *First Snow*. Knopf, 1974. Death as seen from the **Buddhist** point of view. Ages 5-8.

De Paola, Tomie. *Nana Upstairs and Nana Downstairs*. Putnam, 1973. The story of a boy who is heartbroken by the **death of his great grandmother**. The story continues through the death of his grandmother. Ages 3-7.

De Paola, Tomie. *Now One Foot, Now The Other*. New York, NY: G.P. Putnam's Sons, 1980. When a **grandfather has a stroke**, his grandchildren struggle to understand the changes in him. Ages 5-8.

Douglas, Eileen. *Rachel and the Upside Down Heart*. Los Angeles: Price Stern Sloan. When four-year-old Rachel's **father dies**, her life feels turned upside down. A true story. Ages 5-9.

Erling, Jake, and Erling, Susan. *Our Baby Died. Why?* Maple Plain, MN: Pregnancy and Infant Loss Center, 1986. A boy tells us about his thoughts and feelings after a **brother is stillborn**—and later twin siblings are born. For reading and coloring. Ages 4-10.

Farley, Carol. *The Garden is Doing Fine*. Atheneum, 1975. Corrie resists the impending **death of her father** by denying its reality. Ages 11-15.

Fassler, Joan. *My Grandpa Died Today*. Springfield, IL: Human Sciences Press. David and his **grandfather** have a loving relationship that lives on even after death. Ages 3-7.

Ferguson, Dorothy. *A Bunch of Balloons*. Omaha, NE: Centering Corporation, 1992. Helps children understand **loss and the power of memory**. Ages 5-8.

Frost, Dorothy. *DAD! Why'd You Leave Me?*. Scottsdale, PA: Herald Press, 1991. A story about a boy, 10, grieving the **death of his dad**.

Grollman, Earl. *Talking About Death*. Beacon, 1971. Intended as part of a **dialogue to take place between parent and child**. Ages 5 and up.

Gunther, John. *Death Be Not Proud*. Harper, 1949. The author writes of the courage of his 17-year-old son, who is facing death. Ages 12 and up.

Hammond, Janice. *When My Mommy Died* and *When My Daddy Died*. Flint, MI: Cranbrook Publishing, 1980. These **workbooks** are written for young bereaved children after the **death of a parent**. Ages 5-8.

Harris, Audrey. *Why Did He Die?* Lerner, 1965. A mother's heartfelt effort to **speak to her child about death**. Ages 3-7.

Heegaard, Marge. *When Someone Very Special Dies*. Minneapolis, MN: Woodland Press, 1988. This wonderful **workbook** uses art and writing to help children in their grief journeys. Ages 5-12.

Hunter, Mollie. *A Sound of Chariots*. Harper, 1972. A story of a girl in Scotland during World War I and the **death of her father**. Ages 12 and up.

Johnson, Joy and Johnson, Marvin. *Tell Me Papa*. Centering Corporation, 1978. A narrative by a beloved grandfather answers **young children's questions about dying and funerals**. Ages 3-9.

Jordan, MaryKate. *Losing Uncle Tim*. Niles, IL: Whitman Niles, 1989. A poignant story of how a boy copes with his uncle's **death from AIDS**.

Kantrovitz, Mildred. *When Violet Died*. Parents', 1973. The story of funeral preparations and ceremony for a **dead bird**. Ages 3-7.

Klagsbrun, Francine. *Too Young to Die: Youth and Suicide*. Houghton Mifflin, 1976. A comprehensive examination of **youth suicide.** Ages 12 and up.

Klein, Stanley. *The Final Mystery*. Doubleday, 1975. Comparative religious practices, the life cycle and humanity's fight against death are the focal points of this **cross-cultural study**. Ages 8-13.

Kuskin, Karla. *The Bear Who Saw the Spring*. Harper and Row, 1961. A story of changing seasons and the **changes living things go through as they are born, live and die**. Ages 3-7.

Langone, John. *Death is a Noun*. Dell, 1975. A readable examination of death's dilemmas: **medical death, facing death, euthanasia, suicide, etc**. Ages 12 and up.

Lee, Mildred. *Fog*. Seabury, 1972. Growing up after the **death of one's father**. Ages 12-16.

Lee, Virginia. *The Magic Moth*. Seabury, 1972. A mystical accounting of a **young girl's death.** Ages 7-11.

LeShan, Eda. *Learning to Say Goodbye: When a Parent Dies*. New York, NY: Macmillan Publishing Co., 1975. A compassionate book written directly to children grieving the **death of a parent**. Ages 8 and up.

Levine, Jennifer. *Forever in my Heart*. Burnsville, NC: Mt. Rainbow Publications, 1992. A workbook for kids anticipating the death of a **terminally ill parent**.

Lifton, Robert Jay and Olson, Eric. *Living and Dying*. Preager, 1974. Fascinating, scholarly and intellectually demanding, this historical overview investigates responses to **death through the ages,** concentrating most heavily on the present nuclear age. Primarily for the mature reader. Ages 14 and up.

Linn, Erin. *Children Are Not Paperdolls*. Springfield, IL: Human Services Press, 1982. **Grieving siblings** share their thoughts and feelings through words and drawings. Ages 8-12.

Little, Jean. *Home from Far*. Little, Brown and Co., 1965. Jenny and her family learn to carry on with life after the **death of her twin brother** in a car accident. Ages 8-11.

Lund, Doris. *Eric*. Lippincott, 1974. The story, told by his mother, of a **teenager's death from leukemia**. Ages 12-16.

Mellonie, Bryan and Ingpen, Robert. *Lifetimes: The Beautiful Way to Explain Death to Children.* New York, NY: Bantam Books, 1983. A book about the **lives and deaths of plants, animals and human beings**. Ages 3-10.

Miles, Miska. *Annie and the Old One.* Boston, MA: Joy Street Books, 1971. When a Navajo girl's aging **grandmother prepares to die**, Annie tries to stop her by unweaving a rug. Ages 7-11.

Orgel, Doris. *The Mulberry Music.* Harper and Row, 1971. Coping with the illness and **death of a grandmother**. Ages 7-11.

O'Toole, Donna. *Aardy Aardvark Finds Hope.* Burnsville, NC: Mt. Rainbow Publications, 1988. An **animal story about loss** and eventual hope for healing. Ages 5-8.

Rhodin, Eric. *The Good Greenwood.* Westminster, 1971. The story of a boy whose **good friend has died**. Ages 12 and up.

Richter, Elizabeth. *Losing Someone You Love: When a Brother or Sister Dies.* New York, NY: Putnam Publishing Group, 1986. **Teens** share thoughts and feelings after a **sibling dies**. Ages 11 and up.

Segerberg, Osborn, Jr. *Living with Death.* Dutton, 1976. Drawing on research, the author seeks to **answer questions about death's mystery**, the good death, and the good life which leads to it.

Schectem, Ben. *Across the Meadow.* Doubleday, 1973. The vacation of Alfred, an **old cat**, who leaves his home to go on a "vacation" from which he will never return. Ages 3-7.

Scravani, Mark. *Love, Mark.* Syracuse, NY: Hope For Bereaved, 1988. A collection of **letters written to bereaved children** about ways to express their feelings of grief. Ages 7-12.

Sims, Alicia. *Am I Still a Sister?* Slidell, LA: Big A and Co, 1986. This story, written by an 11-year-old whose **baby brother died**, nicely explores a bereaved child's struggle to define a new self-identity. Ages 8-12.

Smith, Doris B. *A Taste of Blackberries.* Crowell, 1973. Jamie dies of a bee sting and his **best friend** is confronted with grief. Ages 8-11.

Stein, Sarah. *About Dying.* Walker, 1974. Tells of **plant, animal and human death** as well as responses to death. Also explains for parents the psychodynamics of loss reactions. Ages 4-9.

Temes, Roberta. *The Empty Place.* Far Hills, NJ: Small Horizons, 1992. The story of a young boy whose **older sister dies**. Ages 5-9.

Thomas, Jane. *Saying Goodbye to Grandma.* New York, NY: Clarion Books, 1988. A family comes together for a **grandmother's funeral**. Ages 5-10.

Traisman, Enid Samuel. *Fire In My Heart; Ice In My Veins.* Omaha, NE: Centering Corporation, 1992. A useful workbook for **grieving teens**. Ages 12 and up.

Tressell, Alvin. *The Dead Tree.* Parents', 1972. The **lifecycle of a tall oak tree** is poetically described, showing that in nature nothing is ever wasted or completely dies. Ages 3-7.

Turner, Ann. *Houses for the Dead: Burial Customs Through the Ages.* McKay, 1976. **Burial rites, mourning beliefs and practices, funeral customs, ghost myths and superstitions** are discussed across time and many cultures. Ages 12 and up.

Uchida, Yoskiko. *The Birthday Visitor.* Scribner, 1975. A **funeral** needn't be a sad event, as seen in a Japanese family. Ages 5-8.

Vigna, Judith. *Saying Goodbye to Daddy.* Niles, IL: Albert Whitman and Co. A gentle story about a child's grief—and healing—after a **father's death**. Ages 5-8.

Viorst, Judith. *The Tenth Good Thing About Barney.* Atheneum, 1971. **Barney, a cat, has died**, and his owner eulogizes him at a funeral. Ages 4-8.

Warburg, Sandol. *Growing Time.* Houghton-Mifflin, 1969. Coping with the **death of a dog** and learning to understand life. Ages 6-9.

Whitehead, Ruth. *The Mother Tree.* Seabury, 1971. This is the story of a family in which the **mother has died**. Ages 8-11.

Wolfelt, Alan. *Sarah's Journey.* Fort Collins, CO: Center for Loss and Life Transition, 1992. This story of Sarah in this book, which has sections in each chapter written just for adult caregivers, can be **read aloud to bereaved children.** Ages 7-12.

Zim, Herbert and Bleeker, Sonia. *Life and Death.* Morrow, 1970. This is an answer book for **questions young people have about death.** Ages 8-11.

Zolotow, Charlotte. *My Grandson Lew.* Harper & Row, 1973. The shared remembrances between a mother and small child of a much missed **grandfather.** Ages 3-7.

Comprehensive Resources

Bernstein, J. *Books to Help Children Cope with Separation and Loss.* New York: R.R. Bowker, 1989. This useful reference contains a comprehensive list of books by age level related to types of losses encountered in childhood (including death). It's also full of helpful tips on how to use bibliotherapy successfully.

Book Services

Centering Corporation
A service offering resources on a wide range of books for and about children.
1531 N. Saddle Creek Rd.
Omaha, NE 68104
(402) 553-1200, Fax (402) 553-0507, email: J1200@aol.com

Compassion Books
477 Hannah Branch Rd.
Burnsville, NC 28714
(828) 675-5909, Fax (828) 675-9687, www.compassionbooks.com
A service offering resources on a wide range of books for and about children. Catalog available.

Companion Press & The Center for Loss and Life Transition
3735 Broken Bow Road
Fort Collins, CO 80526
(970) 226-6050, Fax 1-800-922-6051, www.centerforloss.com
Offers other publications and videos by Dr. Wolfelt, many of which are specific to the needs of bereaved children. Catalog available.

Comprehensive resource

Mills, J.C. and Crowley, R.I. *Therapeutic Metaphors for Children*
New York: Bruner/Mazel, 1986.
This book will provide you with an understanding of the history, nature and dynamics of metaphor, demonstrating its rich heritage in both spiritual and psychological traditions. This resource provides a framework for the systematic development of storytelling skills.

Selected readings

Bettelheim, B. *The Uses of Enchantment.* New York: Alfred Knopf, 1975.

Crowley, R. and Mills, J. "The Nature and Construction of Therapeutic Metaphors for Children," *British Journal of Experimental and Clinical Hypnosis,* 3 (2), 69-96, 1986.

Gardner, R. *Talking, Feeling, Doing Game.* Cresskill, N.J.: Creative Therapeutics, 1973.

Gardner, R. *Therapeutic Communication with Children: The Mutual Story-Telling Technique.* New York: Science House, 1971.

Gorden, D. *Therapeutic Metaphors.* Cupertino, CA: Meta Publications, 1978.

Potpourri

Talk counseling alone with bereaved children does not help them reconcile death loss into their young lives. It doesn't create a wellspring of hope for healing and a sense of belonging in the world. It doesn't heal the wound of grief that comes with the death of someone loved.

Nature Yet something even simpler than talk counseling often has these desired effects: experiencing nature. The great outdoors is a naturally healing place for children. We all too often think of techniques as something we do to children, yet I believe that the more kids learn to simply experience a love of nature and times of quiet reflection in nature, the more they learn about themselves and about life and death.

To help both my child and adult grief companions, I like to have them spend time outdoors. While the adults sometimes think I'm weird (that's OK), the children seem to naturally understand how our earth is a source of emotional and spiritual healing. As a culture, we believe that thinking is better than feeling and that doing is better than being—therefore we try to control nature and see ourselves as separate from it. Children better understand that we as humans are not separate from nature, but a part of it.

We often alienate ourselves from the healing terrain of mother earth. As adults we are often quick to introduce children to artificial environments and things— T.V., computers, automobiles and credit cards. Our daily lives rarely include interaction with soil, trees, wind, animals, rivers, fields and clouds. As a matter of fact, many adults try to avoid contact with these elements of the earth. We run from the rain, detest getting dirty and prefer shopping malls to mountain hikes. And we are emotionally and spiritually lacking because of it. Perhaps we would be well-served to get our hands into the dirt, our faces into the rain, our feet in open fields, our eyes open to the mystery of clouds and our hearts embracing all of mother earth! Maybe before we help bereaved children move forward we need to return them (and ourselves) to the earth.

The healing gifts of nature

Just this evening I saw five-year-old Jamie for her third counseling session. Her 42-year-old father recently died of a sudden heart attack. Jamie is naturally shy and I could sense that she internally questioned if she could trust me to share her deep feelings.

Spontaneously we left my office and walked outside atop the mountain foothills where the Center for Loss sits. We ambled down a boardwalk that leads to a gazebo set among a stand of beautiful pines. As we approached the gazebo, a mule deer fawn suddenly captured our attention. Jamie stopped. Her eyes opened wide and she smiled a smile the likes of which I have rarely seen. Her face lit up with awe. In the midst of her sadness, she experienced a moment of joy. Cut off from her father through his sudden death, she discovered the healing power of nature, the miracle of mother earth.

Resources

Cornell, Joseph. *Sharing Nature with Children*
Dawn Publications
14618 Tyler Foote Rd.
Nevada City, CA 95959
1-800-545-7475, Fax (530) 478-7541, www.dawnpub.com
This book has a multitude of nature games and activities that can be adapted for your grief gardening with bereaved children.

American Horticultural Society
7931 East Boulevard Dr.
Alexandria, VA 22308-1300
(703) 768-5700, Fax (703) 768-8700
AHS sponsors children's gardening symposiums nationally and provides reference materials on developing children's gardens. On their grounds in Alexandria, designers have created eight small gardens just for kids. The gardens have themes like "Butterfly Garden" and "Imagination Garden." The guiding principle is that giving a child her own piece of earth to nurture can be transformative.

Tips for Exploring Nature with Children

I would like to share with you several guidelines for exploring nature with bereaved children. Underlying these tenets, which I've adapted from Cornell's book referenced on p. 191, are essential attitudes of respect for children and reverence for nature.

1. *Teach less, explore more.* Beyond just telling children the facts of nature (e.g., "This is a cactus"), I enjoy telling them about my respect for the way a cactus can survive and thrive in such dry conditions. Sharing my own sense of wonder encourages the child to pose questions and seek an understanding of nature. And sharing my own thoughts and questions seems to allow, if not inspire, children to explore their own. An amazing trust and helping alliance between adult and child also naturally evolves out of this process.

2. *Be spontaneous and receptive.* The outdoors creates a spontaneous excitement in the child that can be naturally therapeutic. Perhaps one of the most rewarding attitudes you can create in children regarding nature is receptivity—being aware and open to the experience. Discover the unique child's interests in nature. Respect her interests and observe her mood changes. Keep in mind that every question, every comment is an opportunity to communicate with the child. Nature provides many metaphors that may result in fruitful discussions about life and death.

3. *Experience first, talk later.* The bereaved child may have an experience of wonder and joy by simply observing quite ordinary things in nature—a butterfly flying free, a squirrel leaping from tree to tree, a fawn being bathed by its mother. Children have a natural gift for embracing the moment they are experiencing. Allow them to experience the moment; talk, if it comes at all, can come later. Healing in grief can and does occur in quiet moments of rapt attention.

4. *Provide praise and patience.* Praise and patience are two ingredients that children respond well to. As you explore nature with bereaved children, be mindful of both of these. Your interest in their discoveries and reactions will feed their energy and self-esteem. If they appear indifferent to nature experiences, be patient. Nature has a way of inviting children in, but don't try to rush the child.

5. *Be playful and joyful.* Children are naturally drawn to nature if you keep the experience fun and relaxing. Your own joy and enthusiasm will be contagious to the child.

The outdoors creates a spontaneous excitement in the child that can be naturally therapeutic.

Candle ritual This technique can be used to help children see and understand that their love for someone goes on even after a death. In fact, many kids, directly or indirectly, will teach you that this is often a question they have within.

To enact the candle ritual, you hold one candle and say, "When you were born you had a gift to give love and receive love. This gift is like a light; it makes you feel warm and happy."

Then you light the candle that represents the child, and say, "At first you got close to your mom. She probably held you and fed you. You felt very close to her."

Then you take an unlit candle, place it next to the unlit candle representing the mother, touch them together so it lights.

"Your dad also loved you very much. He played with you, he held you, he smiled at you, he played games with you. You felt close to him (put the child's candle next to a candle representing the father until it lights) and you lit a love light with him too."

"Last year your dad had a heart attack and he died. The warm, loving part of him was gone (explain that you will now put out the light representing the dad). But you have kept on loving him even though he is dead, and your light has stayed burning."

"You have helped me understand that you miss your dad and sometimes you feel very sad that he can't be here with you. But, the nice thing is you don't have to blow out your love light that is lit for him. You will always have memories of your dad and be able to remember the love he had for you."

"Your candle of love for your dad will even stay lit as you love other people in your life. You won't want to let anyone try to take the love you have for your dad away from you."

As you enact this ritual, you do want to pause from time to time and be certain the child is following you through the story. Children sometimes have questions or want to add to the story. Watch for nonverbal indications about anxiety or questions they might have. Your natural pauses will invite the child to teach you.

Appropriate closure when using this tool is very important. You don't just quickly end it and blow out the candles. You explain that even though we will now blow out the candles (invite the child to blow out the candles when she is ready), the love the child has for her dad will go on and on.

The beauty of this tool is that it can be adapted to a variety of different situations. By the way, I have also used this ritual with adults and found it to be very healing.

Memory ritual

I often use this technique with the child's entire family or significant others. This is where you place two or three large candles in the middle of a table. Around the outside of the table are small candles (one in front of each person who will participate in the ritual). The purpose of this ritual is to assist in memory work. There is a natural bonding that takes place among the participants as they share memories of the person who died.

"We come together tonight to remember someone you all loved. Let's start by listening to a piece of music that your mom liked very much." At this point everyone is circled around the table with a small candle in front of them. Upon completion of the music, I (or whomever) often read something related to memories. One of my favorites is "We Remember Them."

We Remember Them

In the rising of the sun and in its going down,
    we remember them;

In the blowing of the wind and in the chill of winter,
    we remember them;

In the warmth of the sun and the peace of summer,
    we remember them;

In the rustling of the leaves and the beauty of autumn,
    we remember them;

In the beginning of the year and when it ends,
    we remember them;

When we are weary and in need of strength,
    we remember them:

When we are lost and sick at heart,
    we remember them;

When we have joys we yearn to share,
    we remember them;

So long as we live, they too shall live,
    for they are now a part of us,

as we remember them.

You now invite the person to your left to simply share a memory of the person
you are there to honor. There is often silence, tears and laughter as you progress
around the circle. After everyone has shared a memory you can close with an
additional piece of music. Or, someone may have a reading or poem that is
appropriate for closure.

What an excellent way to include everyone in remembering the person who died!
Children and adults alike often find this to be a powerfully healing ritual.
Because, after all, "When words are inadequate, have a ritual."

A special note: Some people think you should always debrief participants after
this ritual. I disagree! I wouldn't have used it in the first place if I didn't trust that
people could not only survive it but find it healing. Yes, it often creates a safe
place to embrace sadness, but that's OK. With rare exception, I explain that afterwards it's often nice to just have some quiet alone time to be with your memories.
You maintain a supportive nonverbal presence, but don't get in the way of healing by processing the experience to death (no pun intended).

Memory books and boxes

Memory books and memory boxes are naturals in assisting the
bereaved child in doing memory work. *Memory books* can be as creative as the child wants them to be. One way is to collect a series of
photographs of the dead person's life. The photos can be glued into
a regular photo album. Underneath the photos the child can write down memories connected to the photos. The child can then be encouraged to use stickers
and other decorations in the memory book. Some kids will want to draw a series
of photos depicting time before an illness, during an illness and after the death.
Again, let them be as creative as they wish. For children who may be reluctant to
make one, you can show them another child's. This often stimulates interest and
they can see the possibilities with their very own memory box.

A *memory box* is a place for bereaved children to store keepsakes of the person
who died. Using a shoebox or other cardboard box, have the child decorate the
outside and then fill it with photos, keepsakes, poems—whatever will help the

child remember the person who died and memorialize his unique relationship with that person.

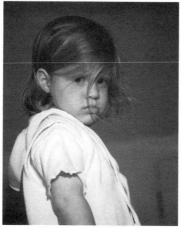

I have had many kids take these boxes to school for show-and-tell. While this can freak out some unprepared teachers, it helps the child integrate her grief into the school setting and, when handled well by the teacher and other caring adults, can help the bereaved child's classmates better understand the bereaved child's thoughts and feelings.

Both memory books and memory boxes become keepsakes that the bereaved child will treasure for the rest of her life.

Remembering makes hoping for the future possible.

The space below is provided for you to note some of your own favorite techniques for use in companioning bereaved children. Obviously, there are hundreds of techniques to consider. I have only noted some of my very favorites here. I'd love to hear from you about your favorite techniques. Drop me a note describing one or two!

Still, remember that grief gardening is an art, and techniques should never be viewed as recipes to resolve a child's grief. Regardless of what combination of techniques is used, a grief gardener stays attuned to the always-evolving process with the unique child. The creative process of helping children reconcile loss is open-ended and ever-changing. As trust builds, bereaved children will teach us what techniques help them heal.

Notes _____

_____

_____

_____

Grief Myth

Bereaved children grow up to be maladjusted adults.

If we create conditions that help children mourn well, they'll go on to live and love well.

Roses are susceptible to disease and insect damage. A fungal disease like powdery mildew can ruin a lovely tea rose if left untreated. BUT, if I intervene soon enough and care for the affected rose properly, it may well grow to be the most vigorous, lushest rose in my garden.

Bereaved children, too, can heal and grow with early intervention and compassionate care. Historical research may have us believe otherwise. Since the 1930s, numerous studies have attempted to establish relationships between childhood bereavement and later adult "mental illness" (depression, psychosis, sociopathic behavior). More recently, however, analyses of the research literature have questioned these results because of methodological problems with the studies.

Still people perpetuate this myth. You may have witnessed this when adults approach bereaved children with this patronizing attitude: "You poor child. You will be forever maimed by this experience."

I repeat: Bereaved children are not damaged goods. In my own experience, if adults create conditions that allow a child to mourn in healthy ways, there's no reason for the self-fulfilling prophecy that the child will be irreparably harmed by the death. I do agree that bereaved children are at risk for emotional problems, but only if they are not compassionately companioned in their grief journeys. If we create conditions that help children mourn well, they'll go on to live and love well.

Have you seen this myth carried out? When and how?

_____

_____

_____

_____

_____

_____

7

Grief Gardening and the Family: A Systems Approach to Healing the Bereaved Child

If I plant a tender orchid in a cachepot and bring it into my home, setting it on a warm, south-facing windowsill where it will receive just the right amount of light, sheltering it from the vagaries of weather, watering it with the fine spray of a watering can rose, pampering it daily with all my love and attention, I can be reasonably sure that the orchid will grow and flourish. Why? Because I control the orchid's environment.

For better or worse, we as grief gardeners do not control the bereaved child's environment. We see a bereaved child one, maybe two hours a week. The child spends his remaining 166 hours a week with his parents, his siblings, his classmates, his friends. All these people influence his mourning; they form his day-to-day environment.

The traditional mental health understanding of grief has, like our culture in general, tended to forget this. Many counselors have been trained to believe that grief is a private, individual crisis. Yet I believe that a family systems approach is the most appropriate one in helping us understand both children's and adults' response to death. In developing my theory of family-oriented bereavement counseling, I hope to inspire you to consider its relevance whether you are working with an individual child and using a family orientation, or working with the entire family as a unit of care.

"I think each family, each individual is a petal opening, each generation is a part of the petal. It is one petal in the great opening flower of human consciousness. Our problems and our pain are not our shame, they are our work. Each of us has certain work to do to grow into our own fullness. Not only for ourselves but for our loved ones and for the whole flower. Beyond us, below, are deep roots into truth. Beyond us, above, is the light of love. We are trying so hard, and we can't do it; it is all happening by grace, and we can't stop it."

Polly Berrien Berends,
Gently Lead

To understand a particular bereaved child's needs we must understand the systems in which the bereaved child operates: the culture, the community, the classroom and most importantly, the family. The caregiver who receives training in a family perspective sees human beings as "belonging to something." The "thing" to which they belong is invariably a larger group of people—a family. Sometimes it is a Ward and June Cleaver-style nuclear family, sometimes it is a nontraditional family and sometimes for children it is a temporary foster family. But regardless

The family is the primary space in which the child's learnings are integrated into day to day living.

of the family make-up, a bereaved child cannot be considered as separate from the social context in which he lives.

The family is the primary space in which the child's learnings are integrated into day to day living. The quality of the family environment (and rules surrounding death, grief and mourning) is a major influence on the bereaved child's capacity to mourn in healthy ways.

Why many of us don't "do" family systems counseling

Despite the best intentions and sound ideological convictions, bereavement counselors and thanatologists' delivery of family-oriented care (across age-groups) is still quite limited in reality. The reasons for this gap are varied and complex, but one of the needs is for a practical, understandable conceptual framework for understanding the counselor's role with the family.

My observation suggests that many grief counselors, often through no fault of their own, have received little if any training in family systems approaches to counseling. New terms, some confusing, like "family adaptability," "family homeostasis," and "structural family interviews" may overwhelm the grief counselor who is brave enough to wander into the family counseling literature. While these concepts may be important to understanding family systems theory, they are not always useful in helping the counselor make practical decisions about helping the bereaved child and family. In actuality, many of the helping approaches developed for family counseling come from specialists in family therapy—who often don't have extensive experience in companioning bereaved children. It seems we might have something to learn from each other.

In addition, most grief counselors are appropriately reluctant to make use of powerful family counseling techniques without special training. The result is that the family systems perspective tends to be talked about more in theory than applied in actual grief counseling. My hope in this chapter is to help try to begin to bridge this gap. (Obviously, another important element in the bridging of this gap is family systems training opportunities for grief counselors.)

201

The illusion of the dyad in child bereavement counseling

If family systems concepts have not been well integrated into grief counseling practices, part of the reason is that the family has been perceived as separate from the counselor's involvement in the system. The counselor has often been taught to be an observer of the family system rather than as a participant in the family system. As leading family therapists such as Haley, Minuchin and Satir have historically emphasized, the central unit in family counseling is not the family alone, but the therapeutic system, which includes both the family and the counselor. Therefore, a logical starting point for a model of the counselor's role in helping bereaved families is that the counselor is part of the system.

A view of the counseling relationship between the counselor and bereaved child can be referred to as "the illusion of the dyad in grief counseling." Why? Because, even when they are not physically present in counseling sessions, family members are very much involved in what goes on between the counselor and the bereaved child.

There can be no doubt that the counselor-bereaved child relationship is multilateral, not bilateral.

Family members (or guardians with whom bereaved children reside) influence, if not outright decide on, the selection of the counselor and expectations the child has of the counseling process. Most also carry out suggested helping principles to assist the bereaved child. Essentially, the family has the "ghost of presence" even when they are not a part of the counseling interaction. Therefore, every counselor who companions bereaved children is involved in a therapeutic triad of counselor-child-family. It's time to acknowledge the ghost!

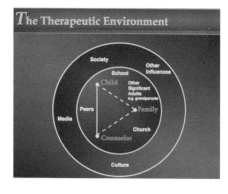

There can be no doubt that the counselor-bereaved child relationship is multilateral as opposed to bilateral. While most counselor-child interactions take place on a one-to-one basis, the therapeutic environment includes not only the child's family, but other influences such as peers, school, media and society in general. See the adjacent graphic for a visual representation of this concept.

You will note that the center of the therapeutic environment is formed by the child, the child's family and the counselor. I will call this the therapeutic triad. Of all the relationships in this triangle, the counselor-child relationship has been given the most focused attention in the bereavement literature. Additional perspectives on the therapeutic triad are introduced below.

• *The family's support of the child*

The family's involvement in and commitment to helping the bereaved child are critical to the child's healing.

While counselors usually counsel children in their own offices, the helping strategies proposed by the counselor are typically carried out at home in the family environment. Consequently, counselors who fail to perceive and make use of the helping role of the family are failing to make use of a systems model of caregiving.

The family's involvement in and commitment to helping the bereaved child are critical to the child's healing. Outside the counseling office, the counselor has little influence over the implementing of proposed helping strategies. My experience suggests that the family generally has the greatest influence.

Does this mean that you can't help a bereaved child except within the four walls of your office? No! But it does mean that to best help the child, you must mobilize the collaborative efforts of the therapeutic triad (as well as other influential elements in the therapeutic environment).

• *The counselor's relationship with the child's family*

Counselors who relate well to the child but not to adult family members will end up with less assistance from the family.

While we need more formal studies, my experience suggests that the quality of the counselor's relationship with the bereaved child's family may determine the quality of the relationship that develops between the counselor and child. It only makes sense that counselors who relate well to the child but not to adult family members (if they relate at all) will end up with less collaborative helping assistance from the family.

Without family assistance, working effectively with the bereaved child may be impossible. Generally, one would anticipate that the more complicated the bereavement circumstances (nature of the death, level and nature of attachment of the child to the deceased, etc.), the more important the counselor-family relationship would become.

• *The counselor's support of the bereaved child-family relationship*

In exploring important concepts of human development more than 15 years ago, Vrie Bronfenbrenner suggested that the quality of primary dyadic relationships (such as husband-wife or parent-child) is influenced by the support given those relationships by significant outsiders. For example, marital relationships are strengthened or weakened by the influence of in-laws; the mother-child relationship depends on the support of the father.

As a significant outsider in family relationships, the counselor invariably has an effect—positive or negative. For example, in supporting the family in coping with the death of one of its member, the counselor may be able to help maintain open, healthy patterns of communication during this naturally stressful period. However, if the counselor over-engages with the bereaved child (perhaps even in a codependent way) to the exclusion of the family, then the counselor is unknowingly undermining the family's internal relationships. The irony is that the most positive relationship between the counselor and the bereaved child may serve to weaken family relationships if the counselor is oblivious to the fact that she is involved in a therapeutic triad.

• *The family's support of the counselor-bereaved child relationship*

The family has the potential to either support or undermine the counselor's relationship with the bereaved child. In an effort to protect the interests of their child, the family is constantly assessing the perceived skill level and caring concern of the counselor. If a child resists going to a counseling session, if a helping strategy suggested by the counselor doesn't seem to actually help, or if a counselor cancels a scheduled appointment or is generally unavailable, the family may grow to distrust the counselor.

The model of the therapeutic triad suggests that a vital element in the continuation of a supportive counselor-bereaved child relationship will be the family's support of the counselor's role. The following are examples of family responses that support the counselor-bereaved child relationship:

"Dr. Wolfelt really seems to want to help you."

"Dr. Wolfelt really seems to want to help you."

"Why don't you tell Dr. Wolfelt about all those mixed-up feelings you've been having?"

On the other hand, some undermining responses:

"He probably doesn't know what he's going to do with you."

"All he does is play with you."

Family systems caregiving strategies

The traditional approach to caregiving with bereaved children has been to focus on the individual child without much involvement (if any) from the family. I am proposing that counseling of the bereaved child should be carried out with direct family involvement when possible. I advocate "family-oriented bereavement counseling." The key difference between a counselor who thinks in family systems terms and one who practices a family systems approach is that the latter regularly integrates the family into the counseling process.

This is not to suggest that the entire family must be present for all counseling sessions. On the contrary, I generally have an initial family session early on in the counseling process and then move the family in and out of sessions depending on the unique needs that evolve over time.

When and which family members to invite depends on the unique needs of each situation. Bringing together the relevant "family" may at times mean inviting the bereaved child's teacher, clergyperson, grandparent or neighbor. The key is to think creatively about the multi-faceted influences on the bereaved child's journey into grief.

When the family is directly involved in the etiology of the bereaved child's need for counseling (e.g., when mom has died and dad remarries a neighbor four months later and says to the child, "This is your new mother; don't talk about your old mother."), then the family's communication pattern may constitute the primary focus of counseling efforts.

Individual, Family or Support Group Counseling?

Counselors often ask me when they should see the bereaved child individually, when they should see the child with his family and when they should refer the child to a support group.

There may be times when you use one or all three of these helping avenues. Even when I'm seeing a child individually, I'm always seeing her world from a family systems perspective.

My own preference is to do some work with the child individually (which helps relieves pressure from the pressure cooker grief can cause in a family) while integrating the family into sessions from time to time.

Individual, family and support group counseling can be effectively used in combination.

The roles and goals of the family-oriented grief gardener

• Create a safe place for mourning.

Perhaps the family grief gardener's most important role is creator of a safe mourning environment for bereaved children and their families. You might think of your counseling office as a greenhouse—a sheltered, warm, nurturing place in which fragile seedlings can go about growing and maturing without the distractions and detractions of everyday life.

The family grief gardener supports growth while embracing the pain of the death and the ripple effect it initiates.

The materials with which you build this greenhouse are the concepts in this book. The family grief gardener uses self, group process and knowledge of family systems to facilitate the six needs of mourning and to help integrate the death into the life of the child and the family. She is a participant-observer—open, honest and direct. She supports growth while embracing the pain of the death and the ripple effect of losses the death initiates.

In sum, this role involves providing security at a natural time of insecurity, emotional and spiritual support at a time when this may be lacking and understanding and acceptance when it may not exist elsewhere.

• Help the family understand grief.

The good grief gardener finds appropriate ways and times to teach bereaved families about grief and the effects it may have on their family system. For example, while children and adults share similar emotions of grief, children are likely to respond with an apparent lack of feelings (see p. 66). Adults often need help in understanding the normalcy of the child's seemingly capricious shifts from acute sadness to apparent indifference and back again.

The family may also need help in understanding that the bereaved child will mourn in doses as she grows older and views her grief anew from different developmental standpoints. Likewise, many adults need help in understanding that people do not get over grief and that while children do not forget their grief, they do not keep it constantly in front of them, either.

Another common grief response families need help in understanding is the "pressure cooker" phenomenon. When death impacts a family, everyone has a high need to feel understood yet a natural incapacity to be understanding. Knowing this often happens lessens adult feelings of guilt about not being as available to the child as they might like to be. Learning about the pressure cooker phenomenon can also free the adults in the family system to do their own work of mourning so they can eventually focus more on the child.

These are but a few of many teachings the family grief gardener might share with bereaved families. Take your own "teacher" cues from the unique needs of the families in your care.

• *Offer an outside perspective.*

Closely aligned with the teacher role is that of helping the family see more clearly what is happening in their individual and family life. The counselor can help by describing or reflecting back to the family observations on the impact of the death on the family. Really, the counselor is providing the family with "new lenses," since the family often may be viewing their situation through tunnel vision. In other words, the grief gardener brings objectivity and a sense of normalcy to the family.

• *Help adults understand the grieving child's behavior.*

Part of the family grief gardener's job is to help other adults in the child's life understand the needs that underlie behaviors.

When a flower wilts, it is telling us it needs water. When its leaves turn yellow, it may be telling us it is getting too much water. When a bereaved child behaves in certain ways, she is telling us something, too.

Part of the family grief gardener's job is to help other adults in the child's life, especially parents, understand the needs that underlie behaviors. For example, an angry, acting-out child feels helpless and in "misbehaving" is expressing her feelings of insecurity. If you can reframe such behaviors for adults, you are helping them to become more supportive and understanding of the child's attempts to alert the family system to her pain.

The Bereaved Family: Ten Realities

1. *Traditional mental health care assumptions about grief have generally reflected those of the broader culture,* e.g., the belief that bereavement is an individual crisis that should be resolved quickly and efficiently. Until only recently, a systems model of understanding bereavement has been, for the most part, absent.

2. *The death of a family member results in special needs for the family as a unit.* Each person in a family has specific functions and roles not filled by anyone else in the family. The death of any member results in the reorganization of adult-child relationships in the system. The healthy reconciliation of grief has long-term implications for the child's and the family's continuing growth.

3. *A bereaved child's grief journey is particularly vulnerable to the help or lack of help provided by significant adults in the child's life.* For example, bereaved children often repress or deny their own grief when they intuit that their parents and other significant adults in their lives do not allow or encourage open mourning. Conversely, bereaved adults will have difficulty supporting and encouraging the child's mourning if they are pushing away or denying their own grief.

4. *Children can cope with what they know.* They cannot cope with what they don't know. When significant adults in the bereaved child's life give them incomplete or false information about the circumstances of the death, they hinder the child's ability to emotionally, cognitively and spiritually integrate the death experience.

5. *Children mourn not just the death, but the changes that death brings about in their world.* Bereaved children have special needs that result from realignment of the family structure and the changed emotional and spiritual environment.

6. *Family rules about death teach children what death should mean to them.* An open family system acknowledges feelings and openly involves children in the events surrounding the death, while a closed family system denies feelings and excludes children from events surrounding the death.

7. *Grief and ways of mourning can be handed down generation to generation.* For example, if parents have unreconciled grief from their own childhoods, it will ripple into the lives of their own children.

8. *New phases of family development result in new acknowledgments of the death and a reworking of the six central needs of mourning.*

Suppose, for example, a mother of two children dies. As those children grow up and reach life milestones, such as a first piano recital or a high school graduation, the family will likely mourn their loss anew from their current perspective.

9. *The counselor who wants to supportively companion bereaved children and families must be aware of her own family systems grief issues.* Ask yourself: What did I learn about grief and how to mourn from my own family? How have I integrated this learning? How do I live this learning both in my personal life and in my caregiving role?

10. *The bereaved child's and family's response to the death, even when complicated, must be respected as the family's best response* given the backdrop of family history, circumstances surrounding the death, cultural beliefs and supportive resources available to the family.

Ask yourself: What did I learn about grief and how to mourn from my own family?

• *Point out discrepancies in communication within the family.*

You can help the bereaved family by pointing out discrepancies in communication.

During a family session, a bereaved child's father says to you, "Sam's doing great!" Yet Sam's extensive acting-out tells you that this is not the case. When discrepancies such as this become apparent to you, it is your role to point them out to the family. For example, you might, after talking with the family, intuit that they have this common, unspoken rule: "Death isn't something we talk about." Yet some members of the family will likely exhibit a need to talk about it. You can help by articulating the unspoken rule and gently bringing the family around to discussing the rule's origin.

• *Help delineate changed roles within the family.*

The family grief gardener helps all members of the family sort out changed roles. If mom died and she usually washed the dishes, someone still has to wash the dishes. You can help families talk such role changes through. At the same time, you must also help guard against inappropriate role assignments within the family. A twelve-year-old cannot and should not be expected to assume a parental role in the family, for example. In other words, you can help counter expectations (stated or unstated) that a child can somehow replace the dead person within the family.

• *Build self-esteem.*

The family grief gardener helps build the self-esteem of all family members. When I observe parents with their bereaved daughter, I might say to them, "I see how Jenny feels cared about and safe with you." Reminders such as these help them feel appreciated as caregivers—something they need during this difficult time. I have found that play is the best way to build the self-esteem of bereaved children. When I allow them to enjoy the moment, they feel good about themselves.

• *Reconstruct the family's loss history.*

The family grief gardener not only assists in mourning the present death, but stays sensitive to the overall family loss history. You can help bereaved families understand that they may not only be mourning this loss, but prior losses as well. Genograms (a format for drawing a family tree that records information about family members and their relationships over at least three generations) can be a helpful tool in understanding the family's loss history.

The family grief gardener helps the bereaved family understand the need to involve children in ritual.

• *Facilitate ritual as a means of healing.*

The family grief gardener explores with the bereaved family how or if they have used ritual to assist both the children and adults in the healing process. He also helps the family understand the need to involve children in ritual. Stepping into his teacher role again, he makes them aware that when words are inadequate, ceremony can assist in the healing process.

One important reminder here: It is never too late to make use of ritual. Families who may have missed the healing benefits of a meaningful funeral ceremony can still be helped by mourning rituals today and into the future. Help them plan a memorial ceremony (even if the death happened some time ago), make a memory table, plant a tree, carry out the candle ritual (see p. 193)—any ritual that will help them acknowledge the reality of their loss and begin to meet the other reconciliation needs of mourning.

• *Act as family advocate.*

Grief gardeners are sometimes placed in the position of suggesting what is in the best interest of the child and family. I was called in to testify in court regarding the needs of one family's children when the mother shot and killed her husband. Rather than sending the children to separate foster homes (which the court was about to do), I said they should be brought back together under the care of someone they already knew and trusted before the tragedy.

In another family advocate situation, I brought a church leader into a counseling session to supportively confront his belief (which was severely complicating the child's and the family's mourning) that mourning and faith are mutually exclusive.

One final, practical way to act as family advocate in times of grief is to write a note to school administrators and even corporate human resource executives requesting additional bereavement leave after a death. The traditional 72 hours off is not nearly enough for children and adults alike to return to school and work.

• *Validate all family members for the courage to mourn.*

The family grief gardener provides support and encouragement for all family members to mourn. While he brings objectivity to the helping process, he also sees himself as a humble guide, a caring companion and a privileged witness to the healing process. See strengths, bring hope and encourage healing!

• *Provide hope for healing.*

The family grief gardener builds individual and family self-esteem.

When a child is referred for counseling, it is not unusual that the entire family system is pervaded by a depressive mood. Obviously, bereavement brings with it sadness and depression. A vital role of the family grief gardener is to nourish hope for not only the child's capacity to heal, but for the entire family's capacity to heal.

The importance of this role cannot be overstated; without hope, healing cannot and will not occur. All members of the family garden may have been assaulted by a hailstorm, yet the family grief gardener looks for strengths in the child's and the family's underlying roots and points out these strengths at appropriate times: "You made some important decisions that resulted in a meaningful funeral for your family."

Basically, the family grief gardener builds individual and family self-esteem, all the while understanding the role of self-esteem in the eventual reconciliation process. He in effect says to the child and family, "See what healing decisions you have already made. See how far you have come. You are making progress and I believe you have the inner strength to survive and to be happy again."

The bereavement literature has long recognized the potential of a family systems approach to caregiving. However, in applied practice the day to day use of this perspective appears to be lacking; too many grief counselors have clung to the traditional individual model of bereavement counseling for too long.

Again, the time has come to acknowledge the ghost and invite it into the counseling setting!

References

Bronfenbrenner, V. *The Ecology of Human Development.* Cambridge, Mass: Harvard University Press, 1979.

Haley, J. *Problem-Solving Therapy.* San Francisco: Josey-Bass, 1976.

Mead, M. "The Individual and Society". Paper read at the International Congress of Mental Health, August, 1948.

Minuchin, S. *Families and Family Therapy.* Cambridge, Mass: Harvard University Press, 1974.

Satir, V. *Conjoint Family Therapy: A Guide to Theory and Technique.* Palo Alto: Science and Behavior Books, 1964.

Wolfelt, A. "Reconciliation Versus Resolution: The Importance of Semantics," *Frontline,* Spring 1995 issue, pp. 3, 4.

Grief Myth

Children are better off if they don't attend funerals.

The funeral provides a structure that allows adults and children to comfort each other, openly mourn and honor the life of the person who died.

Adults who have internalized this myth create an environment that prematurely moves children away from grief and mourning. The funeral provides a structure that allows and encourages both adults and children to comfort each other, openly mourn and honor the life of the person who has died.

Meaningful funerals form the foundation for healthy mourning just as properly prepared soil forms the foundation of a healthy garden. If we skip these crucial first steps, we fail to prepare adequately for the future.

Children, who after all are mourners too, should have the same opportunity to attend funerals as any other member of the family. They should be encouraged to attend, but never forced. I emphasize the word "encouraged" because some children are anxious when experiencing something unknown to them. Through gentle encouragement, loving adults can help bereaved children know they will be supported during this naturally sad and frightening time in their young lives. The funeral can even provide an opportunity for children to express their unique relationship with the person who has died by including a ritual of their own during the service.

(See p. 56 for more on children and funerals.)

Have you seen this myth carried out? When and how?

_____

_____

_____

_____

_____

_____

_____

8

The "Cold Frames" of Grief Gardening: Support Groups for Bereaved Children

In northern climates like mine, gardeners who want a jump start on the season plant seedlings outdoors earlier than the established "last frost" date then protect those tender seedlings from certain death with a contraption called a *cold frame.* A cold frame is a frame of wood or metal sheathed in glass or plastic (picture a mini-greenhouse) that, when placed over a grouping of seedlings, intensifies the sun's warmth and traps heat inside. In this way the seedlings are given a safe, warm place in which to begin their new lives.

Support groups provide a warm, sheltered environment in which bereaved children can mourn.

Support groups provide a similarly warm, sheltered environment in which bereaved children can mourn. Because they offer emotional safety in our mourning-avoiding world (like a cold frame offers safety during a frosty spring), support groups encourage children and teens to reconcile their losses and go on to find continued meaning in life and living.

Support groups help bereaved kids by:

- countering the sense of isolation many bereaved children experience in our shame-based, mourning-avoiding culture.

- providing emotional, physical and spiritual support in a safe, non-judgmental environment.

- allowing them to explore their many thoughts and feelings about grief in a way that helps them be compassionate with themselves.

"The fair-weather gardener, who will do nothing except when wind and weather and everything else are favourable, is never a master of his craft. Gardening, above all crafts, is a matter of faith, grounded . . . on his experience that somehow or other seasons go on in their right course, and bring their right results. No doubt bad seasons are a trial of his faith; it is grievous to lose the fruits of much labour by a frosty winter or a droughty summer, but, after all, frost and drought are necessities for which . . . he must leave an ample margin; but even in the extreme cases, when the margin is past, the gardener's occupation is not gone."

Canon Ellacombe, *In a Gloucestershire Garden,* (1895)

- encouraging members to not only receive support and understanding for themselves, but also to provide help to others. (We know that children do not like to be different from peers and often resist being singled out for purposes of receiving help.)

- offering new ways of approaching problems (e.g., how to respond to the peer who makes fun of the fact that someone in your life has died.)

- helping them trust again in what for many seems like an unsafe, uncaring world.

- providing a supportive environment that can rekindle their love for life and living.

In short, as bereaved children give and receive help, they feel less helpless and are able to discover continued meaning in life. Feeling understood by their peers and effective adult leaders brings down barriers between the bereaved child and the world outside.

Our mourning-avoiding culture often invites children to keep their grief internalized and to adopt ways of avoiding the painful but necessary work of mourning. Support groups instead foster the experience of trusting and being trusted and have the potential of doing wonders in meeting the needs of bereaved children.

This chapter is intended to help grief gardeners with some of the nuts and bolts of creating support groups for bereaved kids. While it is beyond the scope of this book to provide detailed content ideas for these groups, I encourage you to contact hospices, schools and churches to trade ideas and learn from each other.

Getting started: questions to address

Starting a support group for bereaved children can take a lot of time and energy. In fact, I have seen many counselors decide *not* to start groups simply because they foresaw too many roadblocks and details to attend to. I have found the key to be to find another interested counselor who shares your enthusiasm for helping bereaved children in support groups settings! Trying to go this alone may result in not going at all. Besides, it's more fun to do it with someone you enjoy working with.

The Dougy Center

The Dougy Center in Portland, Oregon is a good resource to be aware of if you are going to lead bereavement support groups with children. Here is some info about them:

The Dougy Center is a grief support program providing support groups for children and teens (and separate concurrent groups for their parent(s) or adult family members) who have experienced the death of a parent, sibling or close friend through accident, illness, suicide or murder. The Center is founded on the belief that every child deserves the opportunity to grieve in a supportive and understanding environment. Our society, however, often fails to understand or support the needs of a child and family in grief. This lack of support may result in children and teens acting out their unacknowledged pain through non-constructive behaviors and depression.

The principles of the Dougy Center include the beliefs that 1) grief is a natural reaction to the loss of a loved one, for children as well as adults, 2) within each individual is the natural capacity to heal oneself, 3) the duration and intensity of grief are unique for each individual and 4) caring and acceptance assist in the healing process.

The Dougy Center's support groups are open-ended, and families attend for as long as they feel they need to, in recognition of the uniqueness of each individual. Although the program is therapeutic, the center does not provide therapy, nor teach children or adults how to grieve. We believe children know how to grieve; more often, they are not permitted to do so. In a safe, supportive setting through peer support groups, children share their experience without judgment. The programs of the Dougy Center provide this supportive environment by encouraging the sharing of feelings and self-expression through art, music and other activities to facilitate the process of healing. Our approach is to provide an atmosphere of caring acceptance that acknowledges the individuality of the grief experience and that invites children to share their unique experiences.

The groups at the Dougy Center are age-specific (3-5-year-olds, 6-12-year-olds, teens, adults) and loss-specific (death of a parent, death of a sibling, murder, suicide). Through mutual support, caring and acceptance, the healing process is fostered. Children or families with severe emotional or behavioral problems are referred for therapy, but much of what normal grief looks like is interpreted by the inexperienced teacher, counselor or coach as "crazy." Sometimes it feels that way to the griever, too. Through the sharing of feelings, thoughts and self, the painful grief process is normalized and acknowledged. Children and adults discover their own healing process, in their own timing, and in their own way. We invite them to share this with others on the journey. We believe that, contrary to popular culture's belief that grief is something one "gets over," it is something one "gets through." The griever is forever a changed person because of the impact of the loss of a person he or she loved.

For more information, contact The Dougy Center, 3909 S.E. 52nd, P.O. Box 86852, Portland, OR 97286, phone (503) 775-5683, fax (503) 777-3097, www.dougy.org

Now, let's explore the following bereavement support group start-up tasks:

Performing a needs assessment
Before your commendable enthusiasm causes you to plunge head-long into starting a support group for bereaved kids, step back and formally assess the interest and need for bereavement support groups in your school, hospice or other organization. Questions to address include: What kind of bereavement support groups for kids already exist in your community? What has been the history and success of these groups? What have the leaders of these groups learned about what works and what doesn't work? Who else is willing to commit time and effort to make this group successful? What support group models are being used throughout North America?

Deciding on group membership
Early on you'll need to decide what the group's make-up will be. Will the group be comprised of children who have experienced a specific type of loss or loss of the same kind of relationship (parent, grandparent, etc.)? Or will the common bond simply be that each group member has had someone loved die? In the former, the similarity of losses often creates a tremendous bond for group members and makes relating to each other very easy. However, depending on the size of the population you are drawing from, you may or may not be able to achieve this homogeneity. In smaller towns, children with different types of losses (death, divorce, etc.) are sometimes combined to form a support group. In my experience, however, the needs of children of divorce and bereaved children, while bearing many similarities, are truly different. The main thing is to avoid having a child feel so different from other group members that she feels alone and isolated.

Groups comprised of children with similar losses are especially healing.

Finding a meeting place
Obviously, you hope to find a comfortable, safe place to hold your group meetings. You may already have an ideal place in your school, hospice or church. Try to select a room appropriate for creating a supportive atmosphere, neither too large nor too small. (If too small, it can inhibit play activities in children. It can also violate members' sense of personal space, creating anxiety.) A room with no telephones, away from heavy traffic areas and distraction-free, is preferable. Be certain to modify rooms for different age groups. For example, you can decorate walls with Disney char-

acters for young children and rock stars or athletes for teens. Many children and teens prefer to sit on the floor and often disclose more in this position. Decent carpeting and the availability of large, soft pillows often will help with this. In other words, help make the kids—whatever their ages—feel comfortable in the support group space.

Setting the number of participants

The number of support group members will largely determine the quality of interaction you desire and activities you hope to make use of. When groups get too large, the sense of safety and freedom to be expressive diminishes for many children.

Obviously, numbers are also influenced by age and developmental level considerations. Under ideal circumstances I suggest the following guidelines: preschool groups—six or fewer participants; grade school—six-eight participants; adolescents—six-ten participants. I also think that four is the minimum number of participants; fewer can inhibit group process. (Another bias: I prefer co-leaders so you have someone to plan meetings and to de-brief with.)

Establishing the structure of the group

You must also determine the structure of the support group. Will it be "open-ended," meaning that group members come and go depending on their needs? Or will it be "closed-ended," meaning that the group will meet for a specific number of days or weeks? In my experience, children feel more comfortable and are more likely to stay committed to a group if it is closed-ended. This structure also aids group bonding and the creation of a shared group identity and fosters a more conducive environment for self-disclosure. In addition, the closed-ended structure allows you to integrate the six central needs of mourning (see Chapter 4) into the content of the groups.

Bereavement Camps

Leslie Delp, who coordinates Camp Mend A Heart in York, Pennsylvania, sent me the following explanation of bereavement camps, which are a wonderful form of bereavement support groups. If you'd like more information on starting your own bereavement camp, you can write to her at Grief & Bereavement Services, 1142 Harvest View Court., New Freedom, PA 17349 or call her at (717) 235-4451.

When bereaved children were asked what they minded most about the death in their family, they reported they felt isolated. It was very traumatic to be "different" from their peers.

Bereavement camps address the problem of isolation by introducing children who have something in common . . . a death in the family. At camp, the children have an opportunity to meet and make friends with other children like themselves while they learn all about the process grown-ups call bereavement. And the kids are also treated to fun, games, camping and activities galore!

Bereavement camps range from three-day weekends, complete with overnight stays in cabins, to single days. (Single day camps, while designed to facilitate the bereavement process, are packed full of activity but tend to just introduce children to the concepts of grief.)

Most bereavement camps pair an adult who has experienced a significant loss of their own with a child who has experienced a similar loss. This "grief history" creates a bond between the two. At Camp Mend A Heart, the bonding of the children with their "big buddy" was an essential part of the camping experience.

Camp Mend A Heart includes:

- A camp theme song, tote bag with special toys to take home and a camp t-shirt everyone wears.

- Small group sessions to teach about the feelings that accompany grief.

- Arts and crafts that have special meaning in the child's bereavement process, such as memory scarves, plaques and special heart etchings.

- Physical activities such as swimming.

- A campfire dinner complete with singing and storytelling—and marshmallow-roasting!

- A memory ritual. At the end of camp, we hold a memory ritual near the edge of the lake. Each child is given a candle to take home to light (with supervision) whenever they want to think of their loved one. Songs are sung and poems are recited. After the ritual, a big heart-shaped balloon with the children's names and their loved ones' names written on it is released into the sky.

Creating a camp is an exciting task but one that takes commitment from a group. Ideally, bereavement camps should be overseen by a professional grief counselor, but there is also plenty of work for energetic volunteers!

Determining the length and frequency of meetings

Most research has suggested that for groups to be minimally effective with children, at least ten sessions are necessary. I am aware that six, eight and ten week formats are common throughout North America. When possible, I would advocate for the ten-session model. However, this is not always possible.

Appropriate meeting length depends heavily on the age of the children—for preschool and grade school kids, 90 minutes is usually the maximum. For teens, 90 minutes to two hours usually works well. In addition, some of your length considerations will have to do with the number of participants you have and the activities you plan.

Some support groups for bereaved children meet weekly, some bi-weekly, some monthly. I prefer weekly because children have busy schedules, and the frequency of weekly meetings helps them stay committed to the group and allows for continuity from week to week. However, you should be creative in determining which length and frequency will work best for your group.

Pre-screening group members

Not every bereaved child will be appropriate for support group membership. Children with extensive complications of their grief journeys (traumatic, violent deaths or histories of serious emotional and behavioral problems) are generally better helped by individual counseling.

Participant selection in the bereavement support group is perhaps the most important step. You must feel free to select-in children who you believe will be helped by the group. Conversely, you should select-out those children who may be better served by individual or family counseling. (Which is certainly not to say that the three forms of counseling are mutually exclusive. See p. 206 for more on this topic.)

How do you pre-screen? I recommend you conduct brief, one-on-one meetings with potential group members. You can then determine the child's suitability for your particular group. Pay careful attention to the recency of the loss. I have found that most children (though there are always exceptions) are not ready for a support group for at least three months after the death of someone loved. In fact, bereaved children are typically more responsive to group support approximately eight to ten months (sometimes longer) after the death.

The potential group participant can also be made aware of the purpose of the group, length and frequency of session and potential ground rules. If, after hearing who will participate and what will be involved, a child doesn't want to participate, it is his personal right not to be involved. I have found that when children are coerced or forced to participate, they strongly resist, and unless their resistance is overcome very quickly, little value is gained from the group experience.

Another important question I'm often asked is, "Do I need to seek and receive parental approval for the child to participate in the group?" Yes, by law and as a matter of good ethics, parents (or legal guardians) are responsible for children and need to consent to their involvement in a support group. This contact with parent or guardian has some excellent additional advantages. First, it creates a potential line of communication between counselor and parent, which often results in greater parental involvement on behalf of the child. (See Chapter 7 for more on the therapeutic triad.) In addition, the parent may benefit from some education about group objectives and potential benefits to the child. As noted elsewhere in this chapter, you may want to offer a parent/guardian group that meets at the same time the kids meet. After all, we not only want to help the child but the entire family system.

When bereaved children are forced to participate in support groups, little value is gained from the experience.

It is wise to invite parents or guardians to a personal meeting for further discussion if they want it. A sample parental permission letter can be found on p. 226.

Model Letter of Permission for Support Group Participation

Agency stationery

Date_____

Dear (Parent or Guardian)—

Your son/daughter has been identified as a potential participant for a grief support group that will start next month. The group will consist of eight children who will meet with me and my co-counselor, Susan Johnson, every Wednesday for ten weeks. The purpose of the group is to have children who have had a death in their life benefit from the support of their peers.

During these groups, the children will be involved in open discussion and activities designed to help them understand and teach each other about their grief. I have discussed this group with your son/daughter and he/she has indicated a desire to participate.

If you are supportive of your child's participation in this group counseling experience, please sign below and return this letter to me. If you would like additional information about the support group, please give me a call at _____. Should you desire a personal appointment to discuss this, we can arrange one.

I look forward to the possibility of having your child be an important part of this group.

Sincerely,

Joe Smith, M.S.W.

I give permission for _____ to participate in the group counseling experience described in this letter.

_____

Parent/guardian signature

Parental (or guardian) involvement

This is an area that has all too often been ignored with disastrous consequences. I've heard about many children going home to announce to a parent or guardian that they "went to a support group today." The adult blows up and says, "You did what? What are they doing talking to you about death?" In other words, the family rules about the death may be at odds with the group's objectives. As noted above, always get signed parental permission for the child to participate.

In addition, some group models (such as the Dougy Center's) run parallel parent groups. (Parents meet together in a separate group while children meet.) This model recognizes that the entire family system is impacted by the death.

Creating group ground rules

Through appropriately pre-screening participants and establishing group ground rules, you can create a safe place for children to mourn. Ground rules are also important to your role as leader. You establish expectations for behavior through ground rules.

Children often can help establish the group's ground rules.

The children can help create the ground rules. I simply ask, "Some of you have been in groups before. What kind of rules do you think we need to have for a successful group?" The kids begin to offer up things like, "Don't interrupt when someone else is talking." I sometimes try to re-frame this comment in a positive way by saying, "So maybe we should agree to wait until a person is finished talking before we talk."

Typical ground rules children often help establish are things like:

1. Respect each person's right to talk or just listen.
2. What is shared in this group stays in the group.
3. Be on time for the meetings.
4. Feelings aren't right or wrong, they just are.

With children's' support groups, I always make sure each participating child gets a copy. You might also want to post them in your meeting room.

A special note about confidentiality: Children may not understand the term confidentiality, but they can and do understand, "What we talk about in this group stays in the group." When family members, guardians or friends ask the children what they did in group (and they will), help the children understand that they can talk about what they did in group but should not discuss the specifics of what other group members talked about.

You will run into occasions where you need to remove a group member after the group has begun. For example, you may have a child who is physically or psychologically harmful to other group members. For the benefit of the group and the child, you must act. Misconduct or failure to adhere to group ground rules is often the child's way of saying, "My needs are greater than this group will be able to meet." You should then supportively facilitate a referral for individual or family counseling for that child.

Publicizing your group

The ways in which you publicize your group depends on your situation. Hospices can directly contact potential members through the families they have served. Notification might go out to families through letters, newsletters or personal phone calls. Notices can also be placed—usually free of charge—in local newspapers.

Schools generally have a captured audience, as well. The key is to work with teachers to identify children who would potentially benefit from the support group. You can also post notices on a school bulletin board.

Try ideas that seem appropriate to your setting and unique needs. But do publicize; don't assume bereaved children will naturally find their way to your door.

Sample Support Group Ground Rules

Here's a list of support group ground rules you can use with kids. I do encourage you, however, to let each group come up with its own ground rules. The rule-making process encourages kids to feel ownership of and responsibility to the group.

1. Each kid's grief is unique. None of us will feel exactly the same way. And none of our thoughts and feelings are right or wrong—they just are.

2. Our grief may take lots of time to heal. I'll take as long as I need and so will the other kids in the group.

3. I can talk about my grief when I want to during group, but I won't interrupt anyone else. If someone wants to listen without talking, that's OK, too.

4. Thoughts and feelings shared in this group will stay in this group. I won't tell people outside the group about what the other kids have said or done during meetings.

5. Everyone has a right to talk during group; none of us should hog too much time.

6. I'll come to each group meeting and be on time.

Grief gardeners know that children's grief may take a long time to heal.

Defining Your Leadership Role

A support group leader serves the group by enabling members to achieve the purpose of the support group. That purpose is generally to create a safe place for children to do the work of mourning in a way that allows them to reconcile their losses and go on to find continued meaning in life and living. Sensitive, skilled leadership is often a vital link to a group's fulfillment of its goals.

Obviously, your specific support group may have varying purposes and goals that guide its existence. No matter the goals, however, the group leader's responsibilities remain largely the same. Support group leaders are responsible for assisting the group in:

- determining the group's purpose
- outlining the group's structure and length
- pre-screening potential members
- clarifying expectations and assisting in the development of group ground rules
- organizing details

Now let's explore some of the specific tasks that are often a part of a bereavement support group leader's job description. Again, keep in mind that every group has its own unique requirements.

To model and to be an effective listener, you must really hear what children are saying.

Planning and leading group meetings: Preparing for, organizing and facilitating the group meetings.

Listening: To model and to be an effective listener, you must really hear and allow children to "teach you" and each other what they are thinking and feeling.

Understanding and facilitating group process: Having knowledge of and being skilled in facilitating group process. Working with children in support groups is usually distinctly different than working with adults. For example, as noted throughout this text, children often teach you more through their behaviors than through their words.

Modeling openness and caring: Acting as a role model by being warm, caring and empathetic and by consciously seeking ways to help the group achieve its purpose.

Being responsive to conflicts and problems that evolve: Guiding the group through difficulties that may come up and responding appropriately to destructive behavior in the group.

Learning about effective group leadership roles: Participating in training opportunities that allow you to assess current skills and develop new ones.

Following up with members outside of the group:　Some children will appreciate opportunities to talk individually, while others may need referral for an individual counseling relationship.

Evaluating group progress:　Monitoring the group's capacity to achieve its purpose and make any changes to improve this process.

Let me emphasize how important your job description as a group leader is. It should outline your understanding of the specific responsibilities you have as a leader. If you don't have a job description, create one using the above information as a model. This will help both you and your organization: 1) clarify the details of your role as a group leader, 2) help you get started in your new role, and 3) avoid unstated expectations. A "seat of the pants" orientation to group facilitation is dangerous and minimizes your responsibility as a leader. With appropriate preparation and training, your leadership role will be both satisfying and enjoyable.

My job description as group leader is:

_____

_____

_____

_____

_____

_____

_____

_____

_____

_____

Defining your leadership style

What kind of leader are you? Are you gregarious? Aggressive? Passive? Leaders I have found most effective in bereavement support groups with children lead unobtrusively but firmly. That is, they are warm and responsive at the same time they help the children feel comfortable that someone is "in charge."

One of the most important qualities in an effective group leader of children is flexibility. Being flexible is important because some meetings — especially as the group evolves — will naturally flow without much direction from you. That means that sometimes your meeting plans, no matter how well conceived, should be tossed out the window if the group dynamic takes everyone in a different direction. A good leader is never rigid. And a good leader of children's groups always remembers that children mourn through the use of play. Traditional talk counseling simply doesn't work with bereaved kids.

Understanding the support group's developmental phases

Why is it important to understand that bereavement support groups go through developmental phases? Because knowledge of these phases allows you to both respect and nurture the natural unfolding of the group's development. For example, if you were to expect in-depth self-evaluation of all children at the first meeting, you would not be respecting the reality that this kind of sharing generally does not happen until group trust has been established over time.

Knowledge of the support group's phases allows you to respect and nurture the natural unfolding of the group's development.

Groups tend to develop in a cyclical manner. This means that bereavement needs such as "the telling of the story" tend to be met again and again but at progressively deeper levels of meaning. Of course, individual group members have a vital influence on the process of group development; therefore, the outline that follows is very theoretical.

Phase One: Warm-up and establishing of group purpose and limits

In the beginning of a support group, you can anticipate some normal anxiety about the general uncertainty of "what will happen here." Children may be questioning their capacity to confront their own and others' pain. So, be aware that many group members will attend with a certain amount of hesitancy and some questions about whether or not they should even be here.

Among the questions that may go through their minds during this phase: Who else is in this group? How does their loss relate to mine? Will they understand me or judge me? Will I feel comfortable with these kids? Will I like them? What will we talk about? Are there certain expectations the group will have of me? Will the leader make it "safe" for me to just be who I am? Will I have to talk, even if at times I don't want to? What activities will we do? Can I play and have fun here?

Behaviorally, members will tend to reflect their unique personalities. Some will be more expressive, while others may be silent and withdrawn. This initial period of getting to know each other is critical for what will or will not follow.

The leaders play a critical role in making it safe during this initial phase of the group's development. Here the grief gardener's roles include:

- clarifying the purpose of the group
- gently encouraging each member to "tell his or her story" (who died, the nature of the death, why they are attending this group)
- assisting in the creation of ground rules for the group
- modeling listening and helping everyone feel as if they belong here
- facilitating details such as time of meetings, formats, etc.
- helping children get better acquainted

Phase Two: Tentative self-disclosure and exploring group boundaries

This is the phase where children begin to learn what is expected to happen in the group. Every group has expectations (spoken or unspoken) about what will happen in meetings. Essentially, members are learning how to be participating members of the support group.

At this stage the children begin to see themselves as a group and disclose more about themselves. Often this self-disclosure is rather tentative. It's as if the group is exploring whether it is safe to move to a deeper level of risk. Differences in interpersonal styles and ways of coping with grief also become more apparent during this phase. Some of your activities at this stage should be designed to help the children "feel safe" and give structure to their grief work.

Through increasing self-disclosure and the exploring of group norms or boundaries, members begin to learn more about each other, the leader and themselves. During this phase the grief gardener's roles include:

- continuing to model listening, openness and caring

- continuing to clarify children's expectations of the group

- reminding members of the ground rules established at the first meeting

- providing helpful activities that facilitate children's mourning

- being responsive to conflicts and problems that might evolve

- helping children continue to share feelings and experiences

Phase Three: In-depth self-exploration and encountering the pain of grief

As the group grows and develops, a subtle but important movement takes place. The group begins to move away from the initial discovery of the "why" of the group and toward an increasing involvement in the work of mourning. At this phase, the group has shifted from second to third gear and is beginning to develop group trust at a deeper level. A natural insider/outsider feeling often begins to develop and older children may begin to express how important the group is to them. Now the group is feeling good about itself and the kids look forward to each meeting.

As groups develop, they begin to move toward an increasing involvement in the work of mourning.

A higher rate of self-disclosure and self-expression is now taking place, through words, play or a combination of both. Often, lots of memory work is done as children share the lives of the people who have died. Interactions between members may become more intense and emotional. Also during this phase, group members may begin to work more actively on helping themselves and the other children learn new ways of coping with their losses.

The grief gardener's roles during this phase include:

- continuing to model listening, openness and caring
- being supportive of continued participation of group members
- assisting the group in dealing with any conflicts and problems that might evolve
- making appropriate adjustments to content and format for improvement of the group
- allowing and encouraging the group to be more self-responsible

Phase Four: Commitment to continued healing and growth

During this phase, many children begin to ask for and reach out to others for mutual help and support. The group ambiance takes on a more relaxed tone. Members feel safe and "at home" in the group.

While you should not withdraw as leader, you should be able to share more and more responsibility with group members. You will notice the children modeling empathetic caring responses and even trying to verbalize for the group new insights into the grief journey.

Remember — not every group meeting will go smoothly. You will have good meetings, great meetings, some not-so-good meetings and maybe even some bad meetings. Try using humor to acknowledge a bad meeting.

Phase Four is clearly the most valuable phase in the life of the bereavement support group. In some ways, if the prior phases have been reached, it's like the group is on auto-pilot. Earlier concerns and developmental phases have been achieved and the group is moving at a faster pace. Respect and trust levels are way up, which allows the children to share what they need to share.

At this phase, the group process is typified by much more open-ended expression of thoughts and feelings. Activities you have planned may need to be eliminated as the group seems to need more time for open discussion. By this time the children are genuinely concerned about the well-being of other members. Any missing members become a focus of discussion. The kids will want to know, "Where is Mark?" if Mark is missing.

The grief gardener's roles during this phase include:

- continuing to model listening, openness and caring
- being supportive of continued participation of group members
- modeling of shared leadership principles
- assisting the group in dealing with any conflicts and problems that might arise
- making appropriate adjustments to content and format as the group evolves

Phase Five: Preparation for and leaving the group

Obviously, the bereavement support group that progresses through the above four phases of development creates support and assists bereaved children in ways frequently lacking in our mourning-avoiding culture. Also obvious is that the kind of intimacy developed in the support group environment also creates natural problems of separation when the group must come to an end.

Careful attention must be paid to the importance of this ending. After all, the group's closure is another loss for the group's members. Many grief support groups are so successful they resist ending. However, "graduation" from the support group is an important step toward reconciliation of the death of someone loved.

Expect a certain amount of ambiguity of feelings about the ending of the group. Ending may elicit withdrawal in some, sadness in others, and happiness in yet others. A theme of general optimism and feelings of progress and healing should override these natural feelings of loss. As the group leader, you will need to be sensitive to any and all feelings connected to children leaving the group.

Reflecting on and affirming the growth that has been experienced in the group is a vital part of this phase. One or possibly two meetings should be focused on saying goodbye to each other as a group and supporting hopes for continued healing of the wounds of grief. There will probably be both some tears and some laughter as the group moves toward graduation. Enjoy this and be proud that you have effectively and compassionately led this group toward reconciliation.

The grief gardener's roles during this last phase include:

- creating safe opportunities for children to say goodbye to each other and to the group

- recognizing and understanding the dynamics that occur when a group begins to end

- encouraging reflection on individual and group growth related to the grief journey

- providing referrals for additional resources to those who need ongoing help

- conducting a summary evaluation of the group

A reminder: This five-phase, theoretical model will be influenced by the unique personalities of your group's children as well as by your own leadership style. Some groups will naturally move more quickly through these phases than others. The most important thing you can do as group leader is to ask yourself how you can make it safe for these phases to evolve. If your group is not moving forward or seems to be stuck, try to discern why the children don't feel a sense of trust or safety.

Planning your meetings

The effective group leader is a prepared group leader. I suggest you plan each meeting much in the same way teachers prepare lesson plans: with a flexible structure and a purposeful sequencing of activities. In other words, don't try to "wing it" (while still paying attention to the group's unique gestalt).

Through the years, I have found that a combination of planned activities and open-ended play and discussion time work well for me. I have also found that giving the children "homework" to complete between sessions doesn't always work well. Most of today's children are busy enough with schoolwork, sports and other life activities that support group homework gets forgotten or causes unneeded stress.

If you do want to try having your support group kids do some form of homework between meetings, consider giving them a poem, a short reading on grief or a story about life and death. Other home activities might include making a collage that depicts the bereaved child's grief journey or filling a memory box with photos and other keepsakes of the deceased. Sometimes this type of homework

Suggestions for Leading Discussion

As group leader, your role is to facilitate, literally to "make easier," purposeful discussion and activities about the grief journeys of group members—a task that will require some planning and forethought on your part. Consider the following suggestions:

• *Plan each session*

Write down your goals and expectations for each group meeting. For example, your objective in the first session may simply be to get to know each other. How will you accomplish this? In addition to letting the children tell their stories, you may plan one or two group activities. You might also use music and appropriate readings as prompts for group discussion.

• *Have a routine*

Especially when they're feeling vulnerable, children like the comfort of a routine. You might, for example, open each session with a short reading that you or one of the children has brought. Try to start each meeting slowly; remember, children mourn in doses.

• *Be sensitive to the differences among members*

As group leader and grief gardener, you are probably an outgoing person who feels comfortable sharing experiences in a group setting. Not all children will be so forthcoming, however. Don't force them to talk unless they're ready. On the other hand, you'll also need to be on the watch for the child who likes to talk and monopolizes the group's time.

As group leader and grief gardener, you are probably someone who feels comfortable sharing experiences in a group setting.

238

encourages members to prepare for group and gives them a comforting structure that promotes open discussion. (Of course, it also helps you as leader!) Include the children's parents or guardians and other family members in these activities when possible. You can accomplish this by sending home a note with the children after each meeting that not only tells the parents what you have done in group today, but also requests their assistance in helping the child complete his group "homework." The note might also include supportive tips for the parents to try in helping the bereaved child embrace his grief.

Evaluating your group's progress

"Progress" in grief is difficult to pinpoint. Grief is something we never truly get over; it is an ongoing, recursive process that unfolds over many, many weeks and years. So, if your ten-week support group is finishing up and you feel unable to quantify each child's progress, don't feel discouraged.

First, listen to what your heart tells you about the progress the group has made. Have you felt a growing sense of trust among members? Have the children been able to share their experiences in a way they wouldn't have been able to elsewhere? Have you noticed particular members are able to open up more or cope better than they were when the group began? Have the kids responded to some of your activities with enthusiasm?

Next, ask the children themselves for feedback in the form of an end-of-group evaluation sheet like the one on p. 246. This will help you learn how you can continue to improve with each group you have the privilege of leading.

Continued on page 247.

A Children's Support Group Model

As noted by the inclusion of this chapter in this book, my experience is that many bereaved children benefit from participation in a support group. I have outlined below a ten-session format for a combination education/support group for children ages six-twelve. I urge you to be creative and adapt this model to your situation (a ten-session model that includes age-appropriate activities for teenagers, for example, could be extrapolated from the one that follows), making changes that you think will best meet the needs of your unique group. While this is serious stuff, always remember that it should be fun; you are companioning children who want to play, laugh and have fun, even in the midst of grief.

Obviously, this model is based on my humble, biased opinion that a closed-ended support group model works best. The group meets for ten sessions over ten weeks. (One meeting each week.) No children can join the group after it begins. For maximum effectiveness, the group should be limited to 6-8 children and two adult facilitators.

You will note that I recommend two adult facilitators. This allows you to have a working partner to both plan meetings and debrief with. It also makes it more enjoyable for you as a leader. The leaders can be either professionally trained child counselors or trained lay helpers who have gifts for walking with bereaved children. Often, I have enjoyed the combination of a layperson with a counselor. Everyone learns from each other. Remember, collaborate with your co-leader; don't compete. If your models of helping are too divergent, you may find yourself in trouble.

Bereaved children want to play, laugh and have fun, even in the midst of grief.

Meet with your co-leader several times prior to making use of this model. The key to success is the 3 P's—preparation, preparation, preparation. Then and only then will you be ready to initiate such a group.

As you plan, keep in mind that effective support group leaders use a combination of planned activities and open discussion and play time to keep kids interested and engaged. Be creative as you plan for each meeting. Remember—kids naturally mourn through play, so use this developmental reality to your advantage. In several places I have provided you with more than one idea for the activity for the session, even though you will probably have time for just one. Pick the one that you think may be best for your group. Or, better yet, create one of your own! Follow the lead of the children; they are, as I have said many times throughout this book, fantastic teachers.

You should also note that most support groups will take on a life of their own after the first four or five sessions. Consider your group's unique gestalt when planning later sessions. Be flexible and allow the group's momentum to guide you. Be careful, too, not to prescribe feelings through the use of certain activities. If your group teaches you they are experiencing anger as part of their grief journeys, for example, the pillow fight activity (see Meeting 8) may be very effective. But for those groups that, for whatever reason, are not having trouble with anger, the pillow fight activity might be not only ineffective, it may be inappropriate.

Support Group

Meeting 1

Warm-up time

The leaders provide a welcome to the children. Creative name tags are a nice touch and help the children feel very welcome. Occasionally, I have presented the children with special cups or mugs with their names on them. This is a great way to help them feel welcome. The cup is something they can keep forever as a way to remember their "grief group" of special friends.

The introduction and welcome could include comments such as the following:

• We (introduce your co-leader) are so glad you could come to our special group. All of us here have something in common: someone we care about has died.

• We come together to help each other at this hard time. It can be pretty scary when someone we love dies. We sure hope you will feel safe here to talk, play or do whatever helps you right now. We don't have a magic trick to make you feel better right away, but we are glad you are here. Thanks for coming today.

• Since this is our first time together, we just kinda wanted to get to know each other. Before we can get started, does anybody have any questions?

• Does anybody here have any thoughts about some rules we should make for our group? (Generate some discussion of rules (see sample ground rules on p. 229). Kids are usually really good at coming up with group ground rules, which you can help them flesh out. Tell them you will help them remember the rules each week.

• O.K., let's get to know each other now and understand why we are here. Let's try the "show and tell" activity you were told about last week.

Possible activity

Show and tell

Prior to the first meeting, let each child and his parents or guardians know (through a letter and/or phone call) what will happen at the first meeting. This allows both the children and their families to feel more comfortable about the support group. Have the children bring with them something that captures the unique relationship they had with the person who died. Examples include a picture of the child with the person who died, a poem about the relationship or the person, a special song or piece of music, an item belonging to the person who died or whatever will help the other children learn something about the person who died.

Sitting in a circle on the floor, the children then take turns sharing their object with the other children and explaining what the object means. This activity creates a very natural opportunity for the children to begin to get to know each other and explore how the death is impacting their lives. It also helps meet the fundamental reconciliation need of acknowledging the reality of the death. The more they can "tell the story," the more you will be helping them meet this critical need.

Have children share important linking objects, such as items that previously belonged to the person who died.

Closing

Following the show and tell activity, provide some open-ended play time appropriate to the needs of the children. Take the kids outside if the weather permits. Most love to be outdoors. This is particularly true of bereaved kids, for nature seems to help them be more expressive of who they are as individuals.

Be certain to thank them for coming and help them be glad they came. The first meeting sets the tone and builds safety for them and you.

Support Group Meeting 2

Warm-up time

Open each meeting with some warm-up time. One good way is to welcome everyone and ask how their week went. Sometimes this generates a lot of discussion, but at other times, very little. Always begin with somewhat of an open-ended mindset that allows the children to be your teachers.

Possible activities

Play catch. Stand in a circle and toss a beach ball around. After some free play time at this, have the children state a feeling they've had recently about the death each time they catch the ball.

Nature walk. If the weather allows (and you have parental permission), take the children on a walk around the block or to a nearby park. Have each of them pick up an item (such as a pinecone or a blade of grass) that reminds them in some way of the life or death of the person who died. Then return to your meeting space and talk about these objects.

Take the children on a walk around the block or to a nearby park.

Closing

Discuss the feelings generated by the catch game and the nature walk. Allow for open-ended play time and fun. Right before the children leave each meeting, you might take a minute (literally—be brief) to sum up what you think the group has accomplished that night: "Tonight you shared some of the feelings you've been having about the death. I know it can be hard to talk about, but talking about it helps you feel better. Thanks for sharing and for coming." This kind of statement brings closure to the meeting and affirms the children's grief work.

Support Group

Meeting 3

Warm-up time

Possible activity

Paper masks. Have children make two masks: one showing how they look to others most days, and one showing how they really feel on the inside. Allow time for discussion.

Closing

Open-ended discussion and play time. Closure statement

Support Group

Meeting 4

Warm-up time

Possible activity

Train to heaven. Line up chairs one behind the other and have the children take turns sitting in the front chair (the conductor's seat). Have the lead child "drive" the group to the place where he believes the person he loves is now and explain what the place looks and feels like. This activity can help children articulate their searches for meaning.

Closing

Open-ended discussion and play time. Closure statement.

Support Group

Meeting 5

Warm-up time

Possible activity

Two by two. Part of the reason support groups are effective for kids is that they help them learn to empathize with others' losses. Have the children pair up (you might assign pairs to avoid the "no one wants to pick me" phenomenon) then give the children this instruction: Share with your partner a difficulty you're having with your grief, then brainstorm with your partner some helpful ways to handle this problem. Finally, have the partners tell the whole group what they've learned.

Arm bands. In the late 1800's, mourners wore black arm bands to publicly announce their grief. Bring in some black cloth, elastic and fabric glue and have children make their own arm bands. Encourage them to wear the bands to group. Some kids may also choose to wear them to school, church etc.

Closing

Open-ended discussion and play time. Closure statement.

Support Group Meeting 6

Warm-up time

Possible activity

Feelings collage. Bring a stack of old magazines to group, and have children cut out images that reflect feelings they are having about the death. Glue images onto construction paper or posterboard and have children one by one share their collages with the group.

Closing

Open-ended discussion and play time. Closure statement.

Support Group Meeting 7

Warm-up time

Possible activities

Funeral pictures. Have each child draw a picture of the dead person's funeral, memorial service or grave. Then discuss what the funeral was like and how it made the children feel. Reinforce the purpose and value of funerals.

Freeze game. Play a musical selection, then when you pause the music, have the children freeze. As they're freezing, have them think about different memories: their first memory of the person who died; the happiest time they spent together; the last time they saw the person alive, etc. Then come back together as a group and talk about some of the memories.

Closing

Open-ended discussion and play time. Closure statement.

Have the children "freeze" and think about specific memories.

Warm-up time

Possible activity

Support Group

Support Group

Meeting 8

*Pillow fights.** Anger is a common response to loss. If you're sensing anger among a number of group members, ask them to explain who they're mad at and why. Using pillows they've brought in, have them hold the pillows in front of them (this works well in pairs) and punch the pillows, all the while stating (or shouting!) their feelings of anger. Be sure to spend some time afterwards discussing the feelings this activity brought up.

Closing

Open-ended discussion and play time. Closure statement.

Warm-up time

Possible activity

Support Group

Meeting 9

Musical feelings. Play short excerpts of instrumental pieces of music and ask the children to tell you what the music makes them think about. Is the music sad? Scary? Happy? Ask the children if they've felt any of these feelings since the death.

Closing

Open-ended discussion and play time. Closure statement.

Warm-up time

Possible activity

Support Group

Meeting 10

Then and now game. Have all the children stand on one side of the room. One at a time, a child explains how she felt when the death occurred, runs to the other side of the room, then explains how she feels now, some time after the death. A good activity for the last support group meeting.

Closing

Use the remainder of the group meeting for time to say goodbye to each other and the group. Pizza is almost a must for this last session! Each child can be encouraged (but never forced) to talk about what the group has been like for them. The leaders should then thank each child for being an important part of the group. Hugs are often the order of the day!

*** See the caution about this activity on p. 241.**

Model Support Group Evaluation

Please fill this out and return it in the envelope provided. You don't have to write down your name unless you want to.

1. When you think about this group, what is the first thing that comes to mind?

   _____

   _____

2. What did you like most about the group sessions?

   _____

   _____

3. What did you like least about the group sessions?

   _____

   _____

4. What have you learned by being a member of this group?

   _____

   _____

5. Which of the activities did you like best?

   _____

   _____

6. Which of the activities did you like least?

   _____

   _____

7. What should we change about this group?

   _____

   _____

8. Would you recommend this group to other kids? Why or why not?

   _____

   _____

9. Any other comments or suggestions?

   _____

   _____

Finally, consider the grief needs every bereaved child has and how the group has helped members work through those needs. Using the needs-based model outlined in Chapter 4 is a helpful way of looking at individual and group progression toward reconciliation of the death.

Let's remind ourselves of these needs one more time in the context of group work.

The Mourner's Reconciliation Needs

Need 1. Acknowledge the reality of the death. Members acknowledge the reality of the death just by attending group meetings. Some of your activities are often designed to assist in dosing the children with this important need.

Need 2. Move toward the pain of the loss. Many children need direct permission to mourn. Sometimes what they need most from others is an awareness that it is OK to talk and play out their many thoughts and feelings, both positive and negative. Support groups provide a safe place in which to explore these thoughts and feelings.

Need 3. Convert the relationship with the person who died from one of presence to one of memory. Support groups can help meet this need by encouraging:

- the sharing of memories, both spontaneous and through specially designed group exercises such as memory books & boxes

- the presentation of keepsakes and photos

- journal writing between group sessions (best for teenagers)

Many bereaved children discover some positive aspects of their changed self-identities.

Need 4. Develop a new self-identity. Support groups help meet this need by allowing children to talk and play out their thoughts on identity changes and explore them with others in similar situations. Many bereaved children discover that as they work on this need, they ultimately come to discover some positive aspects of their changed self-identities.

Need 5. Search for meaning. Your support group members will naturally ask many "Why?" questions about the deaths that have affected them. Support groups help by providing a safe, nonjudgmental place in which to search for meaning.

Need 6. Continue to receive support from others. I have already pointed out that grief is an ongoing process that unfolds over the course of many weeks and years. So, while your support group may last for a finite number of weeks, your group members will need infinite support from others.

For some members, this may mean some additional individual or family counseling. (You can help their parents decide if that is appropriate.) For others, it may mean staying in touch with other group members; lifelong friendships often spring from support groups. Still other children will leave your group ready to rely on other people and systems for support. In any case, it is a good idea to for you to compile a list of community resources that children leaving your group can turn to in the months ahead.

Support groups provide one way for children to mourn safely and to begin to reconcile their grief. This does not mean that when the group ends, the children will be fully reconciled to their grief. Indeed, reconciliation is a process that can take many years, especially for kids.

Recommended Resources

Organizations

Association for Specialists in Group Work
Two Skyline Place, Suite 400
5203 Leesburg Pike
Falls Church, VA 22041

This is a professional association for people who specialize in group work. I suggest you obtain a copy of their "Ethical Guidelines for Group Leaders."

Journals

Elementary School Guidance and Counseling
Two Skyline Place, Suite 400
5203 Leesburg Pike
Falls Church, VA 22041

This quarterly journal focuses specifically on the interests of counseling practitioners who work with elementary school-aged children.

The Journal for Specialists in Group Work
Two Skyline Place, Suite 400
5203 Leesburg Pike
Falls Church, VA 22041

This journal publishes full-length articles on group research, innovations and ideas.

The School Counselor
Two Skyline Place, Suite 400
5203 Leesburg Pike
Falls Church, VA 22041

This journal is directed at people working in school counseling settings. Articles focus on implementing theory into practice in counseling research, practical ideas and suggestions and book reviews. Published five times a year.

Small Group Behavior
Sage Publications, Inc.
274 South Beverly Dr.
Beverly Hills, CA 90212

This journal is an international and interdisciplinary journal presenting research and theory about all types of small groups, including but not limited to therapy or treatment groups.

Selected Readings

Baxter, G. & Stuart, W. "Bereavement Support Groups for Secondary Students" in *The Bereaved Teenager*. John D. Morgan (Ed.), Philadelphia: The Charles Press, 1990.

Corey, G., Corey, M., Callahan, P. & Russell, J. *Group Techniques*. Monterey, CA: Brooks/Cole, 1982.

Jones, J. & Pfeiffer, W. *The Annual Handbook for Group Facilitators*. University Associates, Inc., 7596 Eads Avenue, La Jolla, CA 92037.

National Directory of Children's Grief Services. The Dougy Center, 3909 S.E. 52nd Ave., P.O. Box 86852, Portland, OR 97286.

Schaefer, L. Johnson, L., & Wherry, J. *Group Therapies for Children and Youth*. San Francisco: Josey-Bass, 1982.

Grief Myth

Children who cry too much are being weak and harming themselves in the long run.

Tears are not a sign of weakness but a sign of healing.

Crying is the body's natural and cleansing response to sadness. It helps children release internal tensions and allows them to communicate a need to be comforted.

Children may repress their tears (and other emotional releases) either because they have internalized adult demands for repressing feelings, or they have observed that the adults around them repress their own tears. Unfortunately, many adults associate tears of grief with personal inadequacy and weakness. When bereaved children cry, adults often feel helpless. Out of a wish to protect the children (and themselves) from pain, well-meaning, misinformed adults often discourage crying through comments like, "You need to be strong for your mother," or "Tears won't bring him back," and "He wouldn't want you to cry."

Another purpose of crying is postulated in the context of attachment theory, wherein tears are intended to bring about reunion with the person who has died. When a bereaved six-year-old cries, he may be thinking (consciously or unconsciously) that his dead mother will return to comfort him. After all, she always hugged and kissed him when he cried before. The frequency and intensity of crying eventually wanes as the hoped-for reunion does not occur.

Tears are not a sign of weakness in children or adults. In fact, when bereaved children share tears they are indicating their willingness to do the work of mourning. As grief gardeners and other loving adults, we can better assist children by crying ourselves when we feel the need to.

Have you seen this myth carried out? When and how?

_____

_____

_____

_____

9

The Child's Garden:
Helping Grieving
Children at School

In a landscape, a child's garden is usually a learning garden—a place for kids to plant seeds, pull weeds, water their plants and watch them grow. Little may be expected of the garden from an aesthetic or productive standpoint (though in fact a child's garden might spill over with unassuming beauty or produce the biggest pumpkin in town), for the biggest benefit of the child's garden comes in the doing, not the viewing or the harvesting. Through gardening even very young kids learn "adult" lessons. They learn to be responsible for another living thing. And they learn about the mysteries, joys and pains of life and death.

When you think about my grief gardening model, you might think of schools as the child's garden. (Most of you probably know that the word "kindergarten," borrowed from German, literally means "child's garden.") After all, schools, too, are a place a learning and growth. And, like that tangle of weeds, sunflowers and pumpkin vines many of us parent-gardeners set aside for our children, schools, too, are just for kids.

So if schools are the child's garden, how is the garden affected by a death? If you are a teacher or a school counselor, what should you do if a student's family member dies? What happens when a child's classmate (or teacher or other school figure) dies? How can you best help students mourn in healthy ways?

"Nature is man's teacher. She unfolds her treasures to his search, unseals his eye, illumes his mind and purifies his heart; an influence breathes from all the sights and sounds of her existence."

Alfred Billings Street

School is a place for support   As I already pointed out, schools are the child's primary environment during the school year. So, especially in a society looking more and more to its schools as a provider of not just education but also social and emotional guidance, schools are an important source of support for grieving kids. Teachers, especially, are very important to their students. From them they learn not only facts and figures, but behaviors and emotions. Kids also rely on teachers for support during the seven or so hours they are

How can you best help students mourn in healthy ways?

in school each day. In many ways, teachers and counselors are not just imparters of knowledge to children, but also authority figures, role models, friends and confidants during the school day.

School isn't just a place for book learning. It's a home away from home, a place for students to share their lives with others. When a student is grieving, he needs to share his new and scary feelings. He needs to know that like home (we hope), school will be a stable and loving refuge.

Talking to students about death

If you are a teacher or counselor, you are probably good at talking to children. You know that they respond better, for example, when you get down on their level and maintain eye contact. You ask open-ended questions to solicit their thoughts and feelings.

Without talking down to them, you use language that they understand. Keep up the good work. You'll need all these skills as you help students grieve. But you may find that talking about death isn't so easy. That's OK. Our culture as a whole has a hard time discussing death. Actually, what grieving children need most is for someone to listen to and understand them—not to talk at them. Instead of worrying about what to say, try to create opportunities for your bereaved student to talk to you about the death.

Learn about grief

To help your students cope with death and grief, you must continually enhance your own knowledge of childhood grief. You have demonstrated your desire to learn more just by picking up this book. While we will never evolve to a point of knowing "everything there is to know about death," we can always strive to broaden our understanding and degree of helpfulness. Take advantage of resources and training opportunities as they become available.

Another part of learning about grief involves exploring our assumptions about life and death. Think about your own personal losses. Who close to you has died? What did their deaths mean to you? Were you a child when someone you loved died? If so, how did you feel? How did the important adults in your life—including teachers and counselors—help you with your feelings of grief? Thinking about these issues will help you better help your students.

Teach what you learn to students

Don't wait until a student's parents are killed in a car accident to teach your class about death and grief. Make lesson plans that incorporate these important topics into the curriculum. And use natural, everyday encounters with death—a run-over squirrel, a death that made local headlines—to talk about your students' fears and concerns.

Remember the concepts of the "teachable moment," the "nurturing moment" and the "created moment."

The *teachable moment* occurs when an opportunity to teach children about life and death arises through events happening around them. A baby is born; a classmate's grandfather dies. When these events occur, make positive use of them by talking openly about them with all the students.

Create regular opportunities to teach children about death.

During *nurturing moments,* you focus on the feelings of bereaved children. When a student's family member or friend or even pet dies, make yourself emotionally available to that student. Help him understand that mourning is a good thing and that he should feel safe to do it in your presence.

Finally, the *created moment* means not waiting for "one big tell all" about death but working to create regular opportunities to teach children about death. Children who have already been acquainted with the naturalness and permanence of death are more likely to grieve in healthy ways when someone they love dies.

How a grieving student might act

Behavioral problems

As I pointed out in Chapter 3, many children express the pain of grief by acting out. This behavior varies depending on the child's age and developmental level. The child may become unusually loud and noisy, have a temper outburst, start fights with other children, defy authority or simply rebel against everything. Other examples of acting-out behavior include getting poor grades or assuming a general attitude that says, "I don't care about anything." Older children may cut class or run away from home.

Underlying a grieving child's misbehavior are feelings of insecurity, abandonment and low self-esteem. This basic recognition is the essence of artfully helping during this difficult time. My experience as a grief counselor has shown me that the two greatest needs of a bereaved child are for affection and a sense of security. Appropriate limit-setting and discipline, then, should attempt to meet these essential needs. We must let bereaved students know that we care about them despite their present behavior.

Emotional symptoms

Bereaved students will exhibit many of the thoughts and feelings we covered in Chapter 3. But peer pressure may sometimes force students to suppress these healthy thoughts and feelings during the school day. If, through a combination of education, modeling and open communication, you can make your classroom a

Sharing our grief with others is an essential step toward healing.

safe place for mourning, your bereaved students are more likely to share their grief with you and their classmates. And as we've said many times in this book, sharing our grief with others is an essential step toward healing.

Poor academic performance

Grief takes a physical, emotional and spiritual toll on kids, and it may leave them feeling unable (or unwilling) to keep up with their schoolwork. Sometimes poor academic performance in a previously high-achieving student is a symptom that he needs more help with his grief, but sometimes bad grades or academic apathy are normal, temporary grief responses. Allow bereaved children to concentrate on their grief first and their schoolwork second, at least for a while.

When a Classmate Dies

Children aren't supposed to die. But the reality is, sometimes children do die. When a classmate dies, the other children will be profoundly impacted. They will probably feel a deep sense of loss and sadness, especially those who were among the classmate's close friends. Many will be curious. They will want to know what happened to Bobby and why. Some of the children will be afraid. When a classmate dies, children begin to understand that they, too, could die young.

Because the death was part of the children's school lives, teachers are the primary caregivers students look to for help with their grief. The first school day after the death (suspending classes for a day or two immediately following the death is sometimes a good idea), spend some class time explaining what happened. Remember to use simple, concrete language and honestly answer their questions. Model your own feelings. If you want to cry, cry—without apologizing for it.

Later in the day you might have the children make drawings or write letters to give to the dead student's parents. Send a note home with students informing parents about the death. With parental permission, you might also arrange for interested students to attend the funeral. Holding an all-school memorial service is also often appropriate and healing. (The crisis response team model at the end of this chapter provides you and your fellow teachers and administrators a model for handling such news-breaking and follow-up more formally.)

And always remember, grief is a process, not an event. In the weeks and months to come, you will need to provide ongoing opportunities for your students to express their grief. Creating a photo or artwork display on a centrally-located bulletin board will help all the school's students acknowledge the reality of the death. Hang blank sheets of poster board throughout the school on which students can, whenever they feel moved to do so, jot down some thoughts and feelings about the death.

How the School as a Community Can Acknowledge a Death

When a student's family member or close friend dies, acknowledging the death is critical. Timeliness is important. Inform school personnel as well as the bereaved student's classmates of the death and let them know the bereaved student will not be in school for at least several days.

The informing process should occur openly and be a vital part of other "news" that school personnel and students are made aware of. When the death is one that has impacted the entire school—death of a teacher, administrator, school support person or student—everyone in the school should be properly informed. In those schools that have morning announcements through a public address system, I have found that this is an excellent opportunity to inform everyone at the same time. This should be done as soon as possible in that death news often travels fast and is often accompanied by false rumors. Let everyone know when the family is receiving friends at the funeral home, church or family home. Provide the date and time of the funeral service.

When a student's family member has died, peers of the student affected by the death should be encouraged to offer support to their classmate. A group letter from the class to the bereaved student is often one of the most support- ive gestures in the eyes of the child. I have worked with several classes where each student has written a personal note to the student. All of the notes were then placed in a tasteful box and deliv- ered to the bereaved student by one of his better friends and/or the teacher.

When a death impacts the entire school, everyone in the school should be properly informed.

The school counselor and teacher may want to decide together about the appro- priateness of the child's classmates attending the funeral as a group. Be cer- tain to obtain parental permission when doing this because (unfortunately) some parents will think attending a funeral is terribly inappropriate and harmful to their children.

In an effort to help classmates better understand what their peer is going through, I encourage teachers to ask oth- ers in the class who have experienced the death of someone close to them to talk about their experiences. You might even talk to your students about ways of approaching and talking to the newly bereaved student when he returns to school. Help them understand that their classmate will still need friends and fun and that it's important they don't make him feel left out.

School-based peer support groups are another effective, healing forum for bereaved kids. Many students are receptive to this and it aids them in feeling reintegrated into the school setting while at the same time acknowledging their grief.

Getting extra help for the bereaved student When a student seems to be having a particularly hard time dealing with grief, help him get extra help. Explore the full spectrum of helping services in your community. Hospice bereavement programs, church groups and private therapists are appropriate resources for some young people, while others may just need a little more time and attention from their parents or other caring adults.

If you decide that individual counseling outside the realm of school counseling might be able to help the bereaved student, try to find a counselor who specializes in bereavement counseling and has experience working with children. Scan your Yellow Pages for counselors citing grief or bereavement as a specialty. Another credential to look for is certification from the Association for Death Education and Counseling.

Developing crisis response teams For too many children, schools are no safe haven! The reality is that the rate of unexpected, violent deaths in adolescents in the United States has reached epidemic proportions. How sad that in today's world more teens die from violence—especially gun violence—than from any illness. According to the National Center for Health Statistics, homicide by firearms is now the second leading cause of death (after motor vehicle crashes) for 15-19-year-old caucasians. For African Americans in that age bracket, homicide is the leading cause of death.

Without a doubt, nothing can disrupt a school setting as quickly as the death of a member of that community. Fortunately, in the past decade, school systems throughout North America have developed crisis response protocols that address tragic events. Crisis teams have been created to provide practical guidelines and staffing when a tragic event impacts the school.

The formation of crisis response teams is now (in most circles) seen not just as a good idea, but a necessary responsibility. I have had the honor of helping a number of school systems establish these teams and training staff to respond in empathetic, supportive ways to students, staff and the community at large.

This section outlines some of the specifics that must be considered when you are establishing a crisis response team in the school setting. My hope is that this information will inspire schools that have not yet established such teams to move in that direction with haste.

Rationale and goal statements of crisis response teams

Crisis response teams are created in an effort to meet the following needs:

- To provide a written protocol for the school system to respond when someone dies (whether that someone is a student, teacher, administrator, support staff or family member.)

- To create a description of suggested qualifications and training requirements for people who make up the response team.

- To identify individual and group needs and create appropriate individual and group responses.

- To acknowledge the death and create an environment that allows for the need to mourn.

- To assist the people on the site of the death in responding meaningfully to those affected by the loss as well as meeting their own grief needs.

- To provide follow-up and referral services for people who will require and benefit from longer-term support.

Selection and preparation of staff team leaders

It is vitally important to carefully select those persons who will serve as team leaders. Do not assume that the training and education a school counselor, social worker or psychologist has received has adequately prepared him to respond appropriately to the crisis of death. During graduate school many of these caregivers received only a very brief introduction ("Today we will cover death and grief") to bereavement care. The point is that those serving as crisis team leaders should demonstrate not only interest in this area, but the motivation to seek specialized training in grief counseling and crisis response work.

In today's world, more teens die from violence than from any illness.

This training should include, among other things, the following:

- An exploration of personal loss issues and their place in one's life.

- A comprehensive understanding of the grief process, particularly as it relates to children and adolescents.

- An in-depth understanding of the ways in which people naturally respond to traumatic death and the caregiver's subsequent helping roles.

- An overview of the collaborative-consulting role one will have when interacting with school administrators, teachers, support personnel and families.

- An understanding of the various components that make up a school-based crisis response team.
- Assistance in creating teaching components for people who will make up the crisis response team.
- An understanding of relevant ethical and legal issues.

Team members Response team members can be drawn from the population of teachers, counselors, support staff and family members. From an ethical standpoint, I don't think anyone should be forced to serve on a crisis response team, even though for some staff members it may seem a natural fit given their job descriptions.

However, if you commit to a comprehensive training requirement for all team members, you can feel confident that almost anyone can be taught the necessary skills to serve on the team. What often cannot be taught is attitude. By allowing people to volunteer (rather than be recruited) for this special service, you will naturally select-in people who are open to learning about death, dying and loss issues. People not suitable as team members often drop out as they progress through the required training. This is at it should be.

Occasionally a team leader will have to supportively suggest that someone not be a member of the response team. This reality comes with the responsibility of being a team leader.

The training of team members is similar to the content of training outlined above for team leaders. The primary difference is that team leaders may seek even more training than team members, and, over time, become more experienced simply by virtue of the depth of experience.

Responsibility of administration and crisis team leaders

Administration

The school principal is usually the one in charge of the crisis response team at each individual school; however, we can use the word administrator here to indicate whoever is in the position of leadership in the school at the time of the death.

- To contact the crisis response team leader when a death occurs.
- To schedule a meeting of the crisis response team in collaboration with the team leader.

- To arrange classroom coverage for any teacher team members.
- To prepare a memo to staff to communicate the facts surrounding the death or deaths.
- To arrange for informational notes to be sent home with students.
- To coordinate staff and student funeral attendance.
- To designate (when needed) a contact person for the media.

Crisis team leader

- To contact team members through a phone chain.
- To coordinate team response by providing leadership.
- To work with administration in gathering facts and preparing memos to staff and notes that go home with students.
- To assign team members and rooms to be used for crisis intervention and support.
- To assist in identifying primary survivors with special needs.
- To contact the family of the dead person to communicate support and provide assistance.
- To assist in the creation of meaningful rituals appropriate to the situation.
- To arrange for longer-term support systems (individual counseling, family counseling, support groups) to be available to those in need.

Implementation and communication issues

Anyone with initial knowledge of a death contacts the administrator.

The administrator contacts the crisis response team leader.

The team leader will contact team members.

The administrator and team leader work to gather facts about the death in preparation for initial team meeting.

The meeting will be held as soon after the notification of the event as possible.

Response team meeting agenda.

Administrator and team leader will give facts as known at this time.

Team leader will outline plan of action.

General outline for potential plan of action

- How and when death notification will occur.
- Assign team members to their individual responsibilities (e.g. who will go to what room to provide support).
- Coordinate communication with the family of the person who has died.
- Create awareness of who the primary survivors are.
- Review statement of procedure for any student who requests to go home.
- Review specific plan for remainder of the day in responding to the crisis.
- Team leader and administrator continue to monitor and supervise additional response team actions.

Create ways for students to give testimony to the life lived.

Follow-up considerations

- Plan for the inclusion of students and staff in the funeral or other mourning ritual (the school may decide to hold its own funeral or memorial service).
- Allow time after any funeral ritual for students to talk about the experience.
- Teach those who are impacted by the death (may include the entire school system) that healing in grief is a process, not an event.
- Create ways and means for students to give testimony to the life lived. For example: creating a scholarship in the name of the dead person, planting a tree, coordinating donations to family-specified organizations, writing a memorial for the yearbook.
- Provide ongoing grief support services and referrals to anyone in need.
- Assess the effectiveness of the crisis response team's efforts and revising the response protocol to make ongoing improvements.
- Schedule a structured follow-up assessment to be held three months from the tragic event to determine additional needs of survivors.

Recommended Resources

Cassini, Kathleen K. and Rogers, Jacqueline L. *Death and the Classroom: A Teacher's Guide to Assist Grieving Students.* Cincinnati, OH: Griefwork of Cincinnati, Inc.

Cobbs, S.L. "Guidelines for Dealing with Traumatic Events in the School Community," *The Dying and Bereaved Teenager*. John D. Morgan (Ed.), Philadelphia: The Charles Press, 1990.

Fairchild, Thomas N., Editor. *Crisis Intervention Strategies for School-Based Helpers*. Springfield, IL: Charles C. Thomas, Publisher, 1986.

Hoff, L.A. *People in Crisis*. Menlo Park, CA: Addison-Wesley Publishing Co., 1984.

Roberts, A.R. *Crisis Intervention Handbook: Assessment, Treatment and Research*. Belmont, CA: The Wadsworth Publishing Co., 1990.

Stevenson, Robert G., Editor. *What Will We Do? Preparing a School Community to Cope with Crises*. Amityville, NY: Baywood Publishing Co., 1994.

Grief Myth

Children are too young to understand death and religious beliefs about death.

We must strive to teach concepts of death and religion to bereaved children.

Teaching abstract concepts about death and religion is no easy task, but it's one we must take seriously as we try to help bereaved children.

Good gardeners understand that gardens have different needs at different stages. When their gardens are very young, they water frequently and blanket bare spots with mulch. As their gardens mature, they may need to water less and forego mulching altogether; instead their time will be spent deadheading and pruning and pinching back.

Like new gardens, bereaved children need age-appropriate care. It is true that children are too young to completely understand death and the religious and spiritual belief systems surrounding death. Only over time will children assimilate these beliefs, and this developmental limitation must be respected. But no matter the specific beliefs of the family, the child must first be helped to understand that the person has died and cannot come back. It is a mistake to suggest that children need not mourn because the person who died "is in a better place anyway."

Many children naturally become frightened when they hear that after death people go to some poorly defined place (such as "the sky") for some poorly defined reason. For example, several times after a child has died I have learned that the surviving children—siblings and friends—had been told by their parents or church pastor that God needed a little boy or girl in heaven, so the child was "taken." I have counseled several children who were counting the days until they too would be "taken."

In sum, caring adults need not feel guilty or ashamed if they cannot give specific definitions of God and heaven, or what happens after death. Openness to mystery is valuable not only in teaching about death, but in teaching anything about life. On the other hand, neither should we proffer pseudo-explanations that may frighten or confuse children.

Have you seen this myth carried out? When and how?

_____

_____

_____

_____

10

Grief Gardening in June:
The Grieving Adolescent

The June garden is an exuberant garden, lush and full in flower. Many perennials are at their peak and colorful annuals are plumping up nicely. If the gardener has cared well for the garden in spring, weeds are not a problem, nor is the beastly, impending drought of Colorado's July and August.

But the June garden—no matter how lovely and seemingly autonomous—still requires the gardener's attention. Many of the annuals need regular deadheading if they are to flower into the fall. Some spring-flowering perennials must be cut back hard. And insects and disease must be headed off now, in their infancy, before they gain a foothold.

Grieving adolescents remind me of the June garden. They, too, can seem so exuberant, so autonomous, so mature, that they don't need our help—or certainly not as much help as younger children. Yet bereaved teens do need our time and attention and vigilant understanding if they are to heal and grow into the summer of their lives.

Grieving adolescents can seem so exuberant, so autonomous, so mature, they don't need our help.

Still, we grief gardeners and researchers have a long way to go in understanding the grieving adolescent. Teen grief is an area in need of much more research. In fact, those studies that have been done have had some inherent problems:

1) The biggest issue has been that researchers have used different operational definitions (age-group classifications) for adolescence. The lack of agreement on what constitutes adolescence limits our ability to generalize results.

2) The majority of research has tended to be retrospective in nature. Study participants are asked to look back on their responses to a death (usually a parent) at a later period in life. The result is tremendous variability in the time of reported responses from when the death took place.

3) Many of the clinical samples used in studies use a captured population. The

studied adolescents were often those either referred for counseling or receiving counseling at the time of death. We have not had as much access to teens who do not seek counseling assistance. Obviously, this makes for somewhat of a biased sample and affects our ability to generalize results.

4) In some research, loss has been seen generically. In other words, there has been a failure to isolate how different losses (death, separation, moves, divorces) impact the teen differently.

These and other methodological problems suggest there is a real need to encourage more research in this important area.

Having acknowledged a dearth of research in this area, I can say this: I've worked with hundreds of grieving adolescents, and they have taught me that, because of their already difficult life stage, their experience with grief is unique. They are not children, yet neither are they adults. Instead, teens constitute a special group of mourners who, like the June garden, deserve a special kind of care and consideration from the adults around them.

Adolescent developmental tasks complicated by grief

With the exception of infancy, no developmental period is so filled with change as adolescence. One of the primary changes teenagers must go through is separating from their families. Leaving the security of childhood, adolescents begin to separate from their parents and siblings and establish their own identities. This process is very normal and necessary; without it, teens would never be able to leave home, establish careers or have families of their own.

But separating isn't always easy. With it comes the rebellion associated with adolescence. Fights with parents and siblings are common. So, when a parent or sibling who the teen has been at odds with dies, the teen may feel a sense of guilt or unfinished business.

Moreover, even though teens need to separate from their families, they still want to feel loved and secure. This ambivalence can complicate grief. The teen may

Leaving the security of childhood, adolescents begin to separate from their families and establish their own identities.

think, "If I mourn, that means I need you. But my stronger need right now is for autonomy so I don't want to mourn."

As teenagers separate from their families, they attach more to their peer group. Friends, including love interests, may become the teen's most important source of affirmation and acceptance. So, if a teen's friend should die, the hurt can be particularly painful. And it can be difficult for grieving teens to turn to their parents for support when they are in the very process of separating from them. Finally, remember that for a teen, the death of a friend or sibling is the death of another young person. Not only will the teen probably feel despair and outrage at this injustice, but the death can also raise the frightening specter of the teen's own mortality.

Because early adolescence is often accompanied by awkward physical development, many teenagers feel unattractive. This can compromise their self-esteem and make them feel that much more overwhelmed by their grief. Adolescents' changing outward appearance can also make them look like men and women. Too often adults take this to mean that grieving teens are emotionally mature and can "handle" their own grief. Not so. No one, especially a young person, should have to cope with their grief alone. Grieving teenagers need the love and support of adults if they are to become emotionally healthy adults themselves.

Just because some teenagers look like adults doesn't mean they can or should "handle" their grief alone.

School and sometimes jobs are also normal and necessary parts of the teenager's world. In fact, both help them hone their individuality and move toward independence. The death of someone loved, however, can put school and jobs on hold for a time. This, too, is normal. Grieving teens should not be asked to continue on with school and work as if nothing has happened. Actually, the work of mourning must take precedence if a teen is to heal. Parents, teachers and other concerned adults should understand and even encourage this temporary shift in priorities. On the other hand, some teens channel their feelings of grief into their schoolwork. These young people may see their grades or job performance go up.

One last point here is that teens, like children, often do "catch-up" mourning at developmental milestones. Important events like prom or high school graduation may cause the bereaved teen to feel particularly sad because the person who died isn't there to share that moment. This occurrence is normal not only shortly after the death of someone loved, but also years later. In fact, many bereaved teens will continue to do catch-up mourning as they enter adulthood and reach other milestones like marrying or having children.

Nature of the death

In Chapter 2 we explored at some length how the nature of the death can influence a child's grief journey. Here I would like to revisit this important topic as it applies to teenagers.

For many teens, the first special person in their life to die is a grandparent.

For many teens, the first special person in their life to die is a grandparent. If the teen was close to Grandma or Grandpa, this death can be a very significant loss in the teen's life and should be recognized as such. Too often the teen will hear others say "She was very old and sick anyway" or "He lived a long, full life." The fact that the grandparent was old does not take away the teen's right to mourn.

The death of a pet can also be very painful for adolescents. Sometimes they have grown up with the pet and have spent years caring for it, playing and sleeping with it. Teens who have emotionally distanced themselves from family members may actually be more bonded to the pet than they are to people. As a caring adult, you can validate the teen's need to mourn this loss.

Most of the other deaths that teens experience are sudden or untimely. A parent may die of a heart attack, a brother or sister may die of cancer, or a friend may complete suicide or be killed in a car accident. The very nature of these deaths often causes the teen to feel a prolonged and heightened sense of unreality.

At first, the teen will often feel disbelief and numbness. His survival mechanisms tell him that he must push away this horrible reality if he is to survive. Fear, panic and withdrawal are also common responses to sudden death. The teen may worry that someone else close to him, or even he himself, will die, too.

The adolescent's heightened emotions often take the form of rage after a sudden death. Anger is a way for the teen to say, "I protest this death" and to vent her feelings of helplessness.

Rage fantasies are also common. For example, if a teen's mom was killed in a car crash, the teen may express a desire to murder the drunk driver at fault. Try not to be frightened by this rage. It is a normal grief response, and most teens know not to act upon these feelings. However, some will need help in exploring the distinction between feeling rage and taking action.

If someone loved dies after a long illness, keep in mind that the teen probably began the grief process (often called anticipatory grief) long before the actual

death. The teen's need to push away painful realities is stronger than an adult's, so they sometimes feel a greater sense of shock and numbness when the person who has been ill dies. Young people who have had accurate information about the terminal illness withheld from them are also likely to feel shocked when the person dies. Finally, understand that after the long illness of someone they love, teens may feel a sense of relief. This, too, is normal and in no way equals a lack of love for the person who died.

The teen's need to push away painful realities is stronger than an adult's.

The death of a parent can be especially difficult for all young people. Teenagers look to the future more than younger children do, and expect their parents to grow old and be grandparents to the children they may eventually have. A parent's premature death, then, is the death of the teen's dreams for the future.

As we have already said, teens can also be extremely close to boyfriends, girlfriends and best friends. If one of these important people should die, teens need the opportunity to mourn. Unfortunately, their grief is not always acknowledged because society tends to focus on the "primary" mourners: the dead person's immediate family.

If a teen's boyfriend or girlfriend should die, the teen needs the opportunity to mourn.

My "Sweet Sixteen"

The following is excerpted from an exceptionally articulate essay written by a teenage girl after the death of her mother.

My "Sweet" Sixteen

by Heather Fisher

What do most of us think of when we imagine a sixteenth birthday? Flowers? Candy? A big party with lots of friends? A driver's license? Maybe even a car and that infamous first kiss? I know that my dream had always been a big party, family and friends congratulating me for achieving a perfect score on my driving test, and if I was very lucky, a "someone special" to make the day even more complete. Never in my wildest dream, or my worst nightmare, could I have imagined what that day would really be like.

My story begins in October, 1992. My mom began getting sick all of the time. She described her symptoms as those of a bad cold, but one from which she could not receive any relief. She went to many doctors and all gave her an individual diagnosis: everything from bronchitis, to pneumonia, to the flu. . . Our lives continued in this same pattern until Mom collapsed at her office on February 8, 1993. She was rushed to the emergency room, and once she was stabilized, the tests began. The results were not encouraging. The x-rays had shown a two-inch malignant tumor in her right lung as well as tendrils from the mass reaching into her lymph nodes.

My family and I were shocked. None of us ever smoked, and we lead what we've always believed is a healthy lifestyle. We just could not imagine why Mom of all people was being faced with lung cancer. But this was not the time to ask questions; we had decisions to make. Surgery was scheduled for the following week, during which time the entire right lung and several lymph nodes were removed. Because the procedure went well, a vigorous chemotherapy and radiation regimen was scheduled . . . My mom had a good chance of conquering her cancer because she was only 38 years old, a non-smoker, and an otherwise healthy person.

. . . After school was dismissed for the summer, Mom seemed to improve tremendously. She was allowed to come home, and she began to get her strength back. She was slowly becoming the vibrant, caring person we were all so accustomed to. She and I had many wonderful talks, during which we discussed everything from the cutest boys in school to the best places to shop. We decided to go on a shopping spree in Denver the day she completed her treatments. But, unfortunately, that trip would never occur.

July 28, the day before my birthday, Mom woke up and couldn't breathe.

She had been getting gradually weaker and had increased difficulty throughout the weeks before, but we had all partially ignored it. Yet, on this morning, we called 911. An ambulance was sent to our home and she was rushed to the hospital. I will never forget the fear in her eyes as they wheeled her out of the house, or the deep emotion in her voice when she told my eight year old brother, Matthew, and I that she loved us.

Mom was taken to the intensive care unit and hooked up to a respirator that would breathe for her. By this time she was in a near coma, and she didn't know who we were. My dad, grandparents, aunt, uncle and I all stood around her bed. I clutched one hand, my dad the other.

We stood there for hours. The doctors told us there was a massive amount of fluid accumulating at an alarming rate within her chest cavity. . . All we could do was wait. Wait for my mom, my best friend, to die.

Around 5:00 that evening, Mom woke up and looked very aware. Her eyes were bright, and she even had a partial smile on her face, despite her incredible pain. She made eye contact with each of us, and appeared to be at peace with what she knew was inevitable. She glanced at her family members one last time, mouthed the words "I love you" and fell back into a deep sleep. That was the last time she ever opened her eyes.

My mother's heart finally stopped beating at 7:45 a.m. on July 29, my sixteenth birthday.

. . . This event has changed me in numerous ways. I have tentatively decided to become an oncologist, and possibly even search for a cure for cancer. . . I try never to take anything for granted. Each person I meet is special to me, and I do my best to relay that message through my words and actions. I also have become aware of the many caring people in our medical field, the individuals you do not hear about very often. Last, I will always remember everything Mom taught me. Through her life and especially through this experience, I have learned how to laugh, how to be strong, how to live and how to love. Our time together was short, but I thank God for every moment we had.

The grieving teen's support systems

Many people assume that the grieving adolescent's friends and family members will support them in their grief journeys. In reality, this may not be true at all.

First of all, the teen's surviving parent or siblings may not be able to offer support because they are so overwhelmed by their own grief. This is natural and shouldn't be considered selfish or wrong, but it does mean that the teen will need extra support and caring from non-family members during this difficult time. The grieving teen's lack of support may also relate to the social expectations placed on the young person. Teens are usually expected to be "grown up" and support other members of the family, particularly a surviving parent or younger brothers and sisters. Many teens have been told, "Now you will have to take care of your family." The problem is this: When a teenager feels responsible for "taking care of the family," she doesn't have the opportunity, or the permission, to mourn.

Many bereaved teens are greeted with indifference by their peers.

Sometimes we assume that teenagers will find comfort from their peers. When it comes to death, this may not be true, either. Many bereaved teens are actually greeted with indifference by their peers. It seems that unless their friends have experienced grief themselves, they project their feelings of helplessness by ignoring the subject of loss entirely. Worse yet, some of the teenager's peers may be insensitive or even cruel. It's not unusual to see peers avoid the bereaved teen out of an unconscious fear that death might become a part of their lives, as well. Or, sometimes peers try to force the grieving teen to avoid the pain of grief and just get on with life. I call this "buck-up therapy." Teens seem to be more comfortable sharing the good times. You can help by teaching teens what being a good friend in grief means.

The adolescent's mourning needs

In Chapter 4 we explored in depth the six reconciliation needs of mourning, particularly as they applied to younger children. But how are those needs made unique by adolescence?

Need 1: Acknowledge the reality of the death.

Teenagers are not immune from magical thinking. They will sometimes fuel their guilt about the death by literally blaming themselves if they are not helped to reframe this common but devastating feeling. For example, you might hear a teen say, "If I hadn't goofed off so much and made her worry, my mom wouldn't have gotten so sick." To be helpful, you must respect the teen's need to express these "if-onlys," but over time help them come to understand the limits of their own culpability.

Need 2: Move toward the pain of the loss.

Keep in mind that the teen's naturally strong resistance to mourning does not mean that they are not hurting inside or that they are incapable of mourning when given support and understanding. Also remember that because teens don't always articulate their feelings well, they often do as much if not more of their mourning through their behaviors rather than words.

You can help by redirecting inappropriate behaviors. Let bereaved teens know that it's OK to feel angry but that it's not OK to physically hurt themselves or others because of this anger. Find an appropriate way for the angry teen to release his explosive emotions.

Before teens will open up to you, though, you must show them that you care and understand. Grief gardeners can best earn this trust by entering the teen's world first and counseling second. Don't always take teenagers to your office. Instead, shoot baskets with them or go out for a cheeseburger. During these activities, mix small talk with serious talk.

Need 3: Remember the person who died

As you help bereaved teens through their grief journeys, be alert for creative and spontaneous ways to remember the person who died. Journal writing can be particularly effective for adolescents who may not be ready yet to talk openly about their feelings. When words are inadequate, group rituals like planting a tree or dedicating a plaque can be helpful. They also provide concrete memorials that the teens can revisit long into the future. Finally, keep in mind that remembering can be difficult for teens. Some memories are painful, even frightening. But many are joyful and allow the teen to relive the happy times. With your help, grieving adolescents can discover the beauty of memory: through it, the person who died can live on inside them forever.

Need 4: Develop a new self-identity

As social beings, we think of ourselves in relation to the people around us. I'm not just Alan Wolfelt, but a son, a brother, a husband, a friend. Teenagers may be even more closely linked to those around them than adults are because their self identities are just emerging. So, when someone loved dies, teens must begin the difficult process of forming an identity apart from that person.

We should never assign inappropriate roles to young people, especially those that force them prematurely into adulthood. For example, teen boys should not be pressured to financially support their families like dad did. Nor should teen girls have to take the place of mom. This type of role substitution is both unhealthy and unfair to bereaved teenagers. Emotional role changing is equally damaging. For instance, if a teen's father dies, the mother should not rely on the teen for the emotional support her husband once gave her.

The grieving teen's identity is also affected by the realization the he will experience losses in life. Some young people may temporarily evolve a more serious or cautious view of themselves and the world that reflects this vulnerability. Sometimes this seriousness develops as the bereaved teen searches for meaning and often lightens as the grieving process unfolds. As caregivers, we must be watchful that this seriousness does not prevent the teen from having fun and does not develop into chronic depression.

Grieving young people naturally search for meaning after the death of someone loved.

Need 5: Search for meaning

Grieving young people naturally ask "how" and "why" questions about the death of someone loved. We can help by letting the bereaved teen know that these kinds of questions are both normal and important. Remember, normalize but don't minimize.

You should also note that teenagers sometimes act out their search for meaning. Drunk driving and other behaviors that test their mortality are common. While in general you shouldn't judge the ways in which the grieving young person searches for meaning, life-threatening behaviors obviously require intervention.

Need 6: Continue to receive support from adults.

As I've said many times, grief is a process, not an event, and like all of us, bereaved adolescents will continue to need the support of helping adults long after the death.

Mama's Hands

A poem by a fifteen-year-old after her mother's death from cancer.

Mama's Hands

by Angie Sapp

Mama's hands always had love in them.

They held me and comforted me when I was crying.

Everything seemed to go wrong with my mama, but she always made things right for us.

I'll remember watching my mama's hands keeping busy.

But now, I watch my mama's hands lying still and limp on her stomach as she lays in her bed to heaven.

So many things I want to say, but it's so hard.

She still tries to be strong for us. She wants to hold us in her arms again.

But now we hold her.

Why, why does it have to be my mama's hands?

So many times I hear how strong-willed I am, but I feel so weak.

My hands have to be strong for my mama now.

Signs a teen may need extra help

As we have discussed, there are many reasons why healthy grieving can be especially difficult for adolescents. Not only are the deaths encountered by teens often sudden and unexpected, but their lives may be filled with emotional turmoil anyway. Being a teenager is hard enough; being a bereaved teenager can be overwhelming.

Just like any bereaved person, grieving teens need the help and support of those around them if they are to heal. Sometimes, though, bereaved adolescents need extra help.

But how do you tell if a teen needs extra help reconciling her grief? First, don't get caught up in trying to determine which behaviors can be attributed to normal adolescent struggles and which have been precipitated by the death of someone loved. The work of adolescent development and the work of grief are alike in that they both involve mourning losses and accepting changes. Trying to separate them is beside the point.

Being a teenager is hard enough; being a bereaved teenager can be overwhelming.

To determine if the bereaved teen needs extra help, it is more important for you to distinguish between normal behaviors—no matter their cause—and dangerous behaviors. Following are lists of both normal behaviors and those that should be considered "red flags"—warning signs that the bereaved teen is having serious problems that warrant professional attention.

Normal behaviors

- some limit-testing and rebellion
- increased reliance on peers (vs. parents) for support and problem solving
- egocentrism
- increased moodiness
- increased sexual awareness
- impulsiveness, lack of common sense

Teens will be teens, and many of the ways in which they try adults' patience are perfectly normal. Of course, grieving teens are no different; they will exhibit these behaviors, too. Expect some limit-testing and rebellion, like staying out past curfew or arguing with parents. Adolescents also show an increased reliance on their peers for support and problem solving. Egocentrism is normal, too. Young people think the world revolves around them, and they sometimes fulfill their own needs at the expense of others. Teens are also moody. Don't be alarmed by their see-sawing emotions. Of course, adolescence is by definition a period of physical change and increased sexual awareness. At times the teen may seem to think of little else. Finally, young people can be impulsive and may seem to lack common sense.

"Red flag" behaviors

- suicidal thoughts or actions
- chronic depression, sleeping difficulties and low self esteem
- isolation from family and friends
- academic failure or overachievement
- dramatic change in personality or attitude
- eating disorders
- drug and alcohol abuse
- fighting or legal troubles
- inappropriate sexual behaviors

Because teens are going through a developmentally difficult time, we need to give them some leeway. Their frustrating actions are often normal, as we have just pointed out. But adolescents—grieving adolescents, especially—may also exhibit behaviors that are not normal and should be stopped. Suicidal thoughts or actions, such as giving away personal belongings or threatening suicide, are obviously a cry for help and should be taken very seriously. Chronic depression, sleeping difficulties and low self-esteem are also signs that a grieving teen needs extra help. Isolation from family and friends is another red flag behavior. While teens need to emotionally distance themselves from their parents, they should not physically shut themselves in their rooms and prevent all interaction.

Abandoning friends, those all-important people in the young person's life, is definitely a signal that something is wrong. Academic failure can also be a cry for help. As we have said, it's important to let teens mourn first and concentrate on school second. But a total loss of interest in academics, especially for a prolonged period, can signify trouble. (On the other hand, focusing on school to the exclusion of all else, especially the necessary work of mourning, can be a warning sign, too.) You should also look for a dramatic change in personality or attitude. Like everyone, teens are changed forever when someone loved dies, but they should not act like an entirely different person.

Eating disorders are another common manifestation of complicated grief. Be on the watch for symptoms of anorexia or bulimia. Finally, risk-taking such as drug or alcohol abuse, fighting, legal troubles and sexual promiscuity should not be tolerated. Grieving teens sometimes behave in these ways to prove their own invincibility. But no matter the impetus, these actions can harm the teen or others and should be stopped.

As with any checklist, the above lists are not all-inclusive nor are they meant to replace an in-depth assessment by a trained professional. They should, however, help you begin to understand what constitutes a "cry for help" on the part of the bereaved teen. Any behavior that may harm the teen or another person requires immediate intervention. Short of that, be on the watch for severe and prolonged bouts of unhappiness, anger or even indifference.

Also be aware that adolescents who have experienced multiple losses, such as having several friends die in a single car accident or losing a grandparent and shortly thereafter a parent, are probably more at risk for complicated grief. Bereaved teens already dealing with a family problem like alcoholism or abuse will also likely need extra help. These young people, especially, need care and support if they are to heal.

If you think a bereaved teen might need extra help, explore the full spectrum of helping services in your community. Hospice bereavement programs, school counselors, church groups and private therapists are appropriate resources for some young people, while others may just need a little more time and attention from their parents or other caring adults.

Support groups comprised of other teens who have experienced the loss of someone loved can also be a great resource. In these groups, teens can share their unique grief journeys in a nonthreatening, safe atmosphere. And, while the bereaved teen's friends may feel unable to help because they haven't experienced such a loss, support group members offer both compassion and peer support.

Finally, remember that finding a counselor or support group for the bereaved teen is one thing; hospitalizing her is another. Inpatient mental health care can be very beneficial to bereaved people who need to immerse themselves in intense, around-the-clock grief work to heal. But less restrictive therapy options, like out-patient counseling and support groups, should always be considered first. Many professionals feel that hospitalization is overused, especially for teenagers, and the costs can be astronomical. If you're in doubt about hospitalizing a bereaved teen, I recommend you consult professionals with expertise in this area.

Teen Grief Realities

The following statements and follow-up implications are based on my counseling experiences with hundreds of teens. Some are consistent with the available research, others are simply my subjective observations. Use what is helpful; discard what is not.

1. Many teens have a great resistance to counseling and/or support groups.
   Implication: We as grief gardeners must be outreach-oriented in our helping efforts.

2. Several studies have found that a teen's reconciliation of a death is a function of family system issues, and many parents of today's teens grew up in a mourning-avoiding culture.
   Implication: Family systems must be a focus of helping efforts.

3. A differential response has been found between male and female teens. Males tend to have a more aggressive grief response. They may act out physically or use drugs or alcohol. Females in contrast often feel a longing for comfort and reassurance.
   Implication: Be aware of and responsive to these differences.

4. Teens mourn in doses.
   Implication: They need permission to not always be openly mourning. Some teens may need some distractions or "time-outs" from more active mourning. In contrast, others may benefit from encouragement to create "mourning times" or they could get caught up in distractions.

5. While it is important for healthy mourning that adolescents be able to openly express feelings, they may not do so if it sets them apart from their peers.
   Implications: Create opportunities for peer support from teens who have "been there."

6. In times of ongoing stress, many teens report a need for some privacy or "alone time."
   Implication: Don't be threatened by this while at the same time staying available to the teen.

7. Many teens fear loss of emotional control and may be frightened by normal feelings of grief.
   Implication: To help prevent the "going crazy syndrome," we need to help bereaved teens understand the multitude of thoughts and feelings they may have. Teens need to know that sleep disturbances, appetite changes, anxiety and fears, irritability, explosive emotions, etc. are all common responses to death.

8. Most teens are unfamiliar with the intensity and the duration of grief responses.
    Implication: Teens need to know that grief is a process, not an event. The pace of healing will be unique to each person. They need a realistic timeframe for doing the work of mourning. They may be surrounded by adults who are impatient with them and project they should "be back to normal" quickly and efficiently.

9. Shy, quiet teens will naturally have a more difficult time expressing their grief in words.
    Implications: Nonverbal teens may need support in accessing nonverbal means of expressing their grief. Art, music and journaling may be more appropriate avenues of expression than talking for these teens. But watch closely: These teens are easy to miss because they are more withdrawn.

10. Some teens invite adults into defensive interactions (usually through expressing hostility and a sense that "no one understands or cares about me") that serve to distract everyone from the underlying pain of the loss.
    Implication: Recognize that in companioning bereaved teens you may be a whipping post for some who are likely to express their underlying pain through anger. The key is to not get involved in a defensive interaction that might cause you to miss the communication about underlying feelings of helplessness. Appropriate behavioral limits need to be set while the underlying pain is explored and expressed.

Some bereaved teens invite adults into hostile interactions that serve to distract everyone from the underlying pain of loss.

286

Grief Myth

We should help children get over their grief.

Grief, like a garden, is perennial.

Perennial gardens do not have a finite lifespan. Once planted they will return year after year, generation after generation. They may change over time, thriving then faltering as their caretakers come and go, but they rarely disappear altogether. A garden, like grief, is perennial.

Healthy mourning necessarily takes a long time—months, years and even lifetimes. In fact, children never overcome grief; they live with it and work to reconcile themselves to it.

As the bereaved child goes about his work of mourning, he begins to realize that life will be different without the person who died. Hope for a continued life emerges as the child is able to make commitments to the future, realizing the dead person will never be forgotten, yet knowing that his life can and will move forward.

No, children do not get over grief; they learn to live with it. Those who think the goal is to "resolve" bereaved children's grief become destructive to the healing process.

Have you seen this myth carried out? When and how?

_____

_____

_____

_____

_____

_____

_____

_____

_____

11

The Grief Gardener's Gazebo: The Importance of Self-Care

Here at the Center for Loss, many levels of decks and a gazebo connect the redwood pathways that meander the steep, rugged terrain. Nestled as they are among the pines, these tranquil seating areas—overlooking the burgeoning city of Fort Collins to the east and a breathtakingly beautiful canyon and reservoir to the west—invite relaxation and quiet meditation. Simply walk by them and you are pulled, like a magnet, into their restorative purview.

But I must confess that I, like many grief gardeners out there, resist that magnetic pull all too often. Here I am, living and working in this incredible environment, and I spend little time simply enjoying it. I tend to focus on "doing" instead of "being."

How does a grief gardener care well for others while at the same time taking good care of himself?

"A gardener's work is never at an end; it begins with the year, and continues to the next: he prepares the ground, and then he sows it; after that he plants, and then he gathers the fruits . . ."

John Evelyn,
Kalendarium Hortense,
(1706 ed.)

This is the caregiver's conundrum: How does a grief gardener care well for others while at the same time taking good care of herself?

Good self-care is critical for at least three major reasons. First, we owe it to ourselves and our families to lead joyful, whole lives. While bereavement care is certainly rewarding, we cannot and should not expect our work to fulfill us completely.

Second, grief gardening is exhausting—physically, emotionally and spiritually. Assisting bereaved children in movement toward reconciliation is a demanding interpersonal process that requires much energy and focus. Whenever we attempt to respond to the needs of children in grief, chances are slim that we can (or should) avoid the stress of emotional involvement. Each day we open ourselves to caring about bereaved children and their personal grief journeys. And genuinely caring about bereaved children and their families touches the depths of our hearts and souls. We need respite from such draining work.

And third, we owe it to the bereaved children in our care. My personal experience and observation suggest that good self-care is an essential foundation of caring for and meaningfully companioning bereaved children. Children are sensitive to our ability to "be with" them. Poor self-care results in distraction from the helping relationship, and children intuit when we are not physically, emotionally and spiritually available to them.

Poor self-care can also cause the counselor to distance himself from the bereaved child's pain by trying to act like an expert. Because we've been trained to remain professionally distant, some of us stay aloof from the very people we are supposed to help. Generally, this is a projection of our own need to stay distant from the pain of others, as well as from our own life hurts. The "expert mode" is antithetical to the grief gardening model discussed in this book and can cause an irreparable rift between counselor and child.

Bereavement fatigue syndrome

What happens when the child's grief gardener repeatedly ignores his own grief needs? Sometimes, influences such as bereavement overload (experiencing overwhelming loss within a short time span or, in this case, being around loss too much), unrealistic expectations about helping all the bereaved children in one's community or discovering that, at times, one cares more about the child's healing process than the child's family, results in what I call "bereavement fatigue syndrome."

Bereavement fatigue syndrome can be the result of bereavement overload.

Symptoms of this syndrome include the following:

- exhaustion and loss of energy
- irritability and impatience
- cynicism and detachment
- physical complaints and depression
- disorientation and confusion
- feelings of omnipotence and indispensability
- minimization and denial of feelings

Let's examine each of these stress-related symptoms and then explore ways in which we as grief gardeners can strive to take care of ourselves in the face of these symptoms.

Exhaustion and loss of energy

Feelings of exhaustion and loss of energy are usually among the first signals of caregiver distress. For the grief gardener, low energy and fatigue can be difficult to acknowledge because they are the opposite of the high energy level required to meet caregiving demands.

Our bodies are powerful instruments and frequently wiser than our minds. Exhaustion and lack of physical and psychic energy are often unconscious "cries for self help." If we could only slow down and listen to the voice within.

Irritability and impatience

Irritability and impatience are inherent to the experience of bereavement caregiver burnout. As effective helpers we typically feel a sense of accomplishment and reward for our efforts. As stress increases, however, our ability to feel reward diminishes while our irritability and impatience become heightened.

Disagreements and tendencies to blame others for interpersonal difficulties may occur as stress takes its toll on our sense of emotional and physical well-being. A real sign to watch for: You have more compassion and sensitivity for those you work with than you have for your own family.

Cynicism and detachment

As caregivers experiencing bereavement fatigue, we may begin to respond to stress in a manner that saves something of ourselves. We may begin to question the value of helping the bereaved, of our family life, of friendships, even of life itself. We may grow skeptical of the mourner's desire to help himself heal and work to create distance between ourselves and the person. We may work to convince ourselves that "there's no point in getting involved" as we rationalize our need to distance ourselves from the stress of interpersonal encounter.

Detachment serves to help distance ourselves from feelings of pain, helplessness and hurt. I have also observed that a general sense of impatience with the mourner's reconciliation progress often goes hand-in-hand with cynicism and detachment.

Physical complaints and depression

Physical complaints, real or imagined, are often experienced by caregivers suffering from bereavement fatigue syndrome. Sometimes, physical complaints are easier for us to talk about than emotional concerns. The process of consciously or unconsciously converting emotional conflicts may result in a variety of somatic symptoms like headaches, stomachaches, backaches and long-lasting colds.

Generalized feelings of depression are also common to the phenomenon of bereavement fatigue syndrome. Loss of appetite, difficulty sleeping, sudden changes in mood and lethargy suggest that depression has become a part of the overall stress syndrome. Depression is a constellation of symptoms that together tell us something is wrong, and that we must pay attention and try to understand.

Generalized feelings of depression are also common to the phenomenon of bereavement caregiver burnout.

Disorientation and confusion

Feelings of disorientation and confusion are often experienced as a component of this syndrome. Our minds may shift from one topic to another and focusing on current tasks often becomes difficult. We may experience "polyphasic behavior," whereby we feel busy, yet not accomplish much at all. Since difficulty focusing results in a lack of a personal sense of competence, confusion only results in more heightened feelings of disorientation.

Thus, a cycle of confusion resulting in disorientation evolves and becomes difficult to break. The ability to think clearly suffers and concentration and memory are impaired. In addition, the ability to make decisions and sound judgments becomes limited. Obviously, our system is overloaded and in need of a break from the continuing cycle of stress.

Omnipotence and indispensability

Another common symptom of bereavement fatigue syndrome is a sense of omnipotence and indispensability. Statements like, "No one else can provide the kind of grief counseling I can," or, "I have got to be the one to help these people in grief" are not simply the expressions of a healthy ego.

Other people can provide sound counsel to mourners and many do it very well. When we as caregivers begin to feel indispensable, we tend to block not only our own growth, but the growth and healing of others.

Minimization and denial of feelings

When stressed to their limits, some counselors continue to minimize, if not out-and-out deny, feelings of burnout. The caregiver who minimizes is aware of feel-

Am I Experiencing Bereavement Fatigue Syndrome?

A bereavement coordinator for a hospice recently asked me, "How is burnout different from stress?" We might overhear a volunteer or staff person comment, "I'm really feeling burned out today." All of us may have occasional days when our motivation and energy levels are low. While this fluctuation in energy states is normal, burnout is an end stage that typically develops over time. Once a person is burned out, dramatic changes are necessary to reverse the process.

Psychologist Christina Maslach, a leading authority on burnout, has outlined three major signs of burnout (what I'm calling bereavement fatigue syndrome):

- Emotional exhaustion—feeling drained, not having anything to give even before the day begins.

- Depersonalization—feeling disconnected from other people, feeling resentful and seeing them negatively.

- Reduced sense of personal accomplishment—feeling ineffective, that the results achieved are not meaningful.

Step back for a moment and complete the following brief bereavement fatigue syndrome survey. As you review your life over the past twelve months, answer the survey questions:

Bereavement fatigue syndrome survey

1. Do you generally feel fatigued and lacking in energy?

2. Are you getting irritable, impatient and angry with people around you (home and/or work)?

3. Do you feel cynical and detached from the people in your care?

4. Do you suffer from more than your share of physical complaints, such as headaches, stomachaches, backaches and long-lasting colds?

5. Do you generally feel depressed or notice sudden fluctuations in your moods?

6. Do you feel busy, yet have a sense that you don't accomplish much at all?

7. Do you have difficulty concentrating or remembering?

8. Do you think you have to be the one to help all those people experiencing grief?

9. Do you feel less of a sense of satisfaction about your helping efforts than you have in the past?

10. Do you feel that you just don't have anything more to give to people?

In general, if you answered yes to 2-4 of these questions, you may be in the early phases of bereavement fatigue syndrome. If you answered yes to 5-7 of these questions, you are quickly moving in the direction of total fatigue. If you answered yes to 8-10 of these questions, you are burned out!

All of us may occasionally have days when our motivation and energy levels are low.

ing stressed, but works to minimize these feelings by diluting them through a variety of rationalizations. From a self-perspective, minimizing stress seems to work, particularly because it is commensurate with the self-imposed principle of "being all things to all people." However, internally repressed feelings of stress build within and emotional strain results.

Perhaps the most dangerous characteristic of bereavement fatigue syndrome is the total denial of feelings of stress. As denial takes over, the caregiver's symptoms of stress become enemies to be fought instead of friends to be understood. Regardless of how loud the mind and body cry out for relief, no one is listening.

Emotional involvement and stress

The reasons caregivers feel stress are often multiple and complex. When we care deeply for people in grief, we open ourselves to our own vulnerabilities related to loss issues. Perhaps another person's grief stimulates memories of some old griefs of our own. Perhaps those we wish to help frustrate our efforts to be supportive.

Whatever the reason, the natural way to prevent ourselves from being hurt or disappointed is to deny feelings in general. The denial of feelings is often accompanied by an internal sense of a lack of purpose. After all, the willingness and ability to feel are ultimately what give meaning to life.

Of all the stresses grief gardeners are subject to, emotional involvement appears central to the potential of suffering from this syndrome. Perhaps we should ask ourselves what we lose when we decide to minimize or ignore the significant level of emotional involvement intrinsic to caring for the bereaved. We probably will discover that in the process of minimizing or ignoring, we are, in fact, eliminating our potential to help people move toward rec-

If you want to help others, the place to start is with yourself.

onciliation. As the saying goes, "If you want to help others, the place to start is with yourself."

As caregivers to bereaved children, we probably need to remind ourselves that we are our own most important counseling instrument and that what we know about ourselves makes a tremendous difference in our capacity to assist mourners. While the admirable goal of helping bereaved children may alone seem to justify emotional sacrifices, ultimately we are not helping others effectively when we ignore what we are experiencing within ourselves.

Obviously, we cannot draw close to others without beginning to affect and be affected by them. This is the nature of the helping relationship with the bereaved. We cannot help others from a protective position. Helping occurs openly where we are defenseless—if we allow ourselves to be. My experience suggests it takes practice to work toward an understanding of what is taking place inside oneself while still trying to grasp what it taking place inside others. After all, these thoughts and feelings occur simultaneously and are significantly interrelated.

Involving yourself with others, particularly at a time of death and grief, requires taking care of yourself as well as others. Emotional overload, circumstances surrounding death and caring about bereaved children will unavoidably result in times of bereavement fatigue syndrome. When this occurs, we should feel no sense of inadequacy or stigma if we also need the support and understanding of a caring relationship. As a matter of fact, we should be proud of ourselves if we care enough about "caring for the caregiver" that we seek out just such a relationship!

The codependent grief gardener

The evolutionary cycle of codependency

The codependent grief gardener often confuses caregiving with caretaking. Caretakers (rescuers) often become overattached to the people they attempt to help.

If the bereavement caregiver focuses all of her energy on people and problems outside of herself, little time is left for self-understanding. As a consequence, one of the primary symptoms of the codependent bereavement caregiver is a lack of awareness of the dynamics of codependency. This lack of awareness may result in feelings of helplessness and frustration, which are in turn sometimes expressed in the form of obsessing and worrying about one's clients.

Now a vicious cycle is set in motion. The more the helper ruminates about the bereaved children's problems (obviously, worrying doesn't really change anything), the higher the need becomes to rescue. Therefore, more inappropriate overinvolvement occurs, with the focus staying outside of oneself.

Evolutionary Cycle of Bereavement Caregiver Codependence

- Confuses Caregiving With Caretaking (becomes Rescuer)
- Cycle Continues to Repeat Itself
- Multiple Signs and Symptoms of Bereavement Caregiver Codependence
- Obsessing, Worrying About Clients
- Experiences Helplessness, Frustration
- Denial of Problem of Overinvolvement
- Focus of Energy Outside of Oneself (lack of self-awareness)
- Overinvolvement (caring too much)

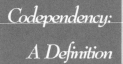

Codependency: A Definition

Do you care too much about bereaved children? Do you care more about helping them than they do themselves (or than their parents or other guardians do)? Do you feel it is your duty to worry about all bereaved people and get involved with their problems? On the other hand, do you feel "used" by some bereaved families?

If you've answered yes to some or all of these questions, you may well have codependency issues that need attention.

The term "codependency" was originally coined in the addictions field and was first used to describe the person whose life was affected as a result of being involved with someone who was chemically dependent. The codependent was seen as someone who developed an unhealthy style of coping in response to another person's alcohol or drug abuse.

So what is a codependent bereavement caregiver? I define it this way: someone who continually puts the needs of the bereaved before her own, ultimately to the caregiver's detriment.

The codependent grief gardener may appear to feed on providing support and comfort to others; however, self needs are often minimized, denied or completely overlooked. He in fact does help the bereaved, but usually wonders if he helped enough or "did it right."

Perhaps Melody Beattie described characteristics of codependency best when she wrote, "If concern has turned into caretaking; if you are taking care of other people and not taking care of yourself, you may be in trouble with codependency."

Signs and symptoms

Multiple signs and symptoms of grief gardener codependency can result from the evolution of this cycle:

- A lack of awareness of the phenomenon of codependency, as well as indifference, and sometimes unwillingness, to learn about it.
- A tendency to try to please others instead of themselves. A need for approval and a tendency to feel safest when giving.
- A desire to "solve" children's problems rather than create conditions that allow them to move toward reconciliation.
- A tendency to overextend and overcommit.
- A desire to do things for people that they are capable of doing themselves.
- A denial of own need for support and understanding, resulting in the myth of "super-caregiver" or "being all things to all people."
- A tendency to "feel different" from or "more special" than other people.
- A desire to be and act extremely responsible. May like to be on 24-hour call and enjoy having a beeper while trying to give the appearance of resenting it.
- A tendency to want to continually "check on" children.
- A desire to be "in control" and a belief that they know how to "make things turn out well" for bereaved children.
- A tendency to need the bereaved child as much, if not more, than the children need them.
- A tendency to neglect their own intimate relationships in favor of helping "needy clients."

Causes of grief gardener codependency

Unreconciled personal grief. As my research on this phenomenon progresses, it becomes increasingly obvious that many people enter into bereavement caregiving as a conscious or unconscious act of healing their own grief. The desire to "fix" someone else's grief is often a projection of a need to "fix" one's own grief. When this occurs, it is a classic form of displacement. The displacer is the person who takes the expression of grief away from personal loss and displaces the feelings in other directions. In this situation, the focus is on the caretaking of other people.

Family of origin issues. I've found that many codependent caregivers were helpers in their families of origin. They may have assumed the responsibility of resolving family conflicts or disciplining other children. In adulthood, they are often those who sponsor family reunions or organize holiday gatherings.

Socially learned personality characteristics. Many bereavement caregivers are particularly sensitive to the needs of others. Sometimes this sensitivity goes beyond empathy to over-identification with the suffering of others. It's almost as if they feel most comfortable when they are with people in emotional pain.

Consequences of grief gardener codependency

There are a wide variety of fall-out consequences when the bereavement caregiver struggles with issues of codependency:

- A broad constellation of stress-related symptoms, such as exhaustion and loss of energy, irritability and impatience, cynicism and detachment, physical illness (real or imagined), omnipotence and feeling indispensable, minimization and denial of feelings.
- Deterioration in relationships with family and friends.
- Symptoms of depression, sleeping difficulties and low self esteem.
- A displacement of compulsive behavior into other areas of life, such as spending money, overachievement, or drug and alcohol abuse.

Prevention and intervention strategies

Perhaps we should remember that just as healing in grief is a process, so is recovering from grief gardener codependency. Remember—having some characteristics of codependency does not mean you are a bad, evil or inferior person. Don't blame yourself if you recognize some parts of yourself herein. Be compassionate with yourself as you acknowledge any potential problems and be hopeful that you might be able to make some positive changes.

The important idea here is that the time has come for us to discuss the need for prevention and intervention strategies:

Create an awareness of codependency and its impact on your life. Once an awareness is present, the process of recovery can begin. This is the important first step in breaking down the denial of self-defeating behaviors.

Reframe yourself as a recovering codependent caregiver, as opposed to feeling good about all the bereaved children you are saving from the cruel world.

Work to acknowledge feelings of helplessness over controlling your codependent behavior. In other words, surrender. Begin your grief work related to a newfound revelation: You do not have to be all things to all people at all times.

Explore issues of your own unreconciled losses in life. Does your need to help others with grief in any way relate to your own unreconciled losses? If so, be certain not to use your counseling relationships to work on your own grief.

Work on unfinished family of origin issues. Attempt to understand how experiences in your childhood may be impacting your need to take care of other people. Were you an arbitrator, parent or therapist to your family?

Stop compulsively taking care of bereaved children. Perhaps you need a vacation from caregiving as you explore your own needs.

Develop ways of caring for and nurturing yourself. Explore your own feelings instead of focusing on everybody else's. Play more and make fun a part of your daily life.

Play more and make fun a part of your daily life.

Be compassionate with yourself when you occasionally slip back into caretaking and martyrdom. Your tendency to want to be in control will not be overcome quickly or easily. Begin to learn the art of healthy detachment.

Stop seeking your sole source of personal happiness through your helping relationships. You don't need the approval of others to have a sense of well-being. While relationships can help you feel good about yourself, they are not what is inside you. Work to attain self-approval and self-acceptance.

Discover the spiritual part of yourself. Spend alone time focusing on self-understanding and self-love.

Helping bereaved children can and should be a healthy activity. Grief gardeners need to counsel, not control. They need to empathize, not overidentify. They need to be responsible to others, not for others. They need to support, not protect. And they need to encourage, not manipulate.

The grief gardener's self-care guidelines

The following practical guidelines are not intended to be cure-alls, nor will they be appropriate for everyone. Pick and choose those tips that you believe will be of help to you in your efforts to stay physically and emotionally healthy.

Remember, our attitudes about stress and fatigue in general sometimes make it difficult to make changes. However, one important point to remember is that with support and encouragement from others, most of us can learn to make positive changes in our attitudes and behaviors.

You might find it helpful to have a discussion among coworkers about bereavement fatigue syndrome. Identify your own signs and symptoms of burnout. Discuss individual and group approaches to self-care that will help you enjoy both work and play.

- *Recognize you are working in an area of care with a high risk for burnout.* While helping other people has its rewards, it also has its dangers. Keeping yourself aware that you are "at risk" for bereavement fatigue syndrome will keep you from denying the existence of stress-related signs and symptoms.

- *Create periods of rest and renewal.* The quickest way to burnout is spreading yourself too thin—trying to help too many people or taking on too many tasks. Learn to respect both your mind's and your body's needs for periods of rest.

- *Be compassionate with yourself about not being perfect!* After all, none of us are! As people who like to help others, we may think our helping efforts should always be successful. Some people will reject your help while others will be invested in minimizing the significance of your help. This is particularly true for survivors who like to see themselves as "being strong." Also remind yourself that mistakes are an integral part of learning and growth, but are not measurements of your self-worth.

Respect both your mind's and your body's needs for rest.

- *Practice setting limits and alleviating stresses you can do something about.* Work to achieve a clear sense of expectations and set realistic deadlines. Enjoy what you do accomplish in helping others, and do not berate yourself for what is beyond you.

- *Learn effective time-management skills.* Set practical goals for how you spend your time. Don't allow time to become an enemy. Remember Pareto's principle: 20 percent of what you do nets 80 percent of your results.

- *Work to cultivate a personal support system.* A close personal friend can be a real lifesaver when it comes to managing stress and preventing bereavement fatigue syndrome. If you have already reached the crisis stage of burnout, realize you may well need the help of others in making lifestyle changes. Many grief gardeners have trouble asking for help. If this is the case for you, practice giving yourself permission to seek outside support. Remember, recent research has demonstrated that human companionship and connectedness helps you live longer.

- *Express the personal you in both your work and play.* Don't be afraid to demonstrate your unique talents and abilities. Make time each day to remind yourself of what is important to you. Act on what you believe is important. If you only had three months to live, what would you do? Use this question to help determine what is really important in the big picture of life and living.

- *Work to understand your motivation to help others with grief.* As grief gardeners, we strive to restore happiness to other people's lives. Does your need to help others with grief relate in any way to your own unreconciled losses? If so, be certain not to use your counseling relationships to work on your own grief. Find trusted resources to help you work with any old and new losses.

Express the personal you in both your work and play.

- *Develop healthy eating, sleeping and exercise patterns.* We are often aware of the importance of these areas for those we help; however, as grief gardeners we sometimes neglect them ourselves. A well-balanced diet, adequate sleep and regular exercise allow for our own physical, mental and emotional well-being.

- *Strive to identify the unique ways in which your body signals you are stressed.* Do you get tightness in the shoulders? Backaches? Headaches? Becoming conscious of how your body communicates stress allows for awareness of stressful situations before they overwhelm you. A constant state of physical tension often results in deterioration, which in turn results in physical breakdown.

Counseling for the Counselor?

The wise grief gardener will find other grief gardeners with whom to explore the ways in which companioning bereaved children impacts one's life. Unreflective work with children in pain can lead to failure in self-care and contribute to the ever-hovering symptoms of bereavement fatigue and depression. Moreover, lack of personal introspection may result in grandiose rescue fantasies and lack of attention to self-needs. Unfortunately, because we as counselors are often taught to appear knowledgeable and "in control," self-care can be more difficult for us than for many others.

The empathetic attachment to bereaved children in pain naturally results in awareness of any pain in the counselor's own life. Added to this is the reality that some counselors' interest in helping children grows from unresolved pains in their own childhoods. Obviously, good self-care in part involves staying conscious of your helping motives and how the counseling experience influences the embracing of your own life hurts, old or new.

How does the child's pain touch your heart? Do you have any "rescue fantasies"? What childhood hurts in your own life might be unreconciled? Do you listen to internal messages of fatigue, sadness, fear? If you do not listen, is the reason that you fear what you may find? If you do listen, what do you do with what you unearth?

So, do I recommend counseling for the counselor? Absolutely. Personal counseling is nothing to be ashamed of; indeed, it should be thought of as part of our ongoing desire to stay in touch with ourselves and others. Supervision and regular debriefing is not only wise, it is invaluable to managing the ongoing demands that come with grief gardening with bereaved children. We understand the importance of regular medical check-ups. Shouldn't we also go in for an occasional emotional and spiritual check-up?

Do you listen to internal messages of fatigue, sadness, fear?

Building support systems for the grief gardener

Grief gardening requires a natural outward focus: on the needs of the bereaved children we attempt to help. Such demands can leave us feeling emotionally and spiritually drained. An important aspect of self-care is to allow us to have sounding boards for how this work impacts our lives.

Friendships can provide the grief gardener with unconditional acceptance and support.

What do support systems provide for us as we tend to gardening? Ideally, supportive colleagues and friends provide some of the following:

Unconditional acceptance and support. In other words, friendships and the need to be nurtured and understood ourselves.

Help with complicated situations. Assistance in ideas that serve to help us in our efforts to help bereaved children and families.

Mentoring. Encouragement to continue to develop new tools to assist us in our work. Models that inspire us and remind us of the importance and value of our work.

Challenge. Encouragement to stretch ourselves beyond our current limits.

Referral. To have connection with additional resources for the children in your care. Good grief gardeners will recognize occasions when it is appropriate to refer those we work with to other, rich sources of support and counsel.

Ask yourself, can I seek support systems when I need to? Who are the people in my life that make up my support system? List five people you could turn to right now for support and nurturing.

_____

_____

_____

Are you involved in any relationships that are damaging to you? What would happen if you placed some boundaries on these relationships?

_____

_____

_____

Review your current support system and make an honest assessment of how well it meets your needs. Identify areas where you could use some change.

_____

_____

_____

Remembering the importance of "spiritual being" time

I have found that nurturing my spirit is critical to grief gardening. Spiritual being time helps me combat fatigue, frustration and life's disappointments. To be present to those I work with and to learn from those I companion, I must appreciate the beauty of life and living.

Spiritual, quiet moments or "down time" (for me, often spent in nature) recharges my spiritual energy. While you may embrace your spirit differently than I do, I encourage you to ask yourself: How do I renew my spirit?

Some people do this through prayer and meditation. Others might do this by hiking, biking, running or other forms of physical alone time. Obviously, there is no one right way to renew your spirit. But one reality is that to be present to others in healing ways, we must each find a way to massage our spirits.

I've always found profound meaning in the words of Carl Sandburg, who wrote the following:

> A man must get away
>> now and then
>> to experience loneliness.

A man must get away now and then to experience loneliness.

Only those who learn how
> to live in loneliness
> can come to know themselves
> and life.

I go out there and walk
> and look at the trees and sky.
I listen to the sounds of loneliness.
> I sit on a rock or stump
> and say to myself
> "Who are you Sandburg?
> Where have you been,
> and where are you going?"

So, I ask you to ask yourself: How do I keep my spirit alive? How do I listen to my heart? How do I appreciate the good, the beautiful and the truthful in life?

_____

_____

_____

_____

_____

Listening to your inner voice

As a caregiver to bereaved children, you will at times become grief overloaded (too much death, grief and loss in your day-to-day life). The natural demands of this kind of work can cause you to have tunnel vision about death and grief. For example, if your own child has a headache, you may immediately think *brain tumor*. If your partner complains of heartburn, you think *heart attack*.

I'll never forget the time I returned home from a three-day lecture series on childhood grief to find my office manager had scheduled the following day full of counseling a variety of bereaved persons and two dying children and their families. Sitting there looking at the schedule, my inner voice called out, "I cannot do any more sadness right now. I need and deserve a spirit break." So, I rescheduled all appointments for the day and went for a drive through nearby Rocky Mountain National Park. I returned home in the late afternoon and spent the remainder of the day playing with my children and being present to my wife.

Grief gardening with bereaved children presents you with the gift of an enhanced awareness of the many tragedies that touch people's lives. Just as the children you companion are changed by death, you are changed by their experiences as well. To embrace our deep appreciation for life and love we must stay grounded—and to do so means caring for ourselves as well as care for others. Our

To embrace our deep appreciation for life and love we must stay grounded.

soil must stay rich and moist, or we will dry up and nothing will grow in our presence! As we all know, the first step to a bountiful and beautiful garden is making sure your soil is healthy!

Final thoughts

Again, be aware that my self-care suggestions are not intended to be all-inclusive. I suggest you and your colleagues develop your own list of ways to prevent and alleviate bereavement caregiver fatigue syndrome. Each one of us has our own unique style of coping with the stress of living. Listen carefully to your inner voice and heed its whispers before they become screams.

Grief Myth

Can you think of any others?

We must work to dispel grief myths for the sake of today's bereaved children as well as future generations.

Throughout this book I have offered a number of grief myths that when internalized, come between the bereaved child and healing. Being surrounded by adults who believe in these myths invariably results in a heightened sense of isolation and alienation in bereaved children. A lack of support in the work of mourning destroys much of the bereaved child's capacity to enjoy life, living and loving. Bereaved children will experience the healing they deserve only when we, as individuals and as a society, are able to dispel these myths.

Can you think of any other myths that when acted upon, inhibit or prevent healing in grief? Take a minute to write down other childhood grief myths you have experienced in your own personal life or in your work with bereaved children. Then take up your hoe and go out into the biggest garden of all—our planet—and work to eradicate these myths.

A Final Word

As you well know by now, I truly believe that nature's own forces and materials can often provide the best conditions for the unfolding of grief's reconciliation in the bereaved child. Sometimes we grief gardeners are tempted to get impatient, forgetting that bereaved children have really just arrived on this earth. As young people, they've been here but a very short time! However, they bring with them innate abilities to grow, to embrace loss, to discover, to feel, to cry and laugh, to get mad. They already know how to love and mourn to the fullest; what they need from us is a nurturing, nonjudgmental, safe place in which to do it.

"A child needs encouragement like a plant needs water."

Rudolph Dreikurs, M.D.

"A book should serve as an axe for the frozen sea within us."

Franz Kafka

Children already know how to love and mourn to the fullest; what they need from us is a nurturing, nonjudgmental, safe place in which to do it.

Obviously, I feel estranged from the familiar doctor-patient model of bereavement counseling. It has the feel of "not me." In fact, I have found the medical model to be a major obstacle to my caring instincts; it limits the full measure of what I have to offer bereaved children. The more we think of ourselves as "doctors" or "therapists," the more pressure we exert (usually unconsciously) on the child to be a "patient."

What different paradigm might undergird our work with bereaved children? The freedom to (re)define who we are as caregivers is a real challenge. It is much easier to go with what we know than to challenge ourselves and others. Indeed, a fearful or complacent ego is most comfortable when it knows specifically what is expected of it.

I hope that my grief gardening model has challenged you. Thinking it through as I wrote this book has certainly challenged me and ultimately increased my flexibility as a caregiver. I have learned that I, too, am a novice grief gardener in many ways. While I have been counseling bereaved children for years, this book is a reflection of my continued growth and need to teach others what I am learning. If this philosophy challenges you, I'm thankful. If it encourages you to be a more open companion to bereaved children, I'm thankful. If it helps you experience that part of yourself that is God's instrument in helping others, I'm thankful.

The opportunity to companion bereaved children is a privilege that has allowed me to be drawn more fully into the richness and beauty of life. Bereaved children, having experienced the death of someone loved, must explore how they will go on to live their own lives and how they will relate to people and the world around them. As companion to them in this process, I have been changed in powerful ways impossible to capture in words. To grief garden for me is to embrace what is good, honest and beautiful.

One way to think of theoretical models is as portraits of the people who developed them. In sharing with you my "portrait" (which has been 20 years in the making and will surely shift and deepen in the next 20), I hope I have engaged your minds and your hearts. For it is in transforming our thinking as we learn that we transform our lives and the lives of those we hope to help.

My Grief Rights*

A Handout for Bereaved Kids

Someone you love has died. You are probably having many hurtful and scary thoughts and feelings right now. Together those thoughts and feelings are called grief, which is a normal (though really difficult) thing everyone goes through after someone they love has died.

The following ten rights will help you understand your grief and eventually feel better about life again. Use the ideas that make sense to you. Post this list on your refrigerator or on your bedroom door or wall. Re-reading it often will help you stay on track as you move toward healing from your loss. You might also ask the grown-ups in your life to read this list so they will remember to help you in the best way they can.

1. **I have the right to have my own unique feelings about the death.** I may feel mad, sad or lonely. I may feel scared or relieved. I may feel numb or sometimes not anything at all. No one will feel exactly like I do.

2. **I have the right to talk about my grief whenever I feel like talking.** When I need to talk, I will find someone who will listen to me and love me. When I don't want to talk about it, that's OK, too.

3. **I have the right to show my feelings of grief in my own way.** When they are hurting, some kids like to play so they'll feel better for awhile. I can play or laugh, too. I might also get mad and scream. This does not mean I am bad, it just means I have scary feelings that I need help with.

4. **I have the right to need other people to help me with my grief, especially grown-ups who care about me.** Mostly I need them to pay attention to what I am feeling and saying and to love me no matter what.

5. **I have the right to get upset about normal, everyday problems.** I might feel grumpy and have trouble getting along with others sometimes.

---

* *My Grief Rights* is available as a 4-color, oversized poster through Companion Press. Call (970) 226-6050 for ordering information.

6. **I have the right to have "griefbursts."** Griefbursts are sudden, unexpected feelings of sadness that just hit me sometimes—even long after the death. These feelings can be very strong and even scary. When this happens, I might feel afraid to be alone.

7. **I have the right to use my beliefs about my god to help me deal with my feelings of grief.** Praying might make me feel better and somehow closer to the person who died.

8. **I have the right to try to figure out why the person I loved died.** But it's OK if I don't find an answer. "Why" questions about life and death are the hardest questions in the world.

9. **I have the right to think and talk about my memories of the person who died.** Sometimes those memories will be happy and sometimes they might be sad. Either way, these memories help me keep alive my love for the person who died.

10. **I have the right to move toward and feel my grief and, over time, to heal.** I'll go on to live a happy life, but the life and death of the person who died will always be a part of me. I'll always miss them.

Wolfelt's Grief Gardening Model

The following explication was written to accompany the landscape watercolor in the full color section. Together these two pieces sum up and tie together the main ideas of Healing the Bereaved Child.

Bereavement caregivers are accustomed to learning about and following "assessment models"—a medical term I dislike. As I explain throughout *Healing the Bereaved Child*, I do not think of myself as assessing grieving children but rather grief gardening with them or companioning them.

So, I wondered as I was writing this book, how could I include the expected assessment model without talking about assessing? Then my editor and I had a fitting idea: Let's render my grief gardening model in garden form. So we turned to Sandy Schlicht, the talented landscape architect who designed the grounds around my house and the Center for Loss, and the equally talented watercolor artist, Cathy Goodale, whose work brightens the interior of my house. The resulting landscape plan, a combination of all our efforts, is printed in lush full color in the color section of this book.

I'd be honored to have you accompany me in a stroll through the garden.

In the lower left corner of the painting you'll find a columbine seedling, which represents the newly bereaved child. As in the parable that sets the tone for this book, the seedling grows at the rocky, untended edge of the garden.

With the grief gardener's help, the bereaved child begins her journey down the reconciliation pathway, encountering the six reconciliation needs of mourning as she goes. (They are numbered for easy reference.) Note that the path is neither smooth nor linear; instead, like grief, it is rocky and it twists and turns. Along the pathway the bereaved child confronts the influences on her unique grief journey: the relationship with the person who died, the nature of the death, her spirituality, her personality, her support systems as well as others.

Near the center of the landscape lies the family garden, for the child's family (and other social groups the child is part of) has a direct and central bearing on the child's ongoing grief journey.

The child's progression down the reconciliation pathway is indicated by the growth of the seedling. Note how small and forlorn the fledgling columbine appears at the beginning of the path. But as we move toward reconciliation, the columbine reappears now and then, growing fuller and stronger each time.

Look, too, for the compost bin; it represents play, which I have emphasized is crucial to a child's healthy expression of grief. Play is indeed the work that feeds the souls of all children. The weed patch, on the other hand, signifies harmful grief myths and other negative influences on the child's grief journey.

Other key elements in the landscape are the greenhouse (representing the counselor's office), the toolshed (representing the counselor's skills and techniques) and the self-care gazebo (representing the counselor's critical need for rest and rejuvenation).

But the focal point in the grief gardening landscape is the reconciliation garden at the upper right-hand corner. Leading up to it are the growth steps, those grief-borne transformations I explored in Chapter 1 (such as change, encountering pain and actualizing our losses). The reconciliation garden itself is awash in brilliant color, signifying the renewed love for life that comes with healing. The splashes of purple-blue symbolize the columbine's breathtaking growth and newfound maturity.

The reconciliation garden is also the clear destination of the reconciliation pathway, for though the pathway meanders back and forth and is never simple and straightforward, the bereaved child who is companioned well through his grief journey will achieve reconciliation and go on to find continued meaning in life and living.

This, then, is my alternative to the traditional grief assessment model. Instead of thinking of the bereaved child as a patient who needs treating, let's think of her as a seedling who needs our love and companionship if she is to survive. Instead of "assessing" her, let's let her guide us (at her own pace) through the garden that is her journey through grief.

Grief Gardening Considerations

Following are the landscape elements that demand your time and attention as you grief garden with a bereaved child:

Identifying information
Child's name, address, age, school, referral source, etc.

Relationship with the person who died
Consider the child's relationship with the person who died. What was the level of attachment in the relationship? What functions did this relationship serve in the child's life? Have you observed any ambivalence in the child's feelings for this person?

Nature of the death
What was the nature of this death? Consider circumstances surrounding the death, anticipated vs. sudden death, the child's sense of culpability for the death, any stigma surrounding the death. Also, who informed the child of the death and how was that done?

The child's unique personality
Consider the child's unique personality. What was the child like prior to the death? How has he responded to the death crisis? Does the child seem to be a dramatically different person now and if so, is this a cry for help?

Unique characteristics of the person who died
What was the person who died like? What role did she play within the family? What does the bereaved child miss most or least about the person who died?

The child's age
How old is the child and what is her unique, developmental level of understanding of the death? What does death mean to this child? Does she understand the finality of the death? How have other factors influenced her understanding of the death? Is this bereaved young person an adolescent and if so, how does his developmental level influence his grief journey?

Social expectations based on the child's gender
Based on his or her gender, how has this child been socially influenced to respond to loss? How can I help the child release emotions he or she may be repressing due to gender conditioning?

Availability of support systems

Consider the child's support system, both within the family and outside of the family. Does this support system allow and encourage her to mourn? How is the child's family system supporting her (or not supporting her) in her grief journey? Does the child have adults around her who model healthy help-seeking?

Cultural/ethnic background

Consider the child's cultural and/or ethnic background and its likely effect on his grief journey. How does that background influence the child's expression/repression of grief?

Religious/spiritual influences

Consider the child's religious or spiritual background and current influences. Does this child participate in any organized religion? If so, are they supportive of the child's need to mourn? What is the family's faith history? How does it influence the bereavement process?

Other crises/stresses in the child's life

Consider other events/conditions in the child's life that may add to or complicate the stress of bereavement. What secondary losses have resulted from the death?

Prior experiences with death

Consider the child's previous experiences with death or other major life losses. Has anyone else the child loved died? Has the child experienced multiple losses in a short time span?

The child's ritual/funeral experience

Consider the child's experience with the funeral of the person who died. Was there a funeral? If so, was the child allowed to be involved? Did the funeral help the child express her grief? Are there other rituals (like making a memory book or planting a tree) that will help this child express her grief?

Physical/health influences

Consider the child's physical health. What has been the child's medical history over the years? Is this child attempting to communicate about underlying needs through the expression of physical symptoms? Do I need to refer this child for a complete physical exam?

School influences

Consider the child's school life. You will probably need to talk to the child's

318

teacher and/or school counselor to answer these questions: How has this child historically done—emotionally, socially, behaviorally and academically—in the school setting? What can school personnel do in their efforts to help me with this child? Is a consultation in the school setting needed in this situation?

Peer influences
Consider the child's peer relationships and their influence on the child's grief journey. Which peers have historically made up this child's support system? Are any of the child's peers expressing concern for the bereaved child? How have the child's peers been impacted by this death? Do I see any changes in peer relationships since the death occurred? How can I involve this child's peers in my helping efforts?

Interests and abilities
Consider the interests, hobbies, favorite school subjects and special abilities of this child. This information will be of great help in involving the child in enjoyable activities in the counseling relationship.

Ten myths of grief
Has this child and family been influenced by any of the ten myths of grief? If so, how?

Child's grief response as observed to this date
Carefully consider the various grief thoughts and feelings (such as shock, guilt, fear, relief) this child is teaching you he has had during his grief journey.

Recommendations for companioning this bereaved child
Consider the ways in which you think you can best help this bereaved child. Will you make use of individual counseling, family counseling, support group counseling or some combination of the above? What involvement will the school, church or other community organization have in the helping efforts? What specific tools or techniques might be of particular help in companioning this child?

The Grief Gardener's Glossary

Following are definitions of some of the key terms used throughout this book:

Actualizing (of loss)	The experiencing and expressing of one's full potential after the death of someone loved. A way of growing through grief.
Bereavement fatigue syndrome	The caregiver's natural response to bereavement overload.
Bereavement overload	The result of experiencing overwhelming loss within a short time span or, for caregivers, being around loss too much.
Buck-up therapy	The societal tendency to move mourners away from their grief through messages such as, "You'll be fine", "You just need to get on with life" and "Think happy thoughts."
Catch-up mourning	Spurts of mourning, often long after the death, in which the mourner lets in some of the pain of grief she may have previously blocked. Often associated with developmental milestones in a growing child's life.
Codependency (of caregivers)	The state in which caregivers continually put the needs of the bereaved in their care before their own needs, ultimately harming the caregiver emotionally, physically, intellectually and spiritually.
Companioning	To "companion" bereaved children means to be an active participant in their healing. Caregiver companions allow themselves to learn from the children's unique experiences and walk with them as they journey through grief.
Complicated mourning	Mourning characterized by absent, distorted, converted or chronic responses to death.
Disenfranchised grief	Grief, often due to a stigmatized type of death, that is not socially acknowledged or supported.
Dosing (of grief)	Children naturally "dose" their grief by allowing just a little of the reality and the pain in at a time. In this way they move toward their grief, at their own pace, instead of away from it.
Forgotten mourners	Children are often "forgotten mourners" because though they naturally grieve, they are often not encouraged to mourn.

Grief	The thoughts and feelings that are experienced within us when someone we love dies. The internal meaning given to the experience of bereavement.
Griefbursts	Sudden, unexpected and strong feelings of sadness, sometimes long after the event of the death. Often very scary for children.
Grief gardening	A holistic bereavement counseling model that, unlike the traditional medical model of mental health care, embraces the naturalness and normalcy of grief and believes in the child's innate capacity to heal and grow through grief. Grief gardeners do not cure the grieving child but instead create conditions that allow the child to mourn.
Magical thinking	The developmental tendency for children to believe that thoughts cause actions. Can cause bereaved children to feel guilty if they think their thoughts somehow caused or contributed to the death of the dead person.
Mourning	The external expression of grief. Sharing one's grief with others. Also "grief gone public."
Multiple loss	The deaths of two or more significant people in the same event or the sequential deaths of two or more significant people within a relatively short time period. Non-death losses can also make-up or contribute to multiple loss.
Pressure cooker phenomenon	A time of great tension within a bereaved family. Everyone has a high need to feel understood yet a natural incapacity to be understanding.
Reconciliation	The process that occurs as the bereaved child works to integrate the new reality of moving forward in life without the physical presence of the person who died. With reconciliation comes a renewed sense of energy and confidence and a capacity to become reinvolved in the activities of living.
Secondary losses	Other losses children experience (such as the losses of identity and emotional security) as a result of the death of someone loved.

Index

loneliness 11, 154, 306-307

lying 13, 51, 86, 91, 104, 280, 308, 315

magical thinking 22, 26, 85, 277, 322

"Mama's Hands," by Angie Sapp 280

medical model of bereavement care x, 2, 5, 11-12, 19, 150, 311, 322

memories 5, 11-13, 19, 25, 27, 34, 39-40, 53-58, 67, 70, 72-74, 79, 83, 87, 89, 92-93, 103-104, 106-109, 124, 129, 132-133, 139-140, 144, 152, 156, 164, 167, 171, 173-174, 184-185, 193-196, 212, 223, 232, 234-235, 237-238, 240-241, 244, 247, 256, 258, 264, 272, 276, 278-280, 283, 293, 295-296, 300, 302-303, 306, 313-314, 318
  ambivalent 73, 109, 278

memory book 54-55, 109, 184, 195-196, 247, 318

memory box 195-196, 237

memory ritual 194, 223

mentally retarded bereaved child 31

mentors 149, 305

metaphors 178, 184, 189, 192

minimization 23, 150, 231, 279, 291, 293, 296, 298, 300, 302

misbehavior 82, 208, 256

modeling 82, 108-109, 145, 173, 230, 233, 235-236, 257, 258

mortality, testing own 35, 279

mourning
  -avoiding culture 8, 10, 40, 59, 155, 218-219, 236, 285
  complicated 47, 49, 52, 72, 95, 109, 115, 271, 283, 321
  definition of 15

despite having faith 44-45, 212
intermittent 63, 104
modeling of 37, 52, 97, 145, 257
normal vs. clinical depression 96
vs. grief 15

multiculturalism 42

multiple deaths (see also multiple loss) 49-50, 52, 318, 322

multiple loss 49, 52, 283, 318, 322

music therapy 169-170
  organizations 170
  selected readings 170

"My Grief Rights" 313

"My Sweet Sixteen," by Heather Fisher 275

myths of grief 7, 3, 15, 63, 99, 119, 144-145, 197, 215, 251, 267, 287, 309, 316, 319

nature, counseling technique 190-192

nature of the death 23, 25-26, 28, 103, 116, 190, 203, 233, 242, 273, 315, 317

nonverbal communication 19, 90, 124, 132-133, 136, 167, 183, 193, 195, 286

numbness 4, 6, 22, 24, 29, 33-34, 36, 52, 66-67, 69, 75, 80, 85, 92, 127-128, 149, 177, 222, 224, 245, 248, 260, 273-274, 309, 313, 315

nurturing moment 256

obituary 57

ossuaries 43

outbursts 80, 256

overprotective 72, 105-106

pain, role of (see also suffering, role of) 6, 105, 114-115

pain of loss, moving toward 11, 28, 91, 105-106, 247, 278, 321
  rescuing from 3, 304

painting (see also art therapy) 79, 162, 166-167, 169, 315

pallbearer 57

paperdolls 186

Pareto's principle 302

pathological 40, 51, 95

patience 19, 112, 133, 192, 281

peers and the bereaved child 26, 29, 59-61, 69, 71, 83, 87, 202, 219-220, 223, 226, 257, 259, 319
  feeling different from 60, 69, 219, 223

perception checking 136

person who died
  age of 23, 25, 28, 317
  characteristics of 32, 317
  personality of 32

personality
  child's 28, 30-32, 89, 95, 138, 170, 317
  person's who died 32

physical health of child 58, 70, 318
  medical examination 58

physical illness 68, 71, 181, 293-294, 300, 303, 307
  identification with person who died 70-71

physical self-expression 156

physiological changes 68

play, use of to express grief 25, 57, 74, 93, 96, 105-106, 244, 247

play therapy 149-160
  journals 160
  material suppliers 160
  organizations 160

poetry 55-56, 172-173, 175, 195, 223, 237, 242, 280

prayer 43, 46, 306, 314

preschool 5, 34, 151, 165-166, 222, 224

pressure cooker phenomenon 206, 208, 322

Also by Alan D. Wolfelt, Ph.D.
RESOURCES FOR AND ABOUT GRIEVING CHILDREN AND TEENAGERS

Healing the Bereaved Child:

Grief Gardening, Growth Through Grief and Other Touchstones for Caregivers

This inspiring, heartfelt book for caregivers to bereaved children contains chapter after chapter of practical caregiving guidelines:

• How a grieving child thinks, feels and mourns

• What makes each child's grief unique

• How the bereaved child heals: the six needs of mourning

• Foundations of counseling bereaved children

• Counseling techniques (play, art, writing, nature and many others; more than 45 pages!)

• A family systems approach to counseling

• Support groups for bereaved kids, including a 10-session model

• Helping grieving children at school, including a crisis response team model

• Helping the grieving adolescent

• Self-care for the child's bereavement caregiver

8 1/2" x 11" format, 344 pages.
Softcover. $39.95
(plus additional shipping and handling)

Wolfelt's Grief Gardening Model

A poster for 'grief gardeners"

This fine art-quality poster not only depicts Dr. Wolfelt's Grief Gardening Model in lush full color, it also contains a written guide to the many metaphors of the garden.
Poster (18 x 24"), $15.00
Or, order Healing the Bereaved Child and receive the Grief Gardening poster for just $5.00 more! *Book and Poster Set, $44.95*
(plus additional shipping and handling)

How I Feel

A Coloring Book for Grieving Children

Dr. Wolfelt's coloring book for kids ages 3-8 explores many of the feelings grieving children often experience. The expressive, easy-to-color drawings clearly depict disbelief, fear, anger, loneliness, happiness, sadness and other normal grief feelings.

24 pages $1.00 (plus $2 S&H per single copy)

25 copies $21.25 (plus regular shipping and handling)

My Grief Rights

A Poster for Grieving Children

This colorful, oversized poster helps grieving kids understand their feelings and empowers them to mourn in healthy ways. Sample headings: I have the right to my own unique feelings about the death; I have the right to need other people to help me with my grief, especially grown-ups who care about me.

Poster (24" x 36") $10.00   (plus additional shipping and handling)

A Child's View of Grief

In this informative, easy-to-read booklet, Dr. Wolfelt explains how children and adolescents grieve after someone loved dies and offers helping guidelines for caregiving adults. A concise resource for parents of grieving kids. The companion videotape, written by and featuring Dr. Wolfelt as well as actual bereaved children and their families, explores several key principles of helping children cope with grief.

Booklet 45 pages. Softcover. $5.95
Videotape 20 minutes. $64.95
(plus additional shipping and handling)

What Bereaved Children Want Adults to Know About Grief

A Companion Press classic, this booklet and audiocassette package offer 15 Principles About Grief and Children and then describe them in language a grieving child might actually use. In the cassette, Dr. Wolfelt's teachings about the 15 principles are interspersed with comments from actual bereaved kids.

35-page, pocket-sized booklet and 25-minute audiocassette. $15.95
(plus additional shipping and handling)

Sarah's Journey

Eight-year-old Sarah had always been her "daddy's little girl"— until the tragic day her father was killed in a car accident. Based on the belief that each child needs to mourn in her own way, this book describes Sarah's grief experience and offers compassionate, practical advice for adults on topics such as regressive behaviors, explosive emotions, children and funerals, the grieving child at school and more.

121 pages. Softcover. $9.95
(plus additional shipping and handling)

A Teen's View of Grief

An Educational Videotape for Bereavement Caregivers

This fresh video on teen grief, written by and featuring Dr. Wolfelt, explodes with in-depth information in its beautifully produced forty minutes: adolescent tasks complicated by grief, nature of the deaths encountered by teens, the grieving teen's support systems and mourning needs, signs a teen may need extra help and practical helping guidelines. Throughout, Dr. Wolfelt's teachings are interspersed with comments from actual bereaved teens.

40-minute videotape $99.95
(plus additional shipping and handling)

RESOURCES FOR ADULT MOURNERS AND BEREAVEMENT CAREGIVERS

Healing Your Grieving Heart:
100 Practical Ideas

Healing The Grieving Heart:
100 Practical Ideas for Families, Friends and Caregivers

Compassionate and eminently practical, our 100 Ideas Books offer specific, here-and-now suggestions for helping mourners heal. (The first book is for mourners themselves; the second book is for families, friends and caregivers.) Dr. Wolfelt overviews the needs of mourners then gives ideas about helping them meet those needs. Also included: what not to do or say, how to listen, how to deal with hurtful advice from others and many other practical tips.

128 pages. Softcover $9.95
128 pages. Softcover $9.95
(plus additional shipping and handling)

SPECIAL SET PRICE
Order both 100 Ideas books and receive 10% off!

100 Ideas Set $17.95

The Journey Through Grief:
Reflections on Healing

This spiritual guide to those grieving the death of someone loved explores the mourner's journey through grief, in particular the six needs that all mourners must meet to heal and grow. Following a short explanation of each mourning need are a series of short meditations written to help mourners work on each need as they feel ready. Bound in hardcover and designed with grace, The Journey Through Grief is sure to be a much-loved, often-referred-to companion on every mourner's bedside table.

160 pages. Hardcover. $19.95
(plus additional shipping and handling)

Understanding Grief: Helping Yourself Heal

A compassionate guide to coping with the death of someone loved, this bestseller helps bereaved people move toward healing by encouraging them to explore their unique journeys into grief and mourning.

Chapter titles include:

- Common Myths About Grief and Mourning
- My Grief is Unique
- What Might I Expect?
- How Am I Doing?
- Taking Care of Myself
- Do I Need Additional Help?
- Helping Guidelines for Support Groups (including a nine-session support group model based on this text)
- Helping a Friend in Grief.

Since its publication in 1992, Understanding Grief has been Dr. Wolfelt's most well-known, well-loved book for mourners.

200 pages. Softcover. $18.95
(plus additional shipping and handling)

Creating Meaningful Funeral Ceremonies: A Guide for Caregivers

Written in an attempt to counteract the current North American trend to deritualize death and to reinstill in us a respect for meaningful funeral rituals, this bestselling booklet explores the ways in which heartfelt funeral ceremonies help the bereaved begin to heal. It also reviews qualities in caregivers that make them effective funeral planners and provides practical ideas for creating authentic, personalized and meaningful funeral ceremonies. An inspiring guide for clergy and others who help grieving families plan and carry out funerals.

65 pages. Softcover. $12.95
(plus additional shipping and handling)

Companion
PRESS

ALL DR. WOLFELT'S PUBLICATIONS CAN BE ORDERED BY MAIL FROM:

Companion Press • 3735 Broken Bow Road • Fort Collins, CO 80526 • (970) 226-6050 • Fax 1-800-922-6051
www.centerforloss.com
All prices are in U.S. dollars and are valid through December, 1999.